# CALL the VET

# CALL the VET

Carl E. and Donna A. Londene

TATE PUBLISHING
AND ENTERPRISES, LLC

Published by Tate Publishing & Enterprises, LLC
127 E. Trade Center Terrace | Mustang, Oklahoma 73064 USA
1.888.361.9473 | www.tatepublishing.com

Tate Publishing is committed to excellence in the publishing industry. The company reflects the philosophy established by the founders, based on Psalm 68:11,
*"The Lord gave the word and great was the company of those who published it."*


*Cover design by Junriel Boquecosa*
*Interior design by Jomel Pepito*

Published in the United States of America

ISBN: 978-1-62854-909-6
1. Biography & Autobiography / Personal Memoirs
2. Biography & Autobiography / General
14.01.30

# Dedication

Dedicated to the memory of Donna A. McCoy Londene deceased February 1, 2013. Her joyous spirit, greatness of heart, and love of life will forever be remembered by her book, her legacy of life.

*Donna and Gene in their "J R" Western outfits ready for the big New Mexico Derby horse race.*

# Acknowledgments

There are so many individuals I need to thank for their support, guidance, and encouragement while writing this book. It is impossible to name all of you here, but you will always be appreciated for the contribution you made.

A special thank you to my husband, Gene, for completing the book when my eyesight failed me, for his help with the publication, and encouraging me during the problematic years.

To my children—Denise, Darlene, and Darrell—for putting up with me as we labored through the completion of the book and their support during my illnesses.

To all the veterinarians and friends we encountered over the years for helping me learn to care for the animals and to Dr. A who without his suggestion and persistence, the book may never have been written.

To my grandfather, D. S. McCoy, who always told me to look for the positive side and said, "Through life always keep your thumbs up 'tis the only way to go." Donna believes it and has lived her life that way.

# Table of Contents

# Writing the Book

For years, Donna had delighted friends with stories about her escapades on the farm. She told the stories many times of her trials and tribulations of adjusting from a city girl to a "farm girl" to the amusement of everyone. She had such a wonderful way of making something ordinary into a hilarious story that fascinated people and kept them coming back for more. She told it like it was even though it was a bit embarrassing to her at the time, which was what made it funny.

In the 1970s, Dr. A, their veterinarian, and his associates encouraged Donna to write a book and name it *Call the Vet.* They said her stories and escapades on the farm were so entertaining when they told them at the veterinary clinics and conventions that each year they waited for the new stories about their favorite customer. They kept them laughing as they told stories about this "city girl turned farmer." They wanted her to put them in writing for everyone to enjoy. There could be a second title for the book, "The Lady Who Talks to Animals."

Gene didn't get involved until she got cancer, and they had lots of time for Donna to dictate and Gene to type. Gene's only regret is that he was not always able to capture the humor on paper that Donna generated verbally. Her enthusiasm, vocal inflections, and body actions added much to the stories. Hopefully, the reader can use their imagination and realize how these stories were related.

The book is part autobiography, part historical, and part hysterical. It is their book done in the manner they lived their lives. The way they wanted to do it!

*Donna's Irish grandfather with his thumbs-up.*

# Dust to Dust

It was only nine o'clock in the morning, and the wind was already starting to pick up. The wind blew every day relentlessly until sundown. The dust clouds boiling up from Eastern Colorado soon covered the sky over Western Kansas, and the dust was everywhere, penetrating every crack in every house, inside the cars and buildings, and covering everything with a fine coat of brown-colored dirt. By midday, huge dust clouds thousands of feet high moved across Kansas and Oklahoma. The wind churned the dirt from the fields into boiling red or black clouds obscuring the sun and turned the day into darkness. Local farmers could not remember the last rain that penetrated the ground. It hadn't rained much in years, and everything was totally dry. The grass, trees, and ground cover were gone from overfarming.

The years following the first world war had been a boon for wheat farmers with an increase in demand and sale price of winter wheat. The availability of tractors with larger plows and disks made it easy for farmers to break up the grasslands and plant everything to wheat. The new crop was much more profitable, which allowed the farmers to buy more equipment and break up more ground. The postwar years turned weapon manufacturers to producing gas and diesel tractors and farm equipment. Rubber tires made the equipment faster. Tractors were replacing the horse-drawn equipment and revolutionizing the farming business. The demand for grain was causing farmers to plow up sod pastures, remove trees, and turn the fields into dryland wheat farms. They gave no thought to conservancy measures to prevent ground erosion.

Very little consideration was given to instigating any government programs to prevent what was to come. By the late 1920s, the prosperous years were over. The rains completely stopped. Wheat fields planted in September failed to sprout, and if the wheat did sprout, it did not stool properly before winter. For wheat to survive and not freeze out, it must stool or develop a root system and multiple blades of green leaves. If it does not, there will be no wheat in the spring to harvest in June.

With thousands of acres lying fallow and no moisture, they could not do a spring planting. Many of the trees and natural windbreaks were gone. Man's greed to make more money had set up a terrible scenario. The worst situation happened. The drought and the winds came. Daily, continuous dry winds swept relentlessly over Kansas. The top soil, which had been tilled and lay barren, was picked up by the wind and moved east in massive dust clouds. The winds coming out of Colorado were also bringing the dust when they arrived in Kansas. Each day the winds came earlier and became more relentless. Dust filled every open crevice—your nose, your ears, your eyes, and your clothes. The dust drifted like snow. Dirt banks and drifts sometimes made it impossible to open doors, and residents were forced to exit from an upstairs window. Cars and equipment were buried under huge piles of tumbleweeds and dirt. Dust entered the oil and filtering system of car and tractor motors and clogged the systems. Animals and people died of dust pneumonia and lack of clean food and water. More died from lack of medical care. Mother Nature had reacted violently to man's greed for money and stupidity in eliminating the natural cover of trees and grass. This terrible situation had developed in a time that the great depression and stock market crash had already driven man back to the farms as his only means of surviving. Now the farm was gone also. The resident homesteaders left Kansas penniless and discouraged. The future of farming in western Kansas was a bleak picture indeed. It would not fully recover for years.

The year was 1932, and it was a terrible time in America. The stock market had crashed three years before. By now, the effects of the depression in the east were being felt in the west. To add to the problems of unemployment and breadlines, the drought and farming decline was causing foreclosures on farms and city dwellers. The run on banks had caused closings and loss of deposits nationwide. The terrible effect was that the people lost the deposits they had in the bank; but if they owed a mortgage, the bank, through the trustee in bankruptcy, foreclosed and confiscated the mortgaged property. These properties were then sold for a fraction of their previous worth to enterprising and often unscrupulous investors who would later profit immensely from the purchase and sale. Often the banker individually, or a selected friend of the trustee, ended up with the property while his bank went bankrupt and the depositors were wiped out. It was a shameful time in American history. The other investors, such as life insurance companies, also profited from foreclosure and later sale of the property.

These were the times and conditions that would welcome our heroine Donna and hero Gene into the world.

Both were born in the later part of 1932, when things were at the absolute bottom, to families severely damaged by the depression. The run on the banks had caused many to close, and people had a complete distrust of the government. The economy was at a standstill.

Sometimes the legend of the phoenix occurs in real life. Rising from the ashes was a person just elected as president of the United States who inherited this faltering nation. His name was Franklin D. Roosevelt. In March 1933, FDR made his first fireside speech. Radios were just becoming common in about 25 percent of the households, and people gathered in the homes that had radios to hear his speeches. He was the first bright light in years, and he started many programs, such as WPA, to employ people and jump-start the economy. His casual and sincere speeches convinced people to reopen their bank accounts by setting up a guarantee of government insurance of their deposits up to a certain amount. History has recorded FDR as the savior of the country, and it is well deserved. Soon, there would be a chicken in every pot and a car in every garage.

It was too late for many to save their farms and property, but soon conditions improved, and a better standard of living would eventually evolve. Good times were coming. Unfortunately, it would be ten years later and World War II to really bring postwar prosperity.

# McCoys to Kansas

The McCoy family, Joseph Alexander and Mary Eva, came to Kansas in the mid-1800s from Illinois and settled in Hugoton, Kansas, in 1883. Their son, Dale S. McCoy married Lillian May Brown. He was a deputy for years, serving in the Dodge City and west Kansas area where the revolver ruled and became sheriff of Stevens County from 1908 to 1912. He had many stories to tell about the lawmen and the lawless. Donna's father, Ronald Lynn "Mac" McCoy, was born May 18, 1904, and married Gertrude Elge Block on April 29, 1924.

When Mac and Gertie had to close their business in Coweta, Oklahoma, in 1932 due to the depression and dust storms and move back to Hugoton, Kansas, Mac's sister had graciously suggested they move into the empty old family homestead farmhouse.

Mac McCoy—a burly, jovial Irishman—paced the floor and anxiously glanced out the window to see if the doctor's car was coming down the road. He had placed a call hours before to come as soon as possible as the labor pains were coming more quickly. His wife, Gertrude, or Gertie, lay in the bedroom of the two-room house. He could see the dust drifts forming, making driving difficult and vision almost blinding.

Mac had done all he could to patch the cracks and windows in the house to keep out the dust from the daily driving winds. He had nailed sheets over the windows and doors and put rugs in front of the doors. He put pans of water on the wood stove to heat and kept the fire going to keep the house warm as possible. He put the children, Dee (age four) and Bobbie (age two) to bed to keep them warm. He gathered towels and everything he thought the doctor would need for the delivery. The dust had come early that day and was now mixing with the snow to make it gray. The house was dark at midday except for the lantern and candles he had lit. He could see only to the end of the lane where the tumbleweeds, dust, and snow were blowing and collecting; and there were no headlights coming.

Gertie's frantic call told him the baby was coming—the doctor wasn't. He was lost in the dust storm. Mac got the four-year-old up to help him with the warm towels as he hurried to help with the delivery the best he could. He had observed the first two children being born and knew a little about what had to happen.

Finally, the doctor managed to find his way through the dust, tumbleweeds, and snowdrifts and arrived at the farmhouse just in time to tell Mac he had done a good job.

Regardless of these miserable times and conditions, on December 20, 1932, a new baby was born and christened Donna Allene McCoy, the heroine of this story.

Many years later, Mac told Donna that when she was born he thought maybe he had saved the wrong thing. She was so hairy she looked like a little ape. Donna retorted, "Well, Daddy, maybe you should have called the vet." Mac and Donna had a very close relationship and good sense of Irish humor. Another family would fortunately survive the dust storms.

# Londenes to Kansas

Four hundred miles east of Hugoton, Fred and Siri Londene lived on a farm near Navarre, Kansas. Fred's Swedish family, with the native name of Lundin, had immigrated from Almhult, Sweden, near the village of Lunden to Samolan, Kansas. Fred's branch of the family changed their name to Londene and moved to Navarre. Fred met and married Siri Helena Boberg after she had immigrated from Motala, Sweden, at the age of sixteen to St. Jo, Missouri.

Fred and Siri had eleven children, the tenth being Carl Eugene "Gene" Londene born in Navarre on October 13, 1932. Since he had various relatives named Carl, his mother decided he would be called Genie. Fred and his brothers operated a large successful farm, and the family was fairly prosperous. They had gone in debt to buy new combines, tractors, and equipment and mortgaged the farm to make the purchase at just the wrong time. The depression in 1929 and the following years of drought and dust storms took their toll, and in 1939 they lost all the farm and equipment to foreclosure. They were evicted, and Fred found a farm near Enterprise where he could operate a farm for a banker who had acquired it in a bank foreclosure.

It was sadly ironic. The Lundin family, crafters or sharecropper farmers in Sweden, traveled nine thousand miles to become successful farmers in Kansas, and now they were back to being sharecroppers again.

The family arrived at the farm in Enterprise, broke and disheartened. The long unoccupied house was discouraging. It had no maintenance since it had been foreclosed. Undoubtedly, Fred, Siri, and the family were mentally defeated by the downturn in their lives. These hardy Swedes had been through a lot, and they would adjust to one more change. They lived on the Enterprise farm until 1949 when they purchased a small farm north of Chapman. Gene lived at home there until 1952 when he entered the military.

# Donna's Arrival in Hugoton

Shortly after Donna was born, the family moved into a house south of town; it was one story and small, but it was still a working farm with a well, barns, and electricity. They acquired chickens, turkeys, a cow, and a big mama sow. Mac took the excess milk, cream, and eggs to town to sell for cash or trade for groceries, which sometimes was only fifty cents a week for flour and beans. Mac picked up some work in town for another fifty cents a week.

The dust continued to blow off and on for seven more years. They were turning on the lights in the middle of the day. In order to get to the barn and back to milk the cows, Mac had to fasten a rope to the house and tie it around his waist. Mac would tug on the rope to tell them he was coming back to the house. He had to put a tea towel over the bucket and strained the milk through it as he milked in order to keep it clean. People had to keep a cow to have fresh milk daily for the children.

As Donna began to walk, Mac often laughed about his little girl with the short legs. He referred to her as his little "Street Sweeper" because her diapers dragged along the ground.

*Donna at McCoy homestead, 1934*

They also had a rope from the house to the outhouse where they kept a broom to sweep off the dust before they could sit down. In the mornings, Mac had to shovel the dirt drift away to get the outhouse door open. It was not a pleasant place to spend much time.

They tried to keep the chickens and turkeys in the barn so they wouldn't be blown away. Donna remembers sitting at the table, and lo and behold, a turkey came flying by; and he had been plucked clean as a whistle by the blowing wind and sand. There wasn't a stitch of feathers left on him. She exclaimed, "Mama, naked, naked turkey." Gertie saw that one or two had gotten out of the barn and they were gone, suffocated and buried by the blowing sand.

During meals, Gertie wet a bedsheet and covered the children so they could eat without dust in their food. They even slept with a wet sheet over them or they had to sleep under the covers. Donna remembers the day her dad took three gingersnap cookie barrels of dirt out of the house. Donna's pictures show the dirt was over three quarters up to the top of the windows, and the fence near the road was almost covered. Hard-boiled eggs were the staple of the day.

When the milk spoiled or the cow went dry, Gertie made homemade beer. As with all German families, Gertie had no problem feeding her kids beer. It was a low alcohol beer heavy on the barley and hops and light on the sugar and considered daily bread in German families. It was food and liquid requirement all in one glass, and it was totally sanitary.

Gertie had beer working, and the minister called on the family. While they were sitting at the table, one of the beer bottles exploded in the closet. Gertie was so embarrassed, but the minister acted like nothing had happened. He was probably secretly wishing he could go home and have some of his own.

Delores, Donna's six-year-old sister, got dust pneumonia, which was the cause of many deaths during the dust bowl days. Dolores slept on a mattress saturated with camphorating oil. They built a tent over her made with oil soaked bedsheets to keep out the dust. The doctor stayed in the house for five days caring for Dolores trying to save her. She was in the bed for more than three months. The doctor came by the house often. When she finally was well enough to get up, she had to relearn to walk. Living in Kansas at that time was an experience that the survivors never forgot.

They lived on the farm for three years until they moved into a house in the city of Hugoton and Donna's farming days were over.

The kids came down with whooping cough and a red sign "Quarantined" was posted on their door. At that time, whooping cough was often fatal, lasted for weeks and was very contagious. School closed until the health inspector said it could resume.

When someone died of whooping cough, small pox, or other very infectious diseases, they were buried immediately on their own farm rather than be transported to the town cemetery. This was done to prevent transmitting the disease and the reason many farms in Kansas have small private graveyards. You can still see them on the hilltops as you drive through.

The family often went to Dodge City to shop where Gertie would dress Donna up like Shirley Temple and stand her on a table. Donna sang all the Temple songs she had memorized and mimicked the actions from the movies. With her hair done up in big ringlets, she was a dead ringer for Temple. The people in the restaurant were always entertained by how cute and talented she was. The owner appreciated the free entertainment and was happy to feed the family for free when they dropped in.

Donna always wandered off and had no fear of strangers. In a visit to Dodge City, she disappeared again. Searching down the alley, they heard the singing of "On the Good Ship Lollipop." They went into the store to the bathroom and there sat Donna, singing at the top of her voice.

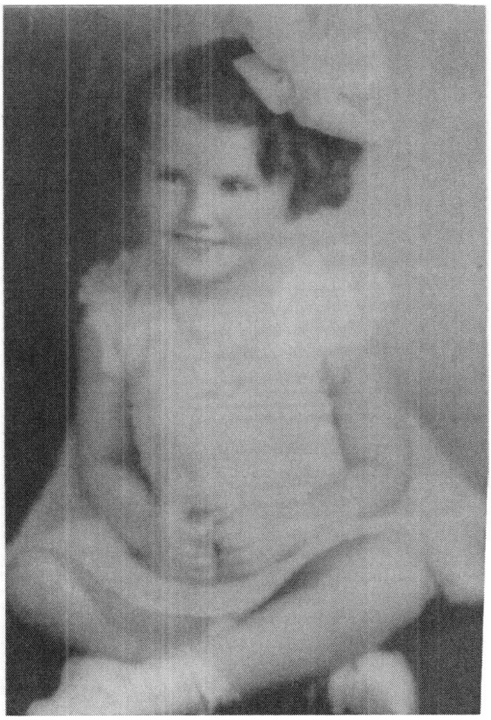

*1936: Donna as Shirley Temple, four years old, singing for her supper.*

The next move in Hugoton was to a house with running water next door to Ella's funeral parlor. The couple had no children and found Donna a joy to have around. Every morning, Donna ate breakfast at home then she scampered off to Ella's kitchen for a second breakfast with ketchup, which was a rare big treat then.

The two morning meals likely contributed to her being a happy, chubby, little girl. Donna sang all the time she was eating. A testament to the capricious spirit in Donna, one day Ella called Gertie and said she had better come get Donna and bring some clothes. Ella said they were having a funeral that morning, and Donna was over there naked. Gertie went over, and there was Donna eating totally nude.

Hugoton was a small town in 1936, but most memorable during a dire time, it had its very own "Lollipop Kid" as Donna became known to everyone.

# Donna Spells Trouble

When Donna was six, the family began a series of moves. Because she was born cross-eyed and almost blind, she began wearing thick glasses at the young age of three. In elementary school, she often saw double and remembers occasions where she would be walking back to her seat, see two seats, and end up on the floor.

The eye doctors recommended that she wear a patch over one eye, which resulted in the left eye becoming dormant. Donna always thought she flunked the first grade for being dumb. Later in life she discovered her first grade report card and found that it was the teacher who recommended that Donna not go to the second grade because of reading difficulties.

So from being a child star, singing for free family dinners and entertaining anyone who came into contact with her, she was no longer the golden child but rather the sickly child as she contacted every childhood disease. During this period, Donna felt like an ugly duckling, and her mother did not help. Gertie would introduce the children as, "This is my daughter, Dolores, and this is my son, Bobbie." Finally someone would say, pointing at Donna, "And who is that?" Gertie would reply, "Oh, that is Donna." Gertie openly displayed favoritism amongst her children and in the end suffered the tragic consequences of that behavior.

As a young girl, Donna received a number of spankings. She was mischievous. After receiving a spanking, it was not uncommon for her to go into a closet and laugh, which got her another spanking. Donna was so solid that Gertie would often break blood vessels in her hand when spanking her. Donna's brother and sister never got spankings, and Donna felt that she was unfairly targeted. Their next move was next to Plum Audrey's house. The Audreys had a teenage daughter who wanted to learn how to dance. Donna made a perfect partner, and while she was only in the fourth grade, her childhood talents returned and she caught on to dance as if she were born to do it. At this point in Donna's life, she could have worn a sign, "Will work for food." She loved to eat. Donna also loved helping people and making them happy and spent many hours just visiting and talking to people of all ages. When her mother couldn't find her, all she had to do was call around the neighborhood, and there would be Donna visiting and helping the neighbors in their house or yard.

Donna was always with her dad at the lumberyard since she got into so much trouble at home. Working in the lumberyard helped Donna learn a lot about the sizes and uses of lumber and nails. She often went on remodeling jobs with her dad after school. Her knowledge of remodeling and decorating would come in useful later in life as she ended up with an old house to remodel.

After the fifth grade, they moved to Russell, Kansas. Within a few years, Mac bought his employer's company and renamed it McCoy Construction Company, which he operated until his retirement.

# Growing up in Russell, Singing, Music, and Art

Donna began life in Russell in the sixth grade. Russell was a former cattle town that became an oil town in the 1940s.

At this point, Donna was a chubby little gal with glasses, a long way from the Shirley Temple protégé. In the seventh grade, her innate talent began to blossom. She was singing in the adult choir at church, studied opera, and hoped to work on Broadway. She loved to perform just like when she was a child dolled up like Shirley Temple. She started to slim down and her love for dance led her to the skating rink in town where she took to skating like a duck takes to water. She skated every time the rink was open and was so good that when a group of professional skaters came from Denver for three summers she was chosen as a partner for one of the skaters.

Back at school, Donna was devoted to her talent. She learned to push a piano around the stage while singing to develop chest strength. She practiced at home by having her brother stand on her chest while she was singing. As time went by, Donna developed into a person who loved life and continued to dream of being an opera singer or in the musical theatre. She took voice lessons every week in Salina with a retired opera singer, had lessons every school day, and sang her way through school.

Donna's life was now filled with singing, music, dancing, and socializing. Starting high school, she was now teaching square dancing. She and her brother did exhibition jitter bugging and performed at the State Elks Convention and other venues. In short, Donna had arrived.

During her senior year, she had an unfortunate interruption in her singing career. Gertie was peeling apples for an apple pie, and Donna walked by the table and snitched a piece of the peeling. As Donna went out the kitchen door, her mother yelled at her, and she took a deep breath, causing the apple peel to lodge in her throat. It wouldn't come out, and she lost her voice for about three months. She was seventeen and wanted to continue with voice in college, so her parents took her to Kansas City. The doctors tried in vain to locate and retrieve the apple peel, but it was lodged in the vocal tissue and they couldn't. She learned to sing again, but it was never the same when trying to make the high notes sound right.

Seventeen years later, a doctor found the apple peel lodged in her vocal tissue with a cyst formed around it. Dr. Lovelace found the cyst when he did the thyroidectomy on her, and after the operation, her voice dropped a whole octave.

Donna became more of a pal to her parents than a daughter. Mac was a thirty-second degree Mason and a member of the Elks Club. Donna accompanied them to the club every Saturday night for dinner and dancing. Donna sang with the band at the Elks Club and for the Masonic meetings. Between songs she was her daddy's dance partner. Donna, Mac, and Gertie loved to dance until two o'clock in the morning and then go to the Saline River fishing for catfish until daylight. For breakfast, they had fried catfish with fried potatoes and onions. The family enjoyed the German/Russian method of putting whole canned tomatoes on their fried potatoes in a cereal dish. Donna's Irish dad had to have lots of potatoes and turnips.

Mac and Gertie often left with friends and went to Wichita or to college ball games. They usually left Friday afternoon and returned Sunday night. Donna was now a freshman in high school, and they were all considered old enough to be trusted to do their own thing.

This weekend, Mac and Gertie were going to Hays for a football game. Donna was home alone as Dee was in college and Bob was gone. Donna invited six of her girlfriends to spend the night and have dinner. They were preparing their dinner and just sitting around the table talking as girls do. Gertie had left a pack of cigarettes lying on the counter. The girls had the house to themselves, so they all had to try one. They sat around the table and each took a cigarette. They all fired up, and they were feeling very grown up and sophisticated. The smoke was filling the room, and they were having a great time puffing and coughing.

Suddenly, the front door opened. Gertie had forgotten her gloves and returned to get them. How many people wore white gloves to games? She wore gloves everywhere. The girls got so flustered they all threw their cigarettes in the trash can, which caught fire. Gertie went into a rage and grabbed the trash can and carried it outside. It was a bad scene.

Donna always worked from an early age. Her sister had asthma and her brother was seldom home. This left Donna as "Cinderella" to do much of the housework washing and ironing for the family. When her brother went to college, he still sent his shirts home for Donna to wash and iron because she did such a good job. She wasn't allowed to do dishes anymore as she didn't see that well and dropped and broke too much delicate china.

Many weekends her mother went to Wichita and Donna and Mac went for dinner and dancing. They danced great together, and when Mac got tired, Donna always had someone eager to dance with her.

Donna always felt her mother disliked her because she had been born when times were really bad. With the depression, dust storms, and lack of income, she was just not a welcome child; and Gertie constantly reminded her of it.

Donna always felt that her mother favored her brother and coddled her sister. Donna undoubtedly aided the problem being a very headstrong, stubborn child while the other two were passive. Donna was absorbed in music and art and pursuing new adventures. She developed a great outgoing personality and confidence in spite of her home life.

# Donna to College

Donna graduated from Russell High School in 1951, followed the McCoy tradition and enrolled at Emporia Kansas State Teachers College, but becoming a teacher was not for Donna.

At Emporia, Donna and Dee were roommates at the Delta Sigma Epsilon Sorority house. Donna found a way to express her love of singing and would leave the sorority house on the pretext of going to practice at the music hall. Instead, she went downtown to a pub and sang with a live band. This worked out very well until her sister Dee discovered her subterfuge and informed the bar owner she was underage.

Donna remained at Emporia State for two years, and in order to pursue art and singing, she transferred to Kansas University. Sadly, Donna›s voice had changed due to the cyst caused by the apple peel. Eventually, so discouraged by having lost her voice, she quit school altogether in the middle of her junior year. Even though she did not finish college, she was confident that her credentials as a member of Delta Sigma Epsilon Sorority and Eastern Star were good enough to get a job.

In 1954, Donna took a train to Dallas, Texas, and discovered it was nothing like Russell. She was hungry when she arrived in Dallas and went into the train station café. There she had her first experience with segregation. She sat down at the counter and was quickly told she should move to the white area. She went to the restroom and didn't see the segregation sign and was promptly thrown out. She had never seen the white dominance of black people in Kansas because of the Green River Law, which prevented black families from settling in the area.

A bus ride to the YWCA was another profound experience with segregation. When she got on the bus, the driver told her to sit right behind him and do what he said because violence among the blacks on public busses was quite common then. She moved out of the YWCA within a week and into a rented room in a private home then continued to look for a job.

She got her first job in the gift wrapping and stationery department at Neiman Marcus. The company was so impressed with her knowledge, work, and personality that they wanted to promote her to a showcase decorator for the fashion windows. Then the company wanted to send her to Paris, France, to further her education in design. She had never been on an airplane, and the thought of going for three weeks on a boat was more than she could fathom. This was not the job for her, and she quit Neiman Marcus, dismissing the opportunities they were offering because of her fear of flying or sailing.

She found a new job at Peat, Marwick, Mitchell & Co., the premier office of the largest accounting firm in the world with some of the wealthiest oil magnets in the world as clients.

It was a far cry from the arts and music field. The office manager she interviewed with sat across the desk and wondered why she applied for a job she had absolutely no experience or qualifications for. He asked if she could type. She replied, "No, sir." He asked if she had any accounting experience. She replied, "No, sir." He asked what she took in college, and he burst out laughing when she said art and music.

Then he unabashedly broke the ice and said he was going to hire her because she was the first honest person who had applied for this job, and he was going to find a spot for her. He was amazed at her truthfulness and bravery for even applying for the job in the first place. She had come to the interview in her plaid square dance dress and her hair down. He requested that she get her hair cut and set at a beauty salon nearby. He advised her that all the women in the office were required to wear hose, heels, hat, and gloves.

She acquired her ensemble and reported to work. She was a receptionist and perfect for the job. She had a great voice and was sent for advanced training on the PBX switchboard. The company saw that her good looks and gift of gab made her an excellent receptionist, and soon she was on a first name basis with all the big clients.

This was a fun job, but to make more money, she had to move up the ladder and soon accepted a promotion managing the mail and filing. She loved this job, and soon had all the files rearranged and a file system that was so impressive the partners adopted her filing system in all their offices worldwide.

Once settled, she worked during the day and in the evenings sang in nightclubs with no one to tell her she couldn't. After a year on the job, she wanted to advance her opportunities and asked about further advancement into the accounting department. He agreed and arranged to give her a year of absence while she took accounting courses. After graduation, she would return to the accounting department. She made arrangements to go home to Kansas where she could enroll in Brown Mackie School of Business in Salina, Kansas.

It was 1955, and she was about to make a career change and become a business student and eventually an accountant. But at Brown Mackie, she was destined to meet Gene, the man who would sweep her off her feet with common interests like dancing, music, and fishing. They were all of Donna's favorites, and she was about to find out why they use the phrase "for better or worse" in marriage and why you always get both.

# Gene's Early Years

Carl Eugene "Gene" Londene was born October 13, 1932, on the family homestead near Navarre, Kansas. He was the tenth of eleven children to Fred and Siri.

Gene attended a one-room country school for six years, went to Enterprise, and graduated from Chapman High School in 1950.

He grew up on the Enterprise farm, which was a young boy's paradise. Except, on the day they arrived, Gene and Freddy had a run in with yellow-jacket hornets.

*Gene and Freddy with bee bites.*

It had a creek running over a mile through the farm with lots of fish. It had rabbits, squirrel, pheasant, and quail for hunting and eating. Gene carried a .22 rifle to school and shot cottontail rabbits on the way home. He furnished many a meal when food was scarce. On weekends, he hunted birds and squirrel in the fall. It was a blessing during the tough war years as Fred was unable to work for a while. Gene's oldest brother, Francis, married and moved; Duane entered the army and went to the Pacific; and Gene and younger brother, Freddy, were left to help with the farm. Dorothy, the oldest sister, went to Wichita to weld airplanes in the Boeing factory, Helen left to teach school, and Virgilee married and moved away. Eileen and Joyce, four and two years older, were still in school and had to help with the milking and household chores.

To make some income, Gene trapped muskrats. He sold the hides for three to five dollars and sometimes made twenty-five dollars a week. It brought in cash for the family food supply and a few personal luxuries. Each morning at four-thirty he was up and off with a flashlight running his traps before school. The Navarre and Enterprise homes were heated during the day with only a potbellied stove in the living room and a cooking stove in the kitchen. The bedrooms had no heat. It was cold going to bed. Siri made sacks filled with shelled corn and at about nine o'clock put them in the oven to heat. The family changed to night clothes in the living room, grabbed a hot corn sack, and ran upstairs to jump in the cold bed. All the kids have a warm feeling forever thinking about the comforting warmth of that corn sack.

The kids' shirts, pajamas, and dresses were made at home from colored flour sacks. Gene and Freddy often wore shirts that buttoned down the wrong side because they were hand-me-downs from a sister.

By the time he was eight, Gene spent many a day sitting behind a team of horses or on the tractor on the farm. He got his first driver's license at age thirteen because the family needed a driver and the girls and Siri didn't drive. He had already been driving for three years taking the girls to church on Sundays in the old unheated '29 Chevy. At fifteen, he got a chauffer's license and drove a school bus part time.

Almost all their food was homegrown and canned. Fruit, vegetables, beef, pork, and all food was butchered at home and canned. Everyone was involved. They went to town only for flour, spices, and necessities.

Gene played football, basketball, softball, and track. To keep in shape, he sometimes ran the three miles home from Enterprise after practice or games and still had to help with the milking and chores after he got home. Since all the older boys were off to fight the war, Gene was the starting left guard in football as a freshman. He weighed only ninety-eight pounds with his uniform on. He was small, but fast.

Gene loved music and played the harmonica, guitar, coronet, bass horn, and french horn. He played the bass horn in the marching band. Since it was a small school, he played football the first half, ran to the bleachers in his football uniform to play in the band during half time, and then back into the game for the last half. He excelled in the french horn and advanced to the state festivals where he brought home some ratings of highly superior. On weekends, he was a member of the Civil Air Patrol marching band and performed all over Kansas at various patriotic parades and functions to sell war bonds.

After high school, he worked with his father remodeling houses and building barns and some new chain stores called Dairy Queen when not working on the farm.

In 1951, with the Korean War now raging, Gene enlisted in the air force conditional on becoming a pilot, passed the exams with flying colors, but couldn't pass the physical because of a cut tendon on his little finger. Instead, he was drafted by the army the next day. They weren't as particular. He finished basic training and luckily shipped out for Augsburg, Germany, instead of Korea.

Gene was in charge of all the weapons and ammunition for the artillery battery and pretty much his own boss. He spent most of his time playing on the battalion basketball, volleyball, and table tennis teams, going to the tournament finals in each. He did a lot of intercompany boxing, which he loved.

*Gene in the army, 1952*

After his service duty, he returned to Chapman. He missed his college entrance time. His father had by now retired and closed the construction company, and Gene didn't have a job. A different life was beginning.

# Donna and Gene Meet

Strange circumstances brought Donna and Gene together. Carl Eugene Londene had a farming and construction background, and Donna Allene McCoy was born on a farm but raised in the city, a former college student and singer, and worked as a designer at Neiman Marcus and an accounting firm in Dallas. The two would seem to have very little in common.

Gene had never been out of Kansas until his military service. His life had been farming and construction work, and he had limited education in etiquette and exposure to the business world. None of his family had ever gone to college. After military, he found his first job with Sunflower Insurance Agency in Abilene. He failed at selling insurance, but the agency needed a bookkeeper. In 1954, he enrolled in Brown Mackie Business College in Salina to study accounting.

This is where Gene and Donna met. They were older students intent upon learning an occupation. In Gene's second year, he was hired as an instructor to teach first semester accounting. He was a natural on the manual typewriters. Learning always came easy, and school was no different.

To earn extra income, Gene graded papers. He gave a new student an F on an accounting paper that he thought was poorly done. Soon he found out from his supervisor that she had discussed it with the student and changed it to an A. He complained to the teacher about the incorrect answer, and she told him to forget it. It happened again, and again Gene was told it was fine. This must be a very special student. Donna was there to learn and was serious about her career. Gene was the instructor for her first year accounting class. Among all the other students, Donna stood out; she was older and came to class dressed up from head to toe in the latest Dallas fashion. She had a touch of class not previously seen at Brown Mackie.

When Gene first set his eyes on her, what sank his boat were her long eyelashes and beautiful smile. He had not met her yet, but the battle was already over. He had lost!

Gene made up excuses to spend time tutoring Donna in accounting. Then they were seated alphabetically next to each other in typing class. Donna was still on her first page when Gene whizzed through four pages with his sixty-nine-words-a-minute speed on a manual. Donna was amazed and embarrassed. He offered to help her again, and it gave him more time with her. Donna didn't seem to mind so they worked closely together.

It turned out that the student who was successfully having her grades changed was Donna. She told the teacher that she had worked with a major accounting firm, and this is the way they did it; and if it was good enough for PMM & Co., it was surely good enough for this idiot grader. When she found out Gene had been flunking her papers, she was furious and didn't speak to him for days. She met him in the hallway and said, "What are you doing, trying to get me kicked out of school? You really don't understand accounting anyway." He wasn't given the opportunity to answer and just stood there with his mouth open while she stormed down the stairs.

They met at the school dance, and after a couple of dances, he asked to take her home. She said no to his surprise since he had never been turned down while at Brown Mackie. "You didn't bring me here, so you aren't taking me home. If you can't ask me in advance, you needn't bother," she told him. He had always gone to the dances and picked up a girl there. It was much easier than having to go to their homes and meet the parents.

It was clear he was going to have to formally ask her out on a date. They went to a movie, and she revealed that she enjoyed dancing with him. The next evening they went to Salina's only nightclub called the Sahara Club. She was an excellent dancer, and he had learned all the Latin American dances while in Germany. The two fit like a glove. They had some ups and downs, but it was not long before the depth of their feelings prompted a conversation about marriage. Donna set the conditions of a marriage by clearly saying, "If you want to marry me, you need to leave Brown Mackie and the insurance business, go to college to earn a degree to become a certified public accountant, and work for PMM & Co." Gene blinked a few times but said he would enroll in college at Kansas State University in Manhattan.

In the following years, they would always maintain they got married because of their dancing, and anytime they had a family feud, they would go dancing to overcome their differences on a dance floor. It's difficult to stay mad at a beautiful woman when you are holding her close dancing and smelling the perfume in her hair.

Soon they were spending all their free time together. Gene lived in a boarding house and didn't have a private room or bath. Donna had a single room and bath but no kitchen. Together they decided they needed privacy, and the only way they could get better living conditions was to get married and live together.

Gene went home and told his parents that he wanted to marry Donna that coming June. Siri was surprised but pleased. Next, Donna and Gene went to Russell and told Donna's folks. Gertie exclaimed, "I am not going to spend a lot of money on another aborted trip to the altar." Donna had already made plans for two weddings and backed out at the last minute. Mac just listened and smiled and let Gertie rant.

They met with Donna's minister who also did not have much confidence that Donna would follow through with this marriage either. He quizzed Donna as to whether she really wanted to schedule the church or just get married privately in the parsonage. He, like Gertie, did not want to go through another cancellation.

Donna's brother and sister both tried to talk her out of it as they had decided it would be Donna who went back to Russell to care for the parents. Gertie proceeded to plan the wedding with great reservations. This time it would be a small family-only wedding. She was going to do this one as simple as possible just in case Donna backed out again. Instead of the huge reception at the Elks Club, it would be in the church basement. There would be only a bridesmaid and a best man; no other attendants except for a ring bearer and ushers.

Gene did not have a suit, but Donna's aunt Gladys came to the rescue and bought him one. Two nights before the wedding, Gene's best man, his younger brother, Freddy, had a car accident and was in the hospital. Now Duane, the older brother, would have to substitute. He had to wear Freddy's suit, which he could barely button, and the pants were a little short. Gene told him if he couldn't zip the pants up, just face the front of the church and not the audience. Lola, his wife, fastened the coat with a safety pin where the button didn't reach. Two hours before the wedding, Gene discovered his car had a flat tire. Was this all an omen? Now it wasn't Donna who was ready to back out.

The wedding hour arrived, Gene and Duane were at the alter, and Donna's sister Dee was brought in from the front door at the last minute as she was almost nine months pregnant and didn't think she could walk all the way down the aisle. Guests still considered it possible that Donna would not show up, but the music started and her dad had her arm and down the aisle they came. When the minister asked if anyone objected to this marriage, Donna looked at her father as if to say, "Save me." Gene also gave him a glance as if to say, "Come on, Pop, jump in there."

He didn't and the minister pronounced them "man and wife" to the joy of all those in attendance.

They left Russell in a shower of rice, tin cans, and a painted-up car. Donna's dad gave them money for a honeymoon in Colorado Springs. But once Donna and Gene removed the tin cans from the car, they decided against the honeymoon road trip and opted for staying overnight in Lindsborg, Kansas. They needed the money more than a honeymoon, and Gene had work and school on Tuesday.

*Donna and Gene's wedding picture, June 3, 1956*

The next afternoon they drove to Salina to start their married life together. Gene went to school in the mornings and worked in a grocery store from noon until six. Donna also continued school.

They rented a house for the summer from some of Donna's friends who were temporarily reassigned. It was a small new house and completely furnished, which was great since Gene and Donna had absolutely no furniture.

Returning from their overnight honeymoon, they set up housekeeping, and the first day Donna boiled hotdogs for lunch, which ended up being a complete disaster with burned food. They didn't know a new pan forms a vacuum, and they couldn't get the lid off. Gene made the remark, "At least it has to get better from here on." Later he would discover Donna was an excellent cook.

Shortly after being in the house, Gene's mom called and wanted to know if they were invited to dinner to see the house. Donna thought this was a little odd that her new parents-in-law would invite themselves to dinner. However, being a good ole girl, she cooked fried chicken, made mashed potatoes and gravy, and prepared a great meal. They had to go through their coats and under the car seats to find money for food. Donna told Gene, "It's your family. You just go buy what I need." At seven o'clock, a great dinner was ready to be served, but no one showed up. Now Donna and Gene were worried there had been a miscommunication. They sat down to wait to see what developed. It wasn't long to find out. There came the knock on the door. There came the entire Londene clan and friends of about thirty folks clear down to the last kid with the ringing cowbells and all the noisemakers. They weren't coming to dinner; it was an old-fashioned Kansas shivaree.

At first Donna was very disappointed and mad that she had slaved all day to make this fabulous dinner, and they weren't coming to dinner at all. She was not aware of the custom of shivarees. This is when all the relatives and friends come to an unannounced housewarming and do all kinds of pranks. They short sheeted the beds so when you got in you could only get your feet down halfway. They put Limburger stinky cheese on your car manifold so that when you started it in the morning it would smell to high heaven; they switched the clothes in the dresser drawers and put peeled grapes in the toe of your shoe. The girls switched the labels on the shaving cream tube and toothpaste tube. At least it wasn't the toothpaste and preparation H. They took out Donna's panties and hid them and in their place were a couple pair that would have fit Dumbo the Elephant. They switched pairs of socks so that nothing matched. They switched the salt and sugar in the bowls. There were so many people it was impossible to watch them all. Everyone had a great time doing their little pranks, and some weren't obvious for weeks. It is a very harrowing experience, but all done in fun. The food didn't go to waste; everything went, including the chicken. Donna was very flustered but took it all in stride until the big Londene boys picked her up, placed her in a wheelbarrow, and pushed her around the block to her desperate embarrassment. Again, she was wondering what kind of family she had married into. It was great relief when everyone left, and Donna and Gene sat down on the couch and breathed big sighs of relief. They were finished meeting family for a while. Time for bed and they would sleep tonight. First, they were finding out all the little things the people had done while they were there.

The next morning Gene was showering and Donna was making breakfast when there came a knock on the door. This strange man, with only one eye, and appearing to be a drunk or an imbecile bum, was at the door. He held his glass eye in his hand that was missing the better part of three fingers and asked Donna if she wanted to hold it and put it back in for him. Donna was trying to get rid of him, but he insisted on coming in, saying he was a repairman there to fix whatever was wrong. Donna told him nothing was wrong, but he insisted and forced himself inside. There he stood, with his eye in his hand, and Donna was getting scared. Next he proceeded to ask Donna how her sex life was.

Donna had enough, now she was really scared. She screamed, "Help, there is a bum here trying to molest me, and he won't leave." Gene rushed to the door ready to do battle, and there stood his brother-in-law Charlie Bean, Dorothy's husband, who worked for the gas company and read meters. Now Donna found out it wasn't just the Londene family that had this weird sense of humor. It was the whole damn tribe of relatives. She eventually becomes great friends with Charlie. He provided humorous situations to the family for years. By now she was wondering what else would surface from this bunch of clowns. Soon she would spend her first Christmas at the Chapman farm, and she would find out the rest of the story.

When Gene got to Kansas State, there was no housing available due to all the new students and the returning Korean veterans going to college. Donna's dad helped them acquire a used eight-by-twenty-one-foot mobile home, which they put on a lot in a new trailer court in a cornfield just east of Manhattan. It was pretty small, but at the time, they were seldom home together except to sleep. Gene would start school Tuesday, and Donna would look for a job.

They moved to a new trailer park occupied with more college students. Here they had a fence, a small grass area, and a beautiful garden where they raised their own tomatoes. In the evening, they sat in the yard with Gene playing the harmonica or guitar and Donna singing. She loved to sing, and her voice carried beautifully; neighbors sat out in their yard listening. People driving on the highway just below the trailer park would slow down and listen. Donna's favorite music was Villa from *Die Fledermaus*, and Gene learned to accompany her. Once or twice a week they went to the Student Union dances, which were free.

Over the next two years, Donna had three miscarriages and was told she would never carry a child. She went through a lot of different jobs before becoming a payroll clerk for the city of Manhattan and singer with a dance band on Friday and Saturday nights. Donna and Gene were both busy with little extra time for more than sleeping.

The last year and a half of school, Gene took all his classes of twenty to twenty-two hours per semester from seven until noon and worked in construction building houses in the afternoons and Saturdays. In the evenings and Sundays, he worked at his cousin's Dairy Queen. Things were financially tough for them, and they had no help from their parents except when they went to the farm and got some eggs. Gene graduated midterm in January 1959, landed a job with PMM &Co in Kansas City, and transferred to Albuquerque, New Mexico. They had made it.

# Donna's Folks to Gene's Folks

When Donna brought Gene home, Gertie was not happy. His first visit to the McCoy house was not a hero's welcome. Gertie had lined Donna up with several rich oil men and did not include a farmer in her repertoire.

Gene was nervous about going to Russell to Donna's home. He had only met her parents once. That was on a Sunday afternoon when Gene and a couple friends stopped by Donna's one-room apartment in Salina to invite her to go driving with them. Gene knocked on her door and Donna answered. She said, "Sure, but let me change clothes." Gene waited just inside the front door of the one-room apartment while Donna went to the bathroom to change.

While she was changing, the door opened behind Gene. There stood this big burly Irishman who immediately inquired in a booming voice, "What are you doing here." This guy looked like a typical oil field worker or Irish barroom brawler, over six feet tall and muscular. He filled the whole doorway and simply said, "I'm Mac McCoy." Gene looked at those huge arms and froze. A cold sweat began, and he felt shivers running up and down his spine.

Donna came out of the bathroom just in time and explained to her father that Gene had just come by to take her driving. She introduced them, and Mac just grunted.

They all went downstairs to the car where Donna's mother sat in the driver's seat in a black suit with a black tam hat and white gloves. She was not overjoyed to see him, and she never got out from behind the steering wheel. After being cordially introduced, she ordered Donna to get in the car, and they left.

All was not lost, and Donna invited him to Russell for dinner with her parents. Gertie, still not pleased, lectured Donna for five minutes on the lack of quality and intelligence of this boy.

Luckily, Mac was an easygoing, jolly Irishman, and easier for Gene to get along with and talk to. He and Gene loved to join in drink, and they were sitting in the living room talking sports. Gertie looked in from the kitchen and told Donna, "Come look, is that boy color blind?" There sat Gene with a red-and-black plaid shirt, blue pants, pink argyle socks, and brown shoes. Gertie never gave up her opinion of Gene, and in spite of this beginning, the marriage happened.

The Londene family having only met the McCoy's at the wedding invited them to their home for a farm dinner. Siri served a roast beef dinner with potatoes and brown gravy and all the trimmings and was well known for being an excellent cook. No one ever left her table hungry or disappointed.

The dinner went off well; they had their dinner, visited a little, and the McCoys left for the hour and a half drive back to Russell. They never came back to the farm, and they made no attempt at any further contact with Gene's family.

They came from two different worlds. The logic of their marriage was like trying to put a square peg in a round hole; it just wouldn't work.

In 1973, Mac and Gertie moved their mobile home to Albuquerque close to the Viola farm until Mac died of cancer at seventy-nine, and Gertie returned to Kansas where she lived out her life in a rest home and died at eighty-two in 1991. Before she died, she disinherited Donna and Dee and left everything to her son, Bob. The girls never believed she signed the papers of her own ability.

When Gertie died, Bob sent Donna a telegram that their mother had died, and he would be handling the estate. The girl delivering the telegram started singing it on the phone when she came to the part that Gertie was dead. Then she said, "Oh my god, they coded this as a singing telegram. I am so sorry." Donna was speechless and shocked that Bob wouldn't even call them. She believed him capable of sending it as a singing telegram. Bob sold all of Gertie's jewelry, investments, and personal items and kept the money. Donna never received a thing from her mother's estate.

Gene's folks lived on the farm in Chapman until 1975 when they moved to Abilene, Kansas, until Siri died in 1972 at the age of seventy-nine. Fred lived there until he entered a home in Abilene and then to a rest home in Chapman, Kansas, where he died at the ripe old age of 105.

# Donna's First Christmas on the Farm

It was Christmas 1956, and all the Londene clan gathered at Fred and Siri's farm north of Chapman. There would be seven families with kids in a small two-bedroom house. Donna and Gene arrived about noon, and she immediately noticed a strange smell. Donna inquired, "Doesn't Fred put lime in the outhouse to control the smell?" As they got closer to the house, the smell got worse. On the porch they passed the wooden kegs of pickled herring, which had their own smell, but the bad smell was coming from the kitchen. Upon entering, they saw all the women gathered around a pot on the stove, and the smell was coming from there. It was Donna's first experience with Swedish cooking and with lutefisk, a Scandinavian fish dish. She was offered a taste but declined. She also declined the Inlagd sill, jellied chicken, and blood pudding. Finally, she found the home made rye bread and feasted on it.

The Londene men were a little ornery. Fred and Siri had both passed on this trait. Francis, Gene's oldest brother, was the biggest practical joker, and Duane was close behind. One of Francis's boys had given him a fart bag for Christmas. They had their fun with it before Donna and Gene arrived, and the stage was set for the next victim. When Donna arrived in the living room where all the men were sitting and talking, there was one chair open. The fart bag was on the chair under the pillow. Gene introduced her to everyone, and Donna accepted the gracious offer from Francis to use the open chair. The sound was loud enough to hear in the kitchen, and Donna jumped up and came unglued. Everyone had a great time about it, except Donna, who was totally shocked in front of all these people she had hardly met and, after expressing some ingratitude, went to the bedroom to cry.

When he quit laughing, Gene finally went into the bedroom to try to talk her into coming out and convinced her it was just a normal Londene Christmas. Gene finally got her back into the living room. Everyone was having coffee. Christmas always called for the traditional smorgasbord of Swedish holiday cooking. There were some of the special Swedish Christmas snacks like cookies, dry bread called knackebrod, and some dried smoked herring. In a little jar on another table was Fred's favorite—small pickled herring. These little fish were about three inches long and were whole fish in a brine sauce. You ate them whole with a piece of knackebrod. Donna got her coffee and sat it down temporarily to be introduced too more arriving relatives.

Setting her cup down was another big mistake. When she picked up her cup and took a drink, there were two little eyes looking at her from the cup. It was a little smoked herring. She had been duped again. She sat her cup down and let Francis have an example of the language she had learned in the oil field working with her dad. Francis made it worse by leading the chorus with his huge laugh.

By now she was beside herself, and after the verbal onslaught she gave to Francis, a truce was called. Siri gave Francis and the boys a sermon that these things would stop and they did. Donna was now officially baptized into the Londene Clan. She survived and wondered what was next.

Donna wondered where the boys got their strange sense of humor and love of playing pranks. On the next trip to the farm she would find out. Fred was a great prankster, but Siri took the cake. Gene and Donna had driven to the farm to play Canasta. Pop had gone to work that day. About six o'clock, he came walking in the door, stopped and without saying a word, threw a wet dishrag at Siri, hitting her right in the face. Gene and Donna were shocked, and expected a battle, but Siri just stood there with her hand over her mouth to conceal the laughter as she always did. It was April Fools' day. She had fixed Fred's lunch that day, which normally consisted of a couple sandwiches, a hardboiled egg, a fruit, and a quart of cold coffee. When he stopped for lunch and bit into this sandwich made of two slices of homemade rye bread, he found it could not be chewed. Siri had wet a dishrag, folded it neatly, and put it in the sandwich.

Donna was amazed Siri had done this. Siri loved pranks, and many of her friends got to know that side of her too. It was unexpected because her outward appearance was of this loveable little four-foot-eleven-inch pixie of a woman. Siri also told about the time she hosted the monthly women's card party. She was known for her great Swedish deserts. She made a three-layered angel food cake and covered the edge with little round chocolates filled with candy. She had also purchased a bag of little onions and dipped them in chocolate and placed them around the edge of the cake so that each piece would have to get an onion. The women all ate the cake, exchanged some quizzical glances among them, but no one said a word. She giggled as she told the story. Then Fred mentioned previous April Fools' Days when she sent hard-boiled eggs for his lunch, he thought until he cracked them and they fell in his lap. He also had not appreciated the little sweet desert cakes filled with mustard and horseradish or the coffee with vinegar in it.

Donna thought Siri was cute and loved hearing the April Fools' Days pranks the family played. Donna began to get the picture of where the boys got their orneriness. It was all inherited from both sides.

After dark, Evelyn played the piano, Gene and Freddy the guitars and harmonicas, Fred the fiddle, Dorothy's husband Charles the spoons, and they made music. Meanwhile, what seemed like hundreds of kids ran wild in the house. Kids were in all the rooms playing games. The grown-ups were all around the kitchen table playing pinochle, pitch, spoons, or pig.

The next summer Donna would realize how deep this love for humor was. Siri's brothers Hugo and Arthur had also emigrated from Sweden with her and came to visit the farm each year. Sunday was a big family dinner, and Donna and Gene drove out to meet them. Donna said to Arthur, "I love to hear you speak in Swedish. It is a beautiful singsong language. Can you teach me some?"

Arthur said, "I will teach you a phrase to tell Siri how wonderful her dinner was." After dinner while everyone was sitting around the table, Arthur announced, "Donna is a smart girl. She has already learned some Swedish." Donna said okay she would try and said her phrase to Siri. Siri immediately yelled things at Arthur in Swedish who just sat and laughed with everyone else, except Donna; she had just told her new mother-in-law her food tasted like crap.

Gene and Donna stayed at the house overnight, and the rest of the families went home since all lived within a few miles. It was so peaceful to have everyone gone and to just sit around the heating stove for a while and have another cup of coffee with Fred, Siri, and maybe Freddy and Joyce. It was nice having all the family together for a day, but it was an unimaginable noisy zoo.

Finally, about midnight, it was time for bed, and Donna survived her first Christmas at the farm. Years later while celebrating Christmas in their own house, Gene and Donna still had great memories of Christmas at Fred and Siri's farm and by now Donna could even smile.

# Arriving in Albuquerque

The day after graduation from Kansas State on January 31, 1959, Donna and Gene said good-bye to their friends and family and left Kansas to drive to Albuquerque. Mac arranged to trade in the twenty-one-foot trailer for a brand-new eight-by-thirty-five-foot Marlette mobile home complete with appliances and furniture and the seller delivered it to Albuquerque.

In Kansas, the hottest thing they ever ate was a bell pepper. Being the curious type at their first meal in Albuquerque, Gene took a whole pepper from this little jar and popped it into his mouth and started to chew. The sensation and results were instantaneous. He was unable to speak and grabbed for a glass of water. His eyes were watering so bad he couldn't find the water glass. Drinking water was his second mistake, now that thing was in his stomach and had burned all the way down. How would he get it out, induce vomiting or light a match and just let it burn out? The waiter saw his suffering and brought a glass of milk. Surely this was not something the natives ate; it must be just for tourists. Wisely, Donna passed on the peppers. The next morning he came to another realization; the hot chili comes out with the same intensity it went in. Welcome to New Mexico, gringo.

After work, Gene picked up Donna at the Blue Spruce Lodge and drove to their new home, which was there and ready, and they moved in. After three months, they decided to live in the mountains and for seventy-five dollars they moved the trailer to a mobile home park in the East Mountains. They loved being outdoors, then Donna discovered she was pregnant. Given her history of miscarriages, the doctor advised that she get back into town to a lower altitude and stay home. They moved again to the North Valley.

In 1959, it took one year as an apprentice to be eligible to get a CPA certificate. Gene's starting salary was $325 per month, and Donna found a job that paid $400 per month. Gene could only rationalize the insult by the fact that he got overtime pay during tax season. Just to make it more demoralizing, the local newspaper headline read "Dogcatcher salary raised to $400 a month."

They were doing well for a while. Donna worked through six months of pregnancy before needing to get off her feet and stay home. A change in altitude increased ones ability to get pregnant. Donna seems to have gotten pregnant on the day they arrived in Albuquerque. It must have been the hot chili Gene ate that night.

The summer of 1959 was not pleasant for Donna; she quit her job and stayed home. She was pregnant and sickly, and there was no air conditioner.

As time got closer to delivery, Gene wanted to name the baby after the Blue Spruce Lodge where it was conceived. Donna decided the names of Dennis for a boy or Denise for a girl. Donna reiterated, "If you want to name the baby, you have one."

With two weeks to go, Donna was now obviously very pregnant, but she still felt good and could still dance and get around. She insisted on joining Gene at the quarterly bank meeting in Santa Fe. After dinner, Gene and Donna went to the ground floor of the La Fonda and found a Mexican band playing dance music. They began dancing and had a great time until the manager came over and requested they not dance anymore. He was worried about a dance floor delivery.

Gene got home from work, and Donna said, "Let's go, now." The hospital was four miles away. The new baby girl was born shortly after arrival.

For Gene, the timing of the birth could not have been worse; it came the evening before he was scheduled to start the four-day CPA exam. The baby had a problem with projectile vomiting and neither Mom nor Dad was able to get much rest. Gene took his exams between running back and forth to the hospital. He ended up getting himself so exhausted that on the last day he fell asleep during the exam and just turned in what he had done up to that time.

When Donna and Denise were released from the hospital, the new parents had a lot to learn. Gene was totally unprepared due to having so many sisters and women in his family; he never did any of the baby stuff. Denise was not being breast-fed and not adapting to the formulas. They sent her home from the hospital with a soybean formula. Day and night they would feed baby Denise, and she would projectile vomit this horrible-smelling stuff. After several weeks of trying different formulas, they called the doctor who readmitted her to the hospital two days before New Year's eve. Gene and Donna went home and slept for sixteen straight hours. Finally, the hospital called and said they had found the magic formula; the baby was eating and sleeping with no more vomiting. The new formula was regular cow's milk right off the Safeway store shelf.

The next day they picked up baby Denise and went home. Remarkably, Gene got his CPA exam results a few months later, and to his surprise, he passed three of the four parts. He failed the theory part by six percentage points taken on the last day when he went to sleep. If he could have stayed awake thirty more minutes, he may have gotten it all. But he was delighted to have passed three of the four parts considering the circumstances. He was determined to get it the next time and he did!

It was nice having a baby in the house, but it was tough getting along on just one salary. They learned to do things that were inexpensive, like playing bridge, canasta, and poker. Their main interests outside the house was still dancing and fishing.

Gene and Donna's favorite was a western nightclub called the Hitching Post with a local band headed by a young singer named Glen Campbell. They went Friday, Saturday, and Wednesday nights on a regular basis. They sat at a table close to the bandstand and became very good friends with the band members who would sit with them during intermission and bum cigarettes. Glen referred to the breaks as a "Wee, wee intermission."

Glen invited Donna to the Sunday afternoon jam session to sing with the band. Years later, when Glen Campbell became rich and famous, Donna would regret not having committed to sing with him on a regular basis. It was a sad day when Glen announced he was leaving Albuquerque to become a star with his own TV show.

They decided that since Gene had now passed the CPA exam and had received a huge $50 per month raise, it might be the right time to consider purchasing a house. They were living the American dream and climbing that social ladder, and they were enjoying life to the fullest.

# Lexington House Purchase 1961

The thoughts of a second child were dictating a larger house. Since Gene was a Korean veteran, they could buy a house with no money down. In the 1960s, the American dream had gone beyond a chicken in every pot to a car in every garage, and now a new house in suburbia for every family. They found a split-level three-bedroom house they loved. Gene changed jobs, and his salary was now an astronomical $500 per month. To qualify for a home loan, all they needed was a job. They now had a huge $108 house payment and their gas, electric, water, and telephone were a total of $25 a month.

They moved in and the first night in the new house they had a bed in the master bedroom and Denise's baby crib in the other, a card table, four chairs, and a rocking chair. This was all they owned since everything was built into the mobile home they sold. They sat on the empty living room floor and decided what they had to buy. A trip to Dial Finance and American Furniture got them started.

When they finished the basement a year later, they had a housewarming party and invited all their friends. While it was a great party, it would be a while before they would do that again. The next morning, Donna's diamond rings were missing, and she had no recollection of taking them off. Now it had become a very expensive party. Days later, she found them on the second story bathroom window ledge outside. What a party?

Donna's yard was a showcase of flowers. They followed Siri's advice to mulch in all the coffee grounds, apple peels, and fruit waste around the plants every week and take cigarette butts from the ashtrays and spread around the plants and rose bushes. When the roses budded, they made a watering can and filled it with cigarette butts and ground garlic and watered the roses weekly. They never had aphids or bugs. In addition, the filters on the cigarette butts make good water-absorbent mulch around the plants.

Darlene, the second child, was born November 22, 1962. Darrell was born February 4, 1965, and the household would never be the same. They felt they had completed their family with the arrival of Darrell, a boy to join the two girls. It was about this time they got new neighbors. Charlie, a geologist, and Eileen, a secretary for the Internal Revenue Service, moved in. In the beginning they seemed unneighborly. Denise broke the ice with her tricycle that had a squeaky wheel. She rode in front of the houses. One day, Charlie could stand it no more; he got the oil and quieted her tricycle.

From here sprang a lifelong friendship. Charlie and Gene both traveled extensively for their jobs, and on weekends, the families became fishing buddies. Charlie refused to have children, so Eileen became very attached to the Londene children becoming a great friend and help to Donna. She often took the kids to church and lunch, introducing the kids as hers.

Eileen had no family except her mother back in Indiana whom she seldom saw. She found a friend to visit with in Donna and told many stories of her mysterious mother. One day during the Cuban Missile Crisis they were showing footage of tourists in Cuba when Eileen jumped up and said to Charlie, "That's my mother." Her seventy-five-year-old mother was walking in the street in Havana carrying her little plaid satchel. Her mother had been employed by the Federal Government for over forty years as a "seamstress" on parachutes. Eileen knew her mother disappeared for weeks at a time, and she always said she was on vacation. One time the children went home to visit her only to find out she had left the day before unannounced and left them only a note to enjoy themselves. A few years later, her mother retired and was given a dinner in Washington, DC. Her plaque read, "For Forty Years of Seamstress Work." Only then did Eileen find out her mother had been a federal agent for all that time. Her many vacations were really assignments, and they took her all over the world. Who would suspect a seventy-five-year-old grandmother of being a spy?

Donna had kids to care for and did not go back to work. The family fell into a routine where Gene got home, had dinner, and enjoyed helping with bathing the kids and putting them to bed by eight o'clock. Donna was exhausted and welcomed his arrival. The kids learned that going to bed meant sleep. Donna and Gene were severely criticized by their friends for child cruelty for letting the children cry themselves to sleep. They followed the example of both their mothers who believed it was good for a child to cry itself to sleep occasionally. This practice allowed Gene and Donna to have quiet time for themselves and friends. Many of their friends couldn't have company because their children were so undisciplined and unbearable. Gene and Donna concluded that the one good use for Dr. Spock's childrearing book was to spank the kids when it was absolutely necessary.

Darrell was now three months old, and Donna had him lying on the living room floor on a blanket while Darlene played next to him drawing on a piece of paper. Darrell was grabbing her paper, and she had enough of his antics. Suddenly, another of those house-filling bloodcurdling screams. It was another rush to the living room for Donna. This time there was no blood. Instead, there lay Darrell with a wooden pencil sticking out of his forehead. Darlene had decided to put an end to this unwanted new arrival and had buried the pencil so deep in his forehead that it just hung there.

It had gone through the skin, and it was buried in the bone. Donna grabbed him up and called the neighbor, Eileen, who by now was always on a "911" status. Eileen drove and Donna sat in the backseat holding the boy, keeping him from grabbing the pencil. They didn't need a police escort to get to the hospital this time as Darrell's screaming was probably louder than any siren. In those days, everyone drove with the window open as air conditioning in cars was not yet for the common folks. The ER removed the pencil and dug out the imbedded lead. It would heal, but it left a permanent mark. Donna realized that if anyone ever kidnapped that boy, or if he got lost, the finder would have no problem identifying him. Once they got to know him, they would probably bring him back anyway.

They had completed building the bar in the basement when Darrell was about two, and somehow Darrell learned how to play king of the mountain at an early age. After accomplishing the climb up the bar, it was a short trip to the aquarium on the end of the bar. Donna had purchased four small goldfish for the new aquarium. She hadn't heard any sounds from the basement for a while, so she went down the steps to see what he had been doing to entertain himself. He was standing on the edge of the bar with both hands in the water of the aquarium peacefully holding the small net for cleaning the pool and swishing both hands through the water.

After removing him from the bar and aquarium, Donna replaced the bubble tube and then noticed there were no goldfish in the water. Fruitless questioning of a two-year-old usually doesn't produce good answers. She couldn't get him to say what happened to the goldfish. She hunted them, and when Gene got home, he hunted them. Darrell finally indicated he had eaten them. Could this be true? They certainly couldn't be found. It was probably true. She would have to feed him more often.

In the mid to late 1960s the favorite program for kids was Batman. Someone had the foolish forethought to buy the boy a batman mask. He had made a cape from a tea towel, and he wore the cape and mask constantly while he played. He even slept and ate in it. All was well until the inevitable happened. The boy was in the basement playing, and Donna was on the phone upstairs. She heard the yell, "Batman," and heard the thud on the floor in the basement. Her worst suspicions were confirmed when the next thing she heard was a bloodcurdling scream from the basement filling the house like darkness. She raced down to the basement, and there he lay in a pool of blood. He had dived headfirst off the bar onto the tile-covered cement floor. He had a long gash under his chin and was bleeding profusely.

He had stopped screaming and was gasping for air for the next assault. Naturally, Gene was out of town in Grants seventy miles away. Donna was in a state of panic. She called her neighbor, Eileen, and the two of them gathered him up and headed for emergency. It took eight stitches under the chin and left him with a lifelong reminder of how Batman really didn't fly. Donna came to the stark realization that there really is no way to return a boy. You made him; you got him.

Sometime before this adventure, Donna and Eileen were sitting out in the back yard having a midmorning cup of coffee. The kids were playing in the backyard on the swing set and sand pile. Darrell had just turned nine months old. Donna had her back to the swing set when Eileen stood up and said to Donna, "Do not panic, do not get excited, but get up very slowly and go to the swing set." This was totally worthless advice. The only part Donna followed was get to the swing set. Her haste was generated by her first glance at the situation. It was a multiple swing set and had a three-inch pipe top about eight-feet long.

There was Darrell, crawling from one end to the other on top of the swing set on the top rail. This rail is about seven feet off the ground, and there is no ladder to get up there. How did he do it? He surely couldn't climb up the leg of the swing set, but he did. He was playing acrobat. He came down willingly and then made the inevitable statement, "Again." Happy hour came early that day.

In 1968, they decided it was time the kids had a dog. It was a pretty little black and white female. Donna named it Nipsy. Their neighbor, an air force captain, had married this nice lady, Solvieg, from Norway. He was sent on an extended tour, and she had remained there with the children and dog. She was in America for the first time and had brought her dog with her.

The dog was a highly registered Norwegian elkhound named Bompsa. A beautiful black and gray that looked much like an Alaskan husky. He was "in the book" of registration. Solvieg decided to take a two-month trip to her home in Norway. She could not take the dog with them. Donna volunteered to keep the dog; it could stay in the backyard and play with Nipsy. Donna and Gene used the same vet, so it would be no problem. Famous last words as usual. The vet was a tax client of Gene's named Jim, just getting started in his practice. Solveig was ready to depart and brought the dog up on a chain.

One extremely cold, icy, snowy winter day, Gene was working in his office. The phone rang. Donna called in a panic, "You have to come immediately. The dogs are frozen together to the swing set. One is pointed one way and the other the other way, and they can't get loose from the leg of the swing set. They are frozen to it."

Gene knew animals, so immediately knew the situation of what had happened. He calmly asked, "How do you know where are they frozen?"

Donna replied, "Their rears are frozen together, and they are both trying to go a different way, and they got wrapped around the swing set, and I think they are frozen to the swing set." Gene decided to have Donna call his client Jim, a veterinarian, who had a very good sense of humor.

He spoke that phrase that followed Donna for the rest of their lives. He suggested that Donna call the vet. Jim received the panic call, and Donna explained the situation and quickly recited in one long breath, "The dogs are frozen together and frozen to the metal swing set leg, and should I take out some hot water to pour on them to free them before they freeze to the post?"

There was silence from Jim as he was trying to regain his composure and come up with an answer that would solve the problem and not offend Donna. Finally, he said in a low official professional voice, "Why don't you pull the drapes, turn on the TV, and then watch the TV uninterrupted for the next two hours?" Donna heard the voices behind Jim at the clinic, as he often used the speakerphone when he was busy, and she heard the guffawing and the snickering. Donna hung up and realized she had been duped. Her first clue was the somewhat humorous tone of voice in Jim's answer and the giggling of the people in the background. She called her friend and boss Fred who raised dogs, and he explained the process of dogs mating.

She phoned Gene and called him every word she had learned from construction workers. By the time Gene returned home from work that evening, it was clear he was in the doghouse again. Donna got over her anger but the phrase "call the vet" would follow this family forever. The episode embarrassed Jim, the veterinarian, enough that he never returned to Gene for his tax services. Also, that night, there was no dinner on the table when Gene got home. It was peanut butter and jelly again. She just didn't appreciate his humor.

*Nipsy and Bompsa. Expecting parents.*

Gene attended district bank meetings regularly, but his company would not pay for wives to attend these out of town trips. Gene found out from other officers that when they took their girl friends, expenses were approved. Gene didn't have a girl friend, and Donna came up with a solution. She dyed her hair blond, bought a new low-cut dress, and enjoyed the weekend bank meeting in Juarez. Donna was the social butterfly of the party. Gene never introduced her by her name, and when word got back to the company president that Gene was there with a girlfriend, his expense report was approved.

Within a few years, all the household projects were done, and they became bored with city life and the poor quality of their neighbors. Their only real friends on the block were Eileen and Charlie, so they all decided it was time to look for a farm.

# Looking for a Farm (1968)

They looked and priced many places in the North Valley. They needed some land for horses, but it had to have a house on it. They could never find the right combination and price range for what they wanted and dreamed about in college—an old house to remodel and a place to have horses.

By 1968, Gene was now making $1,300 per month. They had a comfortable income and enjoyed spending their summers going fishing and going to horse races. They dreamed about having their own farm and horses.

One beautiful April morning, Gene was sitting at the breakfast table finishing breakfast and coffee before work. He flipped through the paper. An AD caught his eye in the farm section listing "Five acres with wells and horse corrals, 4BR Terrone Adobe House, South Valley."

He showed the AD to Donna and suggested she call and inquire about the property. She made arrangements to meet the realtor there. All they knew about South Valley was that it was occupied by a few scattered homesteaders who did not take kindly to intruders moving into their neighborhood.

With a single visit, Donna was convinced. She called Gene told him to take his lunch break and come see the place. Upon arriving at the Viola Road address, he proceeded through the chain-link gate. He drove past a row of large cottonwood trees just budding out. There were spots of green grass and lilacs just ready to bloom. It was very pleasant looking. As he drove in, he glanced to his left, and there was a grove of elm trees in what looked to have been a small lake. Next to it was a dilapidated small old mobile home, which appeared to be inhabited. He drove the two hundred feet from the front of the property to the house and then drove around the big two-story adobe home. It sat up on a little hill with vines and bushes growing up to the eaves of the house and covering two sides of the house completely. It had ivy growing to the top of the north peak of the house. It looked like the abandoned haunted house in Disneyland.

*Rear view of Viola house, porch and upper porch*

It was late April, and the budding trees and greening grass with the occasional flowers and bushes made a beautiful picture. While the house was run-down, they were thrilled to see horses in the corrals and pasture and saw the beauty of the place.

Behind them were open pastures and alfalfa fields clear to the irrigation ditch. The place was isolated and private. The corrals were of old weathered wood. There were some new chain-link pens, and all were full of racehorses. What a beautiful sight. This was the answer to their dreams. It had some acreage, a big old house in need of remodeling, and a place to raise horses. As Gene looked around, he noticed two long adobe buildings, which had never been plastered or finished and had several rooms with many windows.

The house and the two long buildings formed a very large courtyard in old Spanish style. About a hundred feet or more to the west were the corrals and three horse stalls. Next to the house, adjacent to the grape arbor, was a beautiful black stallion in a six-foot chain-link pen and stall with electric wire around the top. It was later explained by the sellers that the two long buildings were built in the 1870s when an Englishman named C. R. Ellis homesteaded the property. In the center of the large courtyard area was a little three-room house covered with tar paper. It was very old and in very bad condition.

It was learned from the realtor that Ellis built this old house and lived in it until they moved into the new house in 1932. It had apparently been rebuilt several times after fires and was now used as a storage building. They looked inside and were amazed by the newspaper used for wallpaper. The first one caught their attention. It was a 1922 AD for cars for sale. It said, "Ford $20 and Chevy $15." It was interesting reading the walls. As a family, they sat on the wooden rails of the corral and admired the horses. They speculated what they could do with this place. The kids were already planning a tree house in the big old cottonwood trees. It had so much possibility, but it was going to be so much work.

*First visit to farm, April 1968*

About that time, the realtor returned, and they were to get a tour of the house. The realtor explained there were twelve or more dogs in the house, but she had talked to Mrs. W, and the dogs would be locked in the bedroom, which meant they would not be able to see the bedroom. This was okay, but they immediately started thinking about how to get the dog smell out of the house. The realtor explained that the house had been listed for over six months for $49,000, and they had not had a single offer after people came to the house. This was getting scary. Maybe the house was haunted. The realtor went in to talk to Mrs. W to make sure the dogs were locked up.

As Gene and Donna nervously waited, they walked to the edge of the house and looked around the farm some more, trying to convince themselves they should stay. Behind the stallion pen was a grove of elm trees very tall and thin. They would find out later this was the grape arbor, which was planted with grapes imported from England in 1877. The grapes were fighting for sunlight, and they were at least thirty feet up in the top of the elm trees.

The outlying areas were piles of junk and weeds. The house had not been painted or given much maintenance in years.

The homeowners were in their seventies and wanted to sell the property in order to retire. Mrs. W had snow-white hair and was very hard of hearing and seeing as she toured them through the house she yelled instead of talked. Her poor eyesight explained the unclean appearance of the house since she could not see the cobwebs and dirt. She explained that the house had been started in 1922 with the building of the concrete basement and foundation. Then each year the adobe mud bricks were cut from the Bermuda grass "colechi" or clays in the pasture, and two feet of wall was laid per year. The bricks were laid wet, and the Bermuda grass grew through the bricks before it died, which held the bricks together. This was most interesting, and Gene was having a tough time convincing himself he was interested in buying a mud house.

This type of adobe block building is called terrone adobe. This contrasted to the commercial adobe blocks, which are made in boxes with straw like the Old Testament people made for the Romans. In the upstairs of the house, the unfinished rooms still had the grass hanging out the sides, which had grown after the bricks were laid, and before the grass died. The walls appeared to need a shave. They got the walls up to the level of three feet above the first floor, or approximately twelve feet, and capped it with a lumber plate. In the unfinished bedroom, Gene could see that the lumber used in the house was rough-hewn full two-by-seven inch. Everything was nailed with what looked like thirty penny nails. They were huge.

The upstairs was a typical English farmhouse style with an attic-type roof. It had a six-foot dormer-type window on each side of the house in the main bedrooms. It was 1920s construction, and the rooms downstairs were plastered with a one-inch hard-plaster finish. The hallway upstairs, which ran the full forty-eight-foot length of the house, and the bathroom were plastered.

The west side had been very roughly finished into an apartment, and the east side was partially finished. The rest of the upstairs remained unfinished, only the studs on the dividers.

Downstairs, the kitchen, bathroom, and master bedroom were painted. The living room and spare bedroom were the original unpainted plaster. The kitchen had a sink and cabinets, and the bathroom was complete. The kitchen lacked plug-ins and the refrigerator was plugged into the bathroom with a long cord lying on the floor. In 1947, they put the water heater outside of the house in a shipping crate adjacent to the screened-in porch. To keep the water heater from freezing, a single light bulb hung inside the crate. It was ironic that Mr. W was the County Fire Marshall, a real life case of the "cobbler with no shoes." The whole house and buildings were undoubtedly unsafe and in violation of every county code on the books. A gross case of neglect.

Mrs. W said that in 1932 the Ellises felt the house was complete enough to move in. The kitchen and bedroom were finished and painted. Mr. and Mrs. Ellis and their three sons began the move into the house, carrying personal items and furniture from the old house. She said Mr. Ellis had worked very hard for years building the house, farming the land and running the dairy. All this while he was working in the railroad roundhouse in Belen. Every Friday night when he came home he would bring a used runner from a wrecked railroad car, and these became the floor joists for the house. A trip to the basement revealed runners from several train lines.

Mr. Ellis was probably in excellent shape for an old farmer. However, while carrying furniture from the old house into the new he had a heart attack and died. He never got to live in his dream house. The widow and children ran the farm and dairy until 1947 when they sold to Mr. and Mrs. W., who did little to improve, finish, or maintain the house after they bought it.

After Mr. Ellis's death parcels of the property were sold off and the last fifteen acres with the house were sold to the Ws in

1947, and they sold off two- and three-acre parcels until all that remained was the house and five acres.

Gene lifted one of the throw rugs, saw the damaged layers of linoleum, and immediately thought this place was mission impossible. It was very creepy. Mrs. W explained the ceiling was black because they roasted pheasants in the fireplace. Since the living room had never been painted the raw plaster absorbed the soot and turned black.

Up to this point, Gene and Donna were not too impressed with the house, and it was obvious why it did not sell. But Gene recognized the quality wood and finish work. He noted the floor, upstairs and down, was all narrow gauge high-quality oak. The landing floor and the steps were all of bird's-eye maple. The posts and trim were of well-finished softwood, probably ash. He was beginning to realize this was not a cheaply constructed house. It was just totally mistreated.

All the original construction was first class. Some washing, and a lot of primer paint, would do wonders. Some of the oak flooring was still in dust-covered bundles lying on the floor of the unfinished rooms upstairs where Mr. Ellis left them when he died in 1932. Again, Gene was amazed at the size of the studs and rafters and the enormous size of the nails. An earthquake would never hurt this house. The oak floors upstairs had never been filled and finished, and again, they were covered with throw rugs.

Mr. W showed them the old adobe buildings and explained they were living quarters for the farm help when the farm and dairy were in their heyday. Most of them now were used as storage and a chicken house.

Gene didn't know if he was up to this challenge or not. After all, he was thirty-five years old, and he didn't know if he had enough time left in his life to clean up this mess. He was thinking of his little maintenance-free new house in the heights and wondering why he would even consider this undertaking.

But when the tour was over, Gene and Donna and children agreed the farm was what they wanted. However, the $49,000 asking price was way beyond what they could afford given how much restoration was going to be required. They went back to their heights home disappointed, and Gene went back to work realizing they would never be able to buy some land with a house on it.

# Purchase of Viola Farm (1968)

That evening, Donna and Gene explained to the kids why they couldn't buy the farm. That weekend, Gene and Donna were going to El Paso to the horse races. Gene had decided to delay making the monthly $108 house payment so they would have money to go to the races. It would normally be a stupid move, but they had a very good record of winning at the horse races and considered it a part-time job. Years before, Gene and Donna had developed a system of betting the horses based on the history that horses that won in the spring would continue to win in the spring. Horses have hay fever and almost all the diseases humans have. Some horses are seasonal and run well only at certain times of the year. Donna had come up with the theory that horses cycle and will win every third or fourth race. Since this was prior to computers, they used a card, and each week with three friends they met on Thursday nights to cut up the race forms and paste the horse's history on the card. They had a lifetime record on every horse that ran in New Mexico.

Friday night they picked out their long-shot horses they would play at the track. and they were off to Sunland Park at El Paso for the weekend. They had refined the system to playing any big money on just a few horses at each track. Some times, they placed bets with a few different bookies, but soon the bookies quit taking their bets because of the consistent payoffs and the long shots they picked. This weekend they were headed to El Paso at Sunland Park to play a horse called Missile Pit.

About 4:30 PM, just as Gene was trying to get out of the office, the realtor called and asked if he was going to make an offer on the property. Gene said no, they could not afford the price. The realtor explained that due to health problems the owners would entertain an offer well below the asking price. Gene was in a hurry to get off the phone so he said sure; he would trade houses even up. The realtor said they would not accept that; they wanted cash money.

Gene knew he could sell his house for over $20,000, so he offered $22,000 with $250 down payment and asked that the owners carry the real estate contract. He did not have the $250, but it was a small matter since he did not think the sellers would consider his offer. At this point, Gene was more interested in getting the realtor out of his office so he could head to the races. The realtor called back and said they needed a $5,000 down payment, and Gene went along sure that none of this was going to work out. He signed a contract and promptly forgot the whole matter. He was so sure that this offer would never fly that he didn't ever remember to mention it to Donna.

They arrived home late Sunday night, counted their hard earned $300 that they had won by playing an old mare named Purple Violet who had won at El Paso in April for three consecutive years and a substantial bet on Missile Pit who also won. The system worked. Purple Violet had returned $54 for each $2 ticket and Missile Pit had paid $4.80. They had done very well by parlaying one horse to the other. All expenses of the trip were paid plus the $300 profit.

Monday morning at about 9:00 AM, Gene's office phone rang; it was Donna. She asked if they had made an offer on the property. Gene said, "Yes, I just forgot to tell you because they will never accept it."

After an eternity, she spoke, "They accepted your offer." The words ran through Gene's spine like a volt of electricity, and he had a little tickling sensation run up his back. Donna told him he was to call the realtor to arrange to pay the deposit of $5,000. His first thought was to grab the wastebasket in case he upchucked. What kind of fraud had he committed?

Gene sat in his office and fumed for half an hour and came to the realization he had to make some arrangement to get the money or figure a way out of this thing before calling the realtor. He had only one solution; he had to go talk to his boss about a pay advance and sign a note with the company or something. He walked into the boss's office as if he was going to his execution. Gene sat down and explained that he had made the $5,000 offer to buy a farm in the valley, and they had accepted the offer. He also explained that he had no possibility of raising the money. Gene explained that he needed to borrow some money from the company, or if the company could help him get a bank loan, and he could pay it back when his Lexington house sold. It was a very embarrassing situation.

The boss was a big man of Italian descent raised in the tough area of Chicago and was not a particularly generous person. Gene was hoping his nervousness wasn't apparent. He was feeling a little squeamish. After what seemed an eternity, without a word, the boss picked up the phone and dialed. Obviously, he was calling the payroll clerk to make out Gene's final check.

Someone answered the phone, and the boss made a very short statement, "Gene is coming out to the bank today. Prepare him an installment note for $5,000 at 5 percent interest payable over five years." Gene's heart started to beat again. He could have jumped up and kissed that big hairy Italian. Well, maybe not that happy.

The company had just bought a bank in Grants, New Mexico, that year; and the bank would make the loan. Gene called the realtor and said he would have the deposit tomorrow. Then he called Donna and explained that all was well; they would own the farm. He knew she was sitting at home more upset at his antics than he was. He got in his car and drove the seventy miles to the bank and came home with the check. This time, there would be dinner on the table when he got home; he was out of the doghouse.

Now the real problems began to bubble up in Gene's mind. They were so happy in their little yard in the heights with all the spare time for recreation. Why did he do this? He didn't get to sleep for a while.

They agreed on a final cost of $23,500 and closed on the property in a week. Mr. and Mrs. W said they would be out, and the buyers could have possession by June 1. They were going to the farm, and they were going to be horse farmers. Actually, horse ranchers sounded better. They were already planning putting up the big overhead log entrance that said, "Londene Horse Race Farm," just like in Kentucky.

Gene had some idea of what it was going to take to get this done, but Donna had a real education coming. He was thinking of the dirt and cobwebs, and she was thinking of all the remodeling she could do. They both loved the thought of getting into that old house and starting the remodel. The next evening they drew up plans on refinishing of the old place.

The family had a party to celebrate the purchase of the farm with Charlie and Eileen who by this time had become part of the Londene family. They celebrated holidays together, traveled with the family, and were legally named guardians of the children. Eileen and Charlie had been going fishing with the family. The two families had become inseparable. So it seemed natural to invite them to buy a mobile home and move to the Viola Farm since there was already a trailer space with utilities there.

Gene had lived with horses all his life and began making plans to acquire a thoroughbred or quarter horse mare. Donna and Eileen got busy with plans for remodeling the house. Charlie had another drink and cigarette and watched.

The kids were getting excited about who was going to get a pony and everything else that walked or swam. The wanted ducks, cats, rabbits, and Donna wanted a pig and a cow. Gene wanted racehorses. Little did they realize that in less than a year, all this would come true, plus turkeys, ducks, sheep, a cow, and a stinking goat. They would inherit about five hundred pigeons, a few skunks, gophers, some pheasant, and at least twenty-four peacocks with the farm.

*First visit to farm, April 1968*

Donna was scared by a chicken as a young girl and was frightened of anything with feathers. While she wanted to have chickens and fresh eggs at the farm, she did not realize the care that would entail.

The family adapted to farm life quickly, but Donna's family was horrified by what they had done in buying this dilapidated property. Gene had taken a picture of the old tar papered house they were going to tear down and sent it to Donna's mother with a note, "Look what I bought for your daughter." The backlash was terrific.

*Hundred-year-old tar paper and wood original homestead house.*

The Lexington house sold quickly, and the family began packing. Friends who were dying to see the place would come to help paint after work. Gene had arranged to be off work for a full week to prepare their new home for living. He hadn't realized yet what he thought would take a few days was actually going to take years.

# Moving to Viola Farm (1968)

Moving from the relatively new house on Lexington in the heights to a run-down farm was a total change of lifestyle. On the weekend before the expected move-in date they visited the farm and found that the owners still had all the furniture in the house, equipment in the sheds, horses in the pens, dogs on the property, and nothing was packed. Gene informed the W's that they had to vacate their Lexington house by the first of the month and that they had arranged for the Viola home to be exterminated that week.

On moving day, Gene borrowed a stock truck, and Donna arranged for her regular cleaning ladies from the Pueblo to help. The cleaning crew arrived at the Lexington house, and Gene took them and the cleaning supplies to the Viola farm in the truck. The house should be empty now, and they hoped to have the house cleaned up before Donna and the kids and some friends arrived after school was out that day.

Arriving at the farm, Gene was surprised to see the sellers were still there hauling personal items from the house. Nothing outside in the yard or in the outbuildings had been moved. The corrals were still full of horses. The kitchen was almost empty, and Mrs. W was yelling at her helpers. The exterminators were coming in thirty minutes. This was not going as expected.

The place was in total chaos; dogs were barking madly while Mr. W supervised the loading of his moving truck. Gene's cleaning ladies refused to go inside while the dogs were there. In addition, there were hundreds of pigeons leaving their droppings on everything. You couldn't walk in the house unless you cleaned the pigeon crap off your shoes, and it wasn't safe to stand under the trees next to the house.

Mrs. W said she did not have room in their new place for all their furniture, and Gene offered to buy what could not be moved out, which included a dining table and chairs with Mr. Ellis carved in initials, he had made them. Gene recognized that the dining set and china cabinet were very old oak and worth keeping. They agreed on a price of $200, and he paid her. The china cabinet had been the Ellis's.

The vet was there euthanizing some of the dogs and was loading the dead carcasses in his pickup. Gene just stood there in the midst of the total confusion and his cleaning ladies huddled in the yard to avoid the pigeon dropping watching the circus in front of them. The exterminator was spraying the house while they finished loading.

When the former owners left with all that could be pulled out of the house, it was time to start cleaning. Empty, the place seemed really big and ugly, and it was almost three o'clock the time Donna would be driving up.

Unfortunately, Gene did not realize that the ten-foot-high stock racks on his truck would make contact with the two electric lines that ran from the utility pole to the house, and they lost electricity. Gene got a ladder and rewired. This was only one of the many disasters to come in that first year.

He looked for his cleaning ladies. Unfortunately, they had walked several blocks to the bus stop and gone home. Later, they called Donna and told her they quit because they were mad at Gene for taking her out of a new house in the heights and dragging her down to what they thought was a hellhole in the South Valley. They told her no one should have to live there, and Gene was a terrible man for forcing her to go there to live like a slave. Donna and Gene never saw these ladies again. They had lost their cleaning crew. Gene had no phone to call Donna and tell her not to come yet.

Mr. W returned and explained they had nowhere to take the horses and asked if he would allow the neighbors to come over twice a day to feed the horses until they got them sold. In addition, he asked to leave all their stuff in the sheds until they could dispose of it. Gene said, "Sure, who is going to notice a little more junk?"

With all the windows exposed, the now-empty house was like a huge fish bowl except for the east side, which was covered with vines and evergreen bushes. The huge living room had five-foot by six-foot windows with sixteen panes each and no curtains. The floor was in terrible shape; the linoleum was peeling and torn away in many places. Mrs. W used muriatic acid to clean the floors, bathtub, and sinks, which had eaten away the linoleum on the floors and pitted the porcelain in the sinks and fixtures.

When Donna and the kids drove in, the house was empty; and for the first time, she saw how filthy the walls and floor were, and she was appalled. She asked, "What have you been doing? Why isn't it cleaned up?" Gene just shook his head and didn't answer. When the friends arrived, the real work began. Several cleaned the kitchen and bathroom while Gene and a helper washed the walls. The walls and ceilings still had the original plaster from 1932 and required several coats of primer to cover the black coating. The painting started.

At around midnight, everyone was exhausted and determined the place was not ready for Donna and kids to move in. Friends took the family home to their house leaving Gene to finish the final coat of primer. Gene continued to work until about two in the morning. He pulled out his military folding cot the family used for camping and placed it in a doorway so his body was in the house and his head was outside getting fresh air. With so many coats of primer, the smell was challenging the bug spray, mice, and dog smell for supremacy.

After the hectic events of the day, it was very peaceful to just lie there in the dark. Gene lived and worked at the house all week from daylight until almost midnight and realized a week would not be enough to finish what needed to be done. By the end of the week, the first floor had furniture. The master bedroom had a bed, and the bathroom was usable. Donna and the kids moved back into the house on Saturday night; the kids slept on couches in the living room and were scared by the dark and stillness of the night.

They ordered pizza for dinner, had to pull the nails out where the front door was nailed shut, and cut a swath about two feet wide in the bushes, so they could open the front door for the first time in twenty-one years. The pizza man came to the front door and was surprised to see this house had a front door. He had lived close by for twenty years.

Soon the kids were moved upstairs into the bedroom on the west side. It took a while to convince them it was safe to sleep up there.

The house had a twelve by twelve porch on the south end of the upstairs with an outside staircase for a separate entrance to the apartment. It had a tapered roof, and the only evaporative cooler for the whole house was on top of this roof. There was no cooler for the downstairs.

Downstairs there was only a single floor furnace next to the main entrance on the east side of the house for the whole area, which included master bedroom, bath, and kitchen. There was no fan for forced air. To compensate, there were built-in wall heaters with cloth-insulated wiring in the bathrooms only, which the family never dared to use for fear of fire.

Mrs. W said his veterinarian was coming by to give Pebbles, the stud horse, and the others their shots and worm them. Next day, the vet arrived and introduced himself as Dr. A. He was talking to Donna while he worked on the horses. She had introduced herself as Donna Londene. Dr. A thought for a while and then said, "Donna Londene. I have heard that name somewhere before. Didn't you have a rabbit at Kansas State University and you brought him by the school veterinary clinic for treatment? I was the one that treated him."

Donna said, "Yes, I thought he had ringworm, and you said I was bathing him too often, and he just had a rash." What a coincidence they would meet here again in Albuquerque. Most of the veterinarians in town were Kansas state graduates.

Then, Dr. A got to thinking, *Donna Londene, Donna Londene, yes that was the name!* "Did you by any chance live up in the heights and know a vet named Dr. Jim?"

Donna was mortified; surely he didn't know about Dr. Jim and the dog story. How embarrassing! Dr. A then proceeded to say that Dr. Jim told this story at the veterinarians' convention every year about this lady that had her dogs frozen to the swing set and every vet in the state loved the story. Donna flushed like a ripe tomato and could have died right there. The two had a long laugh and began a relationship that would last for years. He became their regular vet and with his wife, Evelyn, were friends forever. In the coming years, there would be many more vets and more stories, and the conventions awaited her new escapades.

The fifteen-by-twenty-four-foot cellar under the north side of the house with an outside entrance was not livable, but excellent for storing canned fruit, fresh tomatoes, apples, potatoes, and onions. It was easy to tell that a lot of wine and apple cider had been made in this place. The old cider press and barrels were still there. The cider crocks remained in good shape. They also made wine from the vineyard, which was still on the main property.

Seeing the future, they designed a five-year plan of what had to be accomplished to repair the buildings, fix the fences, and remodel the house and properties. Gene would remark thirty years later that he figured they were finally in the third year of the five-year plan. They took down over 180 trees, mostly Chinese elm. They were cut with handsaws until a friend loaned them a chain saw. There was just so much crap!

Each Saturday, a truck was loaded for a weekly trip to the dump. Wood junk was pushed into a pile by the tractor and burned. Until the untimely discovery that beneath the manure pile was an old trailer complete with tires that one day caught fire from the heat of the fire and created a huge cloud of black smoke. It was about lunchtime, and the neighbor called the fire department upon seeing the rolling black clouds. Since the trailer was underneath the manure, it was a hot fire.

The smell of the rubber mixed with the old dry manure got the attention of the whole neighborhood. The fire department arrived. They hauled water the rest of the day to put out the manure fire under the duress of a terrible smell. The rubber burned out, but it took a lot of water to put out the manure. Not the best way to meet the neighbors but surely a quick one.

One day the kids were helping rake the leaves to a clearing where Charlie would burn them. They let the fire get too close to the building. Donna looked out the kitchen window and saw the fire spreading toward the tack room filled with all the saddles and tack left by the former owners. Gene rushed for a water hose, and it generated another call to the fire department. While they were putting out the fire, the smoke alarm in the house went off. Running back to the house, Gene found a pan of chocolate on the stove had caught fire. He got a wet towel and put it out. Donna had been melting chocolate when the fire started and forgot to turn off the burner when they left the house. The fire department men just stood and looked in shock at the happenings on this place. By now, they were on a first-name basis with the volunteer fire department. They had purchased the farm from the County Fire Marshall after all, and his assistant still lived next door. It was a fortunate association. Now they had two friends in the valley, the vet and the fire department.

Monday came and Gene left for the bank in Grants, New Mexico, for three days work. He left wondering what might go wrong; a habit they both had developed. He had ordered a load of sawdust for horse bedding to be delivered the week before, and they came while he was gone. He had set a stake on the spot where he wanted it unloaded, and Donna directed the driver to dump it there.

When the truck emptied its load, the driver put the truck in gear and started forward before he let the truck bed down. It was a long truck, and when it was tilted, the top of the bed was about fifteen feet in the air. The electric lines to the buildings were twelve feet high at least before he got there. Now he dragged them across the yard. Gene was at the bank in Grants when the panic call came. He somehow expected it.

Donna and the kids were terrorized; the dogs were barking, the horses were running, the truck driver was cussing, and sparks were flying. It was another wild scene. Fortunately, the lines to the house stayed up, and only the water pump and outbuildings were without electricity. Gene had to come home from the bank a day early and rehung the lines. These events were to become typical on the Viola farm, which was marked by calamity.

Another first for them was fighting the cotton from the cottonwood trees. The property had a dozen huge trees and each June they shed cotton, which settled everywhere. In their first year there was no rain and no wind. The cotton fell straight down in huge drifts, a foot or more thick.

Larry, the neighbor showed them how flammable it was and suggested they get out the water hose every night and water down the cotton. Once watered, it was not so flammable. Each day as the sun warmed up the trees, the cotton started to fall. It was everywhere. This went on for about two weeks.

While watering the cotton, someone yelled the house was on fire. Sure enough, smoke was pouring from the roof of the south porch. Everyone panicked and ran for the house, and Gene started pulling the hose toward the house. A neighbor quickly climbed up the water heater enclosure and on to the roof where he unplugged the evaporative cooler motor. It had burned up, but it was enclosed inside the metal case and isolated the fire.

It became natural for Gene and Donna to sit on the front porch and wonder if this nightmare was ever going to end and if they would ever have the free time they did when living in the heights.

Gene asked the people in the little trailer to move so that Charlie and Eileen could purchase a mobile home and again be neighbors.

Donna went into orbit when the first bird met her on the porch and tried to fly past her to get out. She wouldn't go out on the porch anymore until the screens were fixed. Gene patched the screens temporarily. Always, everything was temporary. They didn't have the money to really fix things right, so they patched. There was always tomorrow to do things right.

Gene and Donna sat down and made up a priority list. Items were numbered according to order of necessity. Some of them were big dollar items and were naturally put on the bottom of the list. Items necessary for personal hygiene or comfort were moved to the top of the list. Now when Donna complained about something not being done, Gene could just recite the number on the list. When something broke, it got to the top of the list.

Almost everything they needed was left on the farm, tools, shovels, used screen, wheelbarrows, lumber, etc. The Ws had left all this stuff thinking they would come back and get it. They never did. Mr. W died a year later, and Mrs. W moved to Florida. They had abandoned everything in the sheds and basement. In the sheds were a small fortune of antique tools, small furniture in need of repair, an old gas kitchen stove vintage 1920, a cabinet, and miscellaneous items. They could start their own antique shop.

Now it was time to do something about the pigeons. There were hundreds of pigeons, and they seemed to each contribute their droppings several times a day. Gene had to wash the car before he could go to work.

He got out his trusty .22 caliber semiautomatic fifteen-shot Stevens' rifle. He was shooting in the county, so it was legal. He started shooting pigeons. A neighbor heard the racket and came to help with his rifle. Together, they filled a thirty-gallon trash barrel with pigeons before dark and another the next day.

The next morning in the driveway at high speed came Mrs. W. She got out of the car with her arms flailing and her white hair, what was left of it, waving in the wind. She caught Donna first and started yelling and screaming that Gene was killing her father, and he was a murderer. She became totally hysterical while she was screaming something undecipherable. Donna was scared and the kids, thinking she was a crazy witch or something, ran in the house.

A neighbor friend had called Mrs. W about the shooting of the pigeons. Finally, she calmed down enough that they could understand her. Her parents had lived upstairs until they died. Every morning, her father went out and sat on the upstairs open porch. He had his bag of birdseed and fed all the pigeons while they surrounded him, and he was talking to them. He told Mrs. W when he died he would come back as a pigeon and live on the porch, and she should feed him and say hello. Mrs. W wanted them to stop killing the pigeons. Gene suggested she catch her father turned pigeon and take him with her. That didn't go very far. He offered to catch her father if she could tell him which pigeon it was. He sure didn't want to break up her family. At least this explained why there were so many pigeons.

Gene picked up the nature of the conversation and had carefully slipped the lids on the barrels of pigeons. If she had seen these, it would have been worse. She would have examined every pigeon to see if one was her father. Finally, she left.

The male peacocks were very beautiful, but the bad part was during the night they let out this bloodcurdling scream when they are excited or courting. They sound like a baby screaming, and it took a while to get used to them.

Another night, while they slept, the skunks came to visit. The dogs got their introduction to skunks right under the bedroom window. It was very enlightening to be awakened at two in the morning with the strong odor of skunk. Fresh skunk spray almost makes you sick to your stomach. There were many expressions of phews and yuks, and they all got blankets and covered up their heads. It was June, and all the windows were open. Dr. A told them to get a skunk trap, and they soon solved the problem.

The next was the gophers. They required some expertise to eliminate and were the most challenging and frustrating. There is a small wire trap with a spring and a chain. This will sometimes catch a dumb gopher, but most of the time, you dig out a sprung trap with nothing in it. Most of the gophers are smarter than the person who invented the trap.

Gene decided to do it the easy way. He opened up the tunnel, which is usually about six inches deep. He knew the gopher would come to close the opening. He sat at the end of the hole with a double-barreled twelve-gauge shotgun pointed at the hole.

Gene could see the dirt starting to fill in the hole as the gopher furiously dug too close it. Gene fired both barrels of the shotgun into the hole. Dirt and grass flew everywhere; it had back-blasted into his face, hair, nose, and eyes. It blew his hat off. When it all cleared and Gene could see again, he dug down in the hole, but there was no gopher. It was impossible to escape that blast, but he had. The score was gopher two and Gene zero. The next try would be gopher poison. It was a never-ending war. It was caddy shack all over again on the farm and the war continued forever.

Finally, Dr. A recommended they go to the nursery and purchase some "gopher plants." This is a plant with a strange smell, and gophers will not come near it as the roots are obnoxious to the gophers. It worked.

The first hectic week was over, and the house was livable. It was clean, demoused and debugged, but there was still a lot of painting and cleaning up to do. It still smelled of all the cleaning solvents and bug spray. In addition, there was a remaining mouse smell from the lower kitchen cabinets. New cabinets were coming but were now number 288 on his list. Donna refused to put her silverware, pots, and pans in those cabinets so she kept them in boxes on top. She came up with a unique way to get the priority she wanted. Gene had told her the kitchen cabinets had first priority, but now he had them way down the list. Part of the cabinets was an island that extended out into the room. Eileen came out to visit, and the women got a sledgehammer and an axe and demolished the island. When Gene got home, she told him, "Now if you want to eat, you better start the kitchen remodel." Gene mused it was really unfair; all a woman has to do is refuse to cook or refuse to share a man's bed, and she eventually gets whatever she wants!

The second week they started outside. The cleanup had taken five times their allowed time. Their friends quit showing up after the initial weekend. Gene and Donna had the feeling that some of them thought they were crazy to be here. They were inclined to agree, but they were here and there was no going back.

There was a well house just thirty feet west of the main house. It had been a storm and fruit cellar when the Ellis's lived in the old house. Ellis had drilled a forty-five-foot well in the floor of the cellar and either he or Mr. W had installed an electric water pump and a pressure tank. This provided the house and animals with water. Mr. W had told them the house well was very old and not very deep, maybe forty-five feet.

Donna thought she had better have the water tested, so she called the state engineers office. They condemned the well. Too much iron, magnesium, and bacteria. Donna called the vet, and he recommended she call Ben, a well driller.

Ben rigged up his pile driver. It would be necessary to drive this pipe about seventy-five feet to meet requirements for a drinking well. The first thirty feet went fine. After thirty feet, it began to slow down as he hit clay, then it began to stick completely, and Ben would pound it for ten minutes before it would move.

The next morning, they were down seventy feet, and it would not budge. Ben explained that what he was hitting were tar layers about an inch to three inches thick. Under each tar layer was several feet of river sand. This is how the valley was filled a million years ago. He drove for an hour or better. It had not moved an inch. He vacuum-sucked out some water. It looked good but had a strange smell and little bubbles coming out. Ben decided to pull the pipe from this hole and try another one. No way, it was not coming out. It was embedded in a tar layer.

He pumped the well for hours to clear the water. That evening he said, "Let's connect the water and see if it clears up in a few days." There would at least be water for the bathrooms that night.

Gene got up and prepared to make coffee. He ran some water; it bubbled. He took a glass of water, set a can on top of it, and lit a match to it. It blew the can off. He called Ben and Charlie. The conclusion was they had hit a methane gas pocket. It wouldn't kill them, but it wasn't recommended to use for drinking. They would have to drill a new well. He moved south about sixty feet and drove a new well. This one went down similar to the other through the tar layers but at seventy-five feet when he stopped and blew it out; it blew out about a yard of crystal white quartz sand just like the sand at White Sands National Monument a couple hundred miles south.

The water was completely without taste, and there were no bubbles. They connected to this one and had the water tested. It was fine. It was different from the heights water, no chlorine.

The septic system for the upstairs and downstairs bathrooms ran south toward the grape arbor. They discovered the kitchen drained north into a drain field on the neighbor's property. With three kids and two adults taking baths and washing clothes, it was not long before the drain field "runneth over."

Gene had gone to work and the phone rang. Donna was in a fit with the septic backing up in the bathtub and stool. Gene suggested she didn't take a bath. That kind of help was not exactly what she was after. She hung up, loaded up the kids, and went to friends. Thank goodness, they still had some friends in the heights. Gene could deal with it when he got home.

Mr. W had left him the rotary cables for cleaning out the septic lines. He must have known it would happen soon. They continued to have trouble with the drain fields. Water was coming up in areas different than what Mr. W said was the drain field. It was June, and it was getting hot and windy. It was smelly, but the water would evaporate by noon each day. Then came the rainy period, and there was no more evaporation. Now the excess water just lay, and it smelled. A heavy rain washed it away, but after the rain, it was the same problem.

About that time, Donna's aunt Gladys came through town. She told Donna she was giving a gift of $3,000 to each of the relatives that Christmas, and she would give Donna hers now so she could get a new septic tank and drain. On the farm, the water level was quite high. One could dig a posthole and hit water. Drain fields didn't work too well. It was to be a constant battle until the city sewer and water project came through.

Gene wondered what to do with the old septic tanks. They were old and underground so he just decided to cover the lids and leave them there. He told Donna he had figured out the perfect murder. He would simply open the septic lid and drop someone in. By the time they looked in there, the body would be gone. Nothing could survive in there. Maybe in their old age they could save on funeral costs. When they got tired of living, they could just jump in and pull the lid over them and let people wonder where they had gone.

Upon moving in, they did not have city garbage service. There were two barrels north of the house, and they had to haul their garbage to the dump. They fed all the food scraps to the pigs and chickens. Their first experience with burning trash was also their first experience of what happens when you put hair spray aerosol cans into a burning fire. The kids helped take the trash to the barrel and lit the fire. They had just returned to the house when the explosions came. The flames went so high they burned the cottonwood tree. It was the Fourth of July all over again. Now they started a third barrel for cans.

Eventually, they got city garbage pickup service. Gene was in his office when the panicked call came. The garbage truck had found an old abandoned septic tank in the backyard that had apparently been for the old house. He dropped the whole right rear of his six-ton loaded truck into it. Donna heard the thud and screams of the spinning tire and looked out to see the truck sink deeper into the hole. She wasn't sure what had happened until the smell gave it away. It took the bringing of a D-8 Cat from the city to get that truck out of the pit.

The septic tank saga wasn't over yet. When Gene and Donna arrived at the farm there were over two hundred elm and junk trees growing everywhere. They began taking down trees. The city maintenance people were friends of Mr. W and for years had taken advantage of the big fenced front yard with the ample parking area. When they were working this area, they would park the graders and road equipment in the front yard overnight where they were behind a locked gate and protected by the dogs. After the property changed hands, they continued to park the equipment in the yard at nights.

In addition, when Donna and Gene bought the equipment from Mr. W, there was a caterpillar tow-type road grader with a ten-foot blade. The kind someone stood on the back and adjusted the blade with two big wheels. The county was accustomed to borrowing this grader to maintain the roads that were too small for the big grader. They came to borrow the grader but didn't bring a driver to run it. Donna, of course, was available. She became the new maintenance person and drove the tractor for them.

The maintenance foreman saw the effort they were making digging out the tree stumps. He offered to take his big grader with the ten foot by four foot blade to push out some of the tree stumps. He started on the south side of the house, so they could move the entrance from the east side on Viola to the lane on the south side.

Gene was in the shower, and Donna was cooking breakfast. Donna's mother, Gertie, who had come to visit them, was in the bedroom. Suddenly, a gentle morning breeze blowing in the kitchen window off the newly cut alfalfa field, with the sweet aroma of new cut hay, would take a deciding turn for the worse. The smell was atrocious.

Donna looked out the south door where the grader was. He still was, but now he was in a vertical position. The front end and wheels were sticking up in the air at about a forty-five-degree angle, and the rear of the grader had disappeared into this cavern. Donna immediately thought of the garbage truck and the drain field he located and thought, *Not again*. Yes, it was the same scenario. He had found the main drain field. Gertie came into the kitchen yelling at Donna about that terrible smell and repeating she told them not to buy this stinking place. Gertie had shown up the day before and was sick. Donna had taken her to the medical clinic a couple blocks away for treatment. They gave her a prescription.

Donna's neighbor Maedean said, "Don't you know that is an abortion clinic?" Donna didn't know, and she sure wasn't going to tell Gertie. Gene said to take her back; maybe they could take some of the meanness out of her.

Gene had by now made arrangements to buy the equipment from Mr. W and was using it. Donna had learned to drive the tractor and wanted to learn to plow. There was a small hill in front of the house, and Donna wanted to level it for grass. Since the ground was all sand, the plow could go as deep as the tractor allowed, and it went a little deep. It was suddenly hard to move, it had seemingly stuck on a tree root. She gave the tractor more gas to cut through the root.

The tractor jumped, a geyser of water twenty feet high came up behind her. It looked like Old Faithful. Yes, she had plowed up the water line from the house to the mobile home at the front of the property. They never knew where the water lines and gas lines were as Mr. W had gotten very forgetful. They were finding them one by one. A call to the gas company helped as they came out and marked the lines. They couldn't afford to have this happen to the gas lines.

Not all of the things happening on the farm were pleasant. Ginger, the police dog Donna had received from Dr. A, had puppies. Only one survived and was about two months old. It had the run of the farm. Charlie and Eileen were moving to the farm, and they were making a dirt pad for the new larger mobile home that Eileen had bought.

Gene and Donna had the tractor down to level the pad. Donna got on the tractor to drive it forward while Gene and Charlie tried to excavate a stump. Donna started forward and the chain tightened to pull the stump when they heard a loud pop. It was the worst of scenarios. The little puppy had lain down in front of the large tractor wheel to sleep. When Donna got on the tractor, she could not see over the wheel hub to see the puppy, and it was run over. The kids screamed, and Eileen yelled at Donna to stop the tractor.

Everyone was extremely shocked. Donna was hysterical, and Gene had to pry her from the tractor. The kids were crying. It was a terrible scene. Donna would never forgive herself for this tragedy. She did not get back on the tractor for a long time.

Regardless, the weekend ended and Monday came again. Darrell went out to play in the sand and the girls to school.

Soon, Darrell came running in the house to his mother yelling, "Mommy, there is a big blue man out there." Donna thought he had been reading too many comic books or watching the wrong cartoons on TV. He told her he was scared to go outside again, and she should come see the blue man. She and Darrell stepped around the corner of the house. There he stood, all six feet six of him and the blackest black man she had ever seen. It was a shock, and even Donna's heart missed a beat. Everyone had told her it was too dangerous to live out on the farm by herself. Anything could happen to her. Here was her life already in jeopardy. It was Darrell's first experience with Negroes, and for them to see this huge man standing around the corner of the house had scared him and Donna almost to death. Donna stood there unable to speak, maybe for the first time in her life, and just stared, not knowing what was going to happen next.

Finally, the man spoke with a huge deep voice; he was the county agent who had walked in and was coming up to the house. Gene had asked him to come out and advise on leveling the pasture, but he left town and forgot to tell Donna. It was just a little excitement to start the day. Donna tried to explain to him her son's reaction and calling him a blue man. He just smiled and told Darrell it was all right. The blue man was very helpful on the farm, and he and Darrell became friends. But from then on, he would come to the front door.

On the south side of the house was the stallion pen with a wooden stall only twenty-five feet from the bedroom. It was June and the windows were open. The horse had a cribbing problem. All night long, he was slowly eating up his feed rack and stall. He was grinding all night. Donna was having a fit trying to sleep, and one night she had enough. The horse was cribbing on the board holding the feed rack and had the board in his mouth. Gene had left the sledgehammer on the porch. Donna grabbed the hammer and walked to the horse stall. While the stallion had the board in his teeth, she hit the middle of the board a blow with the sledgehammer. The stallion let out a grunt and almost went over backwards. She thought she had killed him, she didn't, but he didn't crib anymore that night.

People seemed to show up at the farm at unannounced times. One day a realtor from Albuquerque drove in on a Saturday morning just to see the place. He sat down, visited for a while, and said he used to live in the old building to the south with the smoke stack on top. He was going to school and worked on the farm for his rent. He was very helpful with information about the old place. Another woman stopped by and said she used to train horses there and lived upstairs for a year. Everyone seemed to have a piece of history about the farm. Many mornings some neighborhood women came to the front of the property and picked the leaves from a strange little plant growing there. Gene asked them what they did with the leaves, and they simply replied medicinal.

One morning a Texas car drove in. It was one of the Ellis sons who now lived in Orange, Texas. He had relatives in Albuquerque and just stopped in to see the old place where he grew up. He sat and talked to the family for hours and told them all the history of the farm. He had grown up there, and he was very helpful in clarifying the construction of the house and the operations of the farm. He talked a long time about the early days of the farm and the operation of the dairy before it burned. He didn't have much to say about what happened after Mr. Ellis died. Gene asked him if he could confirm the old story of the stagecoach stop in the pasture and the missing gold. He said his father told him the story as he was there when it happened, so he assumed it was true. At least the part about the stagecoach stop because the adobe bricks and foundation were still there and they had found so many pieces of old iron and tack. Some of what Gene and Donna found was still out in the shed. Gene had dug up many bricks and rusted iron while plowing.

So many people had connections to this place. Gene told him people were still digging in the pasture and looking for the gold. Ellis said they had been doing that for a hundred years, and if there was any gold there, he would have found it. But he did confirm that some people had an old map showing the area. Eventually, they quit coming. Maybe they found it?

They were all interested in seeing the clean up and fix up going on. Gene and Donna got the feeling they were living in a local landmark. The history of this old place was fascinating.

# Donna Baling Hay (1968)

The first year on the farm was full of newfound enjoyments and some hard-learned lessons. The sellers were unsuccessful at selling the equipment on the farm and ended up offering it to Gene at a discounted price.

Gene and Donna now became the owners of a tractor, baler, rake, mower, plow, and other useful farm equipment. Their neighbor Larry was happy to show them how to use this equipment and make some extra money. This worked for Gene since he had committed to buying the equipment at $100 a month for the next twelve months. Larry had been baling hay for people in the South Valley for years.

Larry arranged for contracts on four fields to be cut and baled. They contracted twenty-eight acres. When Gene had to go out of town, Donna worked with Larry and learned to operate the equipment.

In New Mexico, the air is so dry that you have to wait on the dew to fall at daylight before you can rake or bale or all the leaves fall off, which meant being at the field by 3:00 a.m. and waiting for the dew to fall. Donna had learned to drive the tractor, but she wasn't able to start the baler and repair the equipment.

*Donna on tractor mowing alfalfa*

By the time of the second cutting, all was going well. Then Larry had a heart attack and could not drive a tractor, and it would be up to Gene and Donna. Donna helped mow and rake, and Gene did the baling. Fields were cut for a share of the hay, a third on large fields, and half on small fields. They sold the hay to make their money. It was a good system because they would stack the hay and sell it in the winter when they got a better price.

Larry was coming to the field to supervise, but he didn't do any physical work. Gene was still going out of town when they needed him most. Then one hot July, with several fields cut and needing to be raked or baled, things got worse. Gene was sick in bed with dust pneumonia.

Larry could not drive the tractor. They had four acres at home down, ready to bale, and a twenty-eight acre field down, and ready to rake. Donna was trapped and trying to figure out how she got into this mess of obligations with Gene sick.

The next morning she and Larry got out the tractor and baler, and she drove it down the street to the field miles away. The baler was wider than half the road and was difficult to maneuver around mailboxes and stoplights. She drove slowly in the early morning traffic.

Larry went to the field, started the baler for her, and did the settings. Now all she had to do was pull it around the field and bale the hay. Sure, it was not quite that easy. She had no more than started when the baler lost its wire feed. Larry told her to get down on the ground and feed the wire back into the knotter and up around the needle. Then on top of the baler to feed from the needle back to the other tie ring. Being short, she had to crawl up on the baler to feed the needles.

With that accomplished, she started back up but the tractor died. Now with Larry's supervision, she had to disconnect the carburetor glass filter bowl and clean it. Then the gas line had to be blown out, and she got gas in her mouth. She knew nothing about engines and gas lines. By now, Donna was ready to cry, greasy and dirty, and thinking why she ever agreed to buy this damn farm. She was developing a farmer's vocabulary when things went wrong. A half hour later, she was settled and back to baling, with dirt in her hair and down her back, she was becoming a real farmer.

They finished the field and she had to haul the baler three miles to the big field. Donna was driving the tractor pulling the baler, and Larry followed with his blinkers going. It was a nerve-racking drive, and she felt like telling Gene where to put his farm! She stuck with it and finished all the fields just before a rainstorm.

With the rain pouring and Donna needing to get the tractor home, she realized the tractor had no windshield. It was raining hard and hailing, so she pulled her hat down over her face and drove with one hand while she held the hat on to ward off the rain. The hailstones were bouncing off the tractor hood and hitting her in the face. She was crying and cussing and got totally soaked by the time she got home. She had performed mission impossible and won. The city girl had now conquered the farm; and she had the respect of Gene, Larry, and the kids. She took her shower that evening, crawled in bed, and died to the world. She went to sleep with a very good feeling about herself.

Donna got so good at threading the baler that one of their neighbors who owned the same baler came over to have Donna come and show him how to thread his baler. It was an interesting situation as he spoke no English, and Donna spoke very little Spanish. Donna would recognize his voice and would hang up, get in her car, and drive over. She climbed up on his baler and threaded his wire. He said thank you in Spanish and both understood.

They had moved to Albuquerque because Donna had rheumatoid arthritis, and it had been so bad in Manhattan it was difficult for her to use her hands and hips. But after the first year on the farm, she was substantially improved. She always wondered if riding the tractor had not jarred the calcium in her hips loose. For sure her improvement had to also include the fact that she was in the sun a lot and living a good healthy life.

When arthritis awareness month rolled around, Donna was referred to the committee by her doctor. They asked if she would be willing to canvas her neighbor raising funds for the committee. She said no because she had twenty-eight acres of hay down again, and she had to bale it.

The lady was interested in her story as how an acute rheumatoid arthritis person could do this. She asked Donna if she could come out and interview her and was amazed at how a person so weak in Kansas could do what she was doing now. Donna had been told by local doctors that she would be in a wheelchair soon, and they would have to begin giving her gold shots in her joints. This woman worked at a local TV station and wanted to feature Donna on the news show. Donna was game, and so they sent out a TV camera crew to film Donna baling hay and planned to prepare a short story documentary for showing during arthritis awareness month.

On the day of taping, Donna was preparing to go to a dinner function that night so her nails and hair were done up. When the TV crew arrived, they asked that she cover her manicured hands and her hair. She agreed, put on her green coveralls, gloves, and cowboy hat and rode around on the tractor baling hay for a ten-minute TV news documentary on what a person could accomplish when they made their mind up to stay active. Unfortunately for one of the cameramen who while backing up for a better shot came into contact with an electric fence. Up until that moment this guy had never heard of an electric fence. He has now! They cleverly filmed her coming to the field and passing by the clothesline full of drying clothes for a "woman's touch."

That evening, Donna got dressed in her formal attire so she and Gene could go to the bank board dinner. They happened to sit across the table from New Mexico Senator Clinton P. Anderson and the president of the bank. There was a TV on the wall behind Donna, and soon Anderson looked up at the TV and then at Donna, back at the TV, and back at Donna.

He finally said, "Young lady, is that you on that tractor?"

Donna responded, "What tractor?" She turned around and looked at the TV, and sure enough, there she was. She was very embarrassed and wanted to crawl under the table. She told him, "Yes, sir, that is me." Donna expected him to say she sure cleaned up nice, but he was very polite and thought it was great of her to do the documentary.

The clip was played on Channel 7 with commentator Dick Knipfing providing a narrative about the benefits of outdoor living for arthritis sufferers. For the entire month of June and during the arthritis drive, the news clip ran during many newscasts.

Gene and Charlie were usually only able to work on the farm on weekends and some evenings and both were out of town on occasion. Until Gene quit his job and became self-employed, he was gone to Chicago a few days every month, to Grants for three days and had to make occasional trips to Denver and Arizona. Each time he left, it was up to Donna and the kids to run the farm. By now, Eileen quit her job and was staying home working on projects and chores with Donna full time.

One day the women decided the elm trees in the lane had to come down. They started with a couple of small trees. Then they decided to attack this large tree with a twelve-inch trunk with a crosscut saw. They began sawing the trunk about six inches above the ground and sawed a little over three-fourths of the way through when they discovered it was time for a coffee break.

In the meantime, Joe, the hay hauler, arrived to put a load of bales in the hay shed. Joe was a big strong six-foot-six black man from Texas who would toss bales onto the stack two at a time, one with each hand. He picked up the bales in the field and stacked them in the haystack for ten cents a bale. Donna and Eileen finished their break and returned to finish sawing down the tree. On the way out to the tree, Eileen had said, "Let's push on the tree and see if it is about ready to fall." Joe and his wife watched as these two women walked up to this twelve-inch tree and started to push. Joe couldn't see the cut they had made or the crosscut saw because of the weeds and grass around it. He did hear Eileen say "Let's push the tree over." All Joe and his wife saw was these two women walk up to a twelve-inch tree and give a push and down went this thirty-foot high tree. Joe stopped dead still with two bales still in his hands and said to his wife, "Whooee, Mama, did you see that? Don't you ever mess with those ladies." They were impressed, and Donna never did tell him about all the sawing they did before giving the tree a push. Joe was a respectful friend for life.

# Remodel Viola House (1970)

Donna and Eileen decided the six layers of linoleum in the house had to go. Gene said it was number 182 on the master to-do list. Donna had other ideas. They were told that the best way of removing it was to burn it off. Donna and Eileen cleared the room of all furniture, drapes, and wall hangings.

Out in the shed, Gene found a butane bottle with a weed burner attachment. They knew there was a wooden floor under the tar and linoleum, and they knew wood burned. They had two fire extinguishers inside and a water hose ready outside. They were all a little nervous about putting several hundred degrees of heat on the floor inside the house, but they were going to try it.

They removed the baseboard and started heating the linoleum. Surprisingly, with a little heat, the linoleum started to smoke, and you could peel it off almost immediately with a sharp shovel or claw hammer. The smell was atrocious, and they wrapped wet bandanas over their mouth and nose.

They had all the windows open and several fans blowing air through the house to get rid of the smell and heat. After the linoleum was gone, the oak wood underneath was fine. They heated and peeled for about four hours, and the floor was stripped of six layers of linoleum. They applauded themselves for a tremendous job accomplished, and the house was still standing.

To their surprise, the oak floor had never been finished, so they were able to sand, scrape, and dig out the dirt. By that evening, the floor was cleaned and sanded. The next day, they wiped it with a cleaner, and it was ready for the base coat and crack filler. Some of the cracks were so deep and dried out it took a couple fillings and sandings. But by the end of the week, it was ready for the first coat of finish. It got five coats in all, with a light sanding in between coats, and eventually, a nice low semi-gloss finish. It was now a beautiful floor and made the house look like new.

They patched the holes in the plaster, repainted the entire room, and revarnished the doorframes and moldings where they had been scorched. When the floor was dry, they moved the furniture back into the room. The antique china cabinet got a few repairs, and it took four people to move it back into the room, probably why Gene was able to acquire it so cheap. The piece was over a hundred years old, and the glass was over a quarter inch thick.

They added new glass chandeliers, new drapes and furniture and the room became very pleasant. Now Donna decided she needed some rugs to protect the floors from the outdoor sand. Gene did not like the idea and preferred the wooden floors, but Donna reminded him of their agreement—his office, her house. He didn't have a vote.

Next, they carpeted the upstairs to cut down the noise and provide some warmer floors for the kids as this was a cold house upstairs and down. That was a great improvement. Darrell liked the carpet so much he took his pillow and blanket and slept in the hall right in front of the wall heater. The kids were all raised in that cold upstairs. Gene was unsympathetic; he was raised in a cold room. The kids sarcastically said they knew that, and they also knew he walked a mile to school uphill both ways.

Lucky for Gene he had many contractor clients who got behind in their bills and he was able to trade out their bills. Some years, Gene would be short on cash because he had traded out too many of his receivables. When this happened, he would remortgage the farm to generate the cash to run the office. In his opinion, it was better than losing the money all together. About 1990, they carpeted the whole downstairs and both stairways. Now there were no more visual oak floors. They are still there, but they are buried under carpet. Some day in the future a new owner will remove the carpet and discover those beautiful oak floors.

The Londenes seemed to do everything in reverse. They started out with an $18,500 mortgage and now had it up to $183, 000. They had a nice house and office and vehicles paid for. Everyone likes to leave something for their heirs when they die. Gene and Donna always said they would do the same; they would leave them a mortgage.

By 1974, Gene's accounting practice was doing very well. He had a junior partner and ten employees, plus Donna in tax season. They bought a new 1975 Chevrolet Blazer, and Donna had a used Cadillac. They bought an interest in a condo at the ski resort in Purgatory, Colorado, and the whole family learned to ski. In 1972, they acquired a lot in Colorado near the Conejos campground, and they wanted to build a cabin there.

They wanted a cabin, and they wanted to remodel the house. They couldn't have both. Donna argued the girls were coming of age, and they should have a house suitable for entertaining. Gene argued the house was sufficient since the girls would be leaving for college soon and the cabin was more necessary. They decided to have a vote. The vote was three women for the house remodel, and two men for the cabin. So in 1974, they began planning for the remodel and modernizing of the house and actually had an architect draw up plans.

During 1974, just as they were to start, the country went into a recession. Over one-half of Gene's clients were in the construction business and the building business came to a halt. His receivables didn't pay, and the house was put on hold. Gene worked out an arrangement with a client that owed him money to send one of their crews out to work on his house and trade it out on their bill.

Gene maintained it was still eighty-seven on the list. Donna replied, "Do want to eat? Start the construction!" Donna wanted to tear down the old screened porch on the west side of the house and build a new dining room, kitchen, utility room, and bathroom. She said, "I can do it for about twenty thousand."

Gene looked at her plans and got a construction loan for thirty thousand and said, "Here you are, go to it." Obviously, some words here he may regret later. Gene was so busy he gave Donna a free rein on the construction. In addition, she invoked the rule, "his office, her house," and she wanted her new kitchen he promised her seven years ago.

Things started okay. The first client put in the foundation, floor, rough in walls and roof, and installed the tile. Next, they nailed on strips to hold the concrete roof tile. This is where the first problem came. Donna walked into the new part of the house and heard this funny sound like wood tearing. She looked up at the ceiling just in time to see a nail coming through her new exposed tongue and groove ceiling. She ran outside to stop the men from nailing. They were all Mexican nationals and spoke no English, so she went into an arm waving session to supplement her verbal assault. The men did not understand, but she knew enough Spanish to say, "No mas," and they stopped nailing. She took the foreman into the house to show him all the nails protruding from her ceiling by over an inch.

She called the contractor who at least spoke English. He came over, and they pulled all the nails. The holes they left are still in the ceiling, but they aren't noticeable unless you know they are there.

About five thirty, just after the workers left, one of those New Mexico mountain storms spilled over the mountain and came roaring down the valley. It rained over two inches at the farm in less than thirty minutes. Soon after it started raining, the water started coming down the walls of the old part of the house and pouring into the new part like little rivers. They had cut up into the old roof and hadn't weather sealed the joint. All the water from the old pitched part of the roof was coming in the house. The bathroom and pantry ceilings were starting to come down. It came into their bedroom and kitchen. It rained hard, and then as is typical in New Mexico, the sun came out and dried up the outside, but not the inside.

There was no sunshine spirit inside, and Donna was beside herself. She emptied the pantry and saved the food she could and got towels and started mopping water. As Gene drove in the yard, the construction foreman followed him in. She met them both at the gate and was not a bit bashful about expressing her feelings on this situation. There wasn't much they could do at this point except clean up the water. They threw out many food packages and had to wash the bedding. They slept upstairs that night.

The next day the crew showed up, finished nailing the strips, and started installing the concrete roof tiles over the entire roof, the new and the old. It looked very nice, and the water in the house was forgotten except for where the rain left stains on the ceilings. Great, now they were ready for the next client to come finish the room.

Donna called Mickey, the second contractor, and since they were good business friends, he and his assistant Randy suggested lunch. At lunch, after a couple martinis, Mickey said, "We will have a crew there right away, and we will finish that thing in two weeks. It will be no problem. You won't even be out of a house for more than a week." It must have been the martinis talking. When he returned to his office, he arranged for the supervisor and crew to start the following Monday. On Monday morning early, Gene went to work. Donna was there to instruct the crew. She had her plans, pictures, and drawings ready. At eight o'clock, a pickup pulled into the driveway and a man got out. Donna met him at the door and he introduced himself as Lawrence, the man to build her house. Donna asked, "Where is your crew?"

He replied, "I am the crew."

She called the company and asked, "Where are the rest of the people?" She was told they had picked up some new jobs, and everyone was busy that week. Lawrence was all she was going to get. Lawrence was a construction foreman for this client, but he was going to do this job himself. He was Spanish, but at least this one was a lifelong Albuquerque resident and spoke English. It was a great improvement over the last bunch.

Lawrence started working, and Donna found out who his crew was. She became a carpenter's assistant for the next six months. She designed and directed and did the "grunt" work to help with the installation. She held the boards for him and helped carry the lumber. She even got up on the scaffolding to help install the wall paneling, and she stained all the panels and woodwork for days.

She got out her picture of the brick kitchen taken in Don Knott›s home in California. They did an exposed beam ceiling with all glass windows running twelve feet on the west side. She had an antique oak fireplace from the old hospital and a huge built in china closet over one hundred years old to build into the dining room. The dividers, fireplace, and arches would be brick.

The brick was a problem; Lawrence didn't do brick. Fortunately, Gene had another tax client, Bill, who was a bricklayer. He was contracted to lay the brick in the kitchen, dining room, and the fireplace. Donna showed him the pictures of Don Knott's kitchen, and he said it was not a problem. He said he could do it exactly like that.

He showed up to work in the morning, and he had a load of brick sand and some cement delivered. He started in the kitchen and completed the arch over the stove. Next was the built-in wine rack and the arch over the cabinets. All was going well except he went out to his truck often, and he usually quit shortly after lunch and went home. Donna was gone many mornings driving kids to school and other functions. When she was home, she thought this was a little strange that he quit work so early. After a few days, she was gone for most of the day and came home to find the vertical brick on the divider arch was straight on one side and leaning a half inch on the other. Donna had a very good sense of level and could sight level within one sixteenth of an inch. Bill would get the level, and she was always right. She made Bill tear it out and do it all over. How could a professional bricklayer not see they weren't level?

Finally, Bill was doing the chimney on the outside. Donna came home and saw him leaning half way off the scaffold with one leg hooked over the support iron, and he couldn't straighten up. She thought he was going to hang himself, and she wondered why he couldn't straighten up and get his balance. Now she noticed he had been drinking. In addition, he got tired of going to his truck so often, and he now had his quart of vodka sitting on the scaffold. Now she knew why his work deteriorated in the afternoon and he went home early. He was totally drunk.

She accosted him and found out he was drinking a quart of vodka by noon every day. She told him to leave, and he was fired if he couldn't stay sober. He finally got his leg loose from the scaffold, made it down off the scaffold, dumped the cement, got in his truck, and left. He almost hit the gate with his pickup, so he backed up toward the house. Donna ran out yelling at him to stop and go forward. He got the pickup straightened up and headed out the lane about three miles an hour.

Each day when his quart of vodka was empty, he just closed up and left weaving. She looked in their trash barrel and noticed several empty vodka bottles. Whatever cement was still in the wheelbarrow when the bottle was empty, he just dumped on a pile, and the pile of hardened cement was now over two feet high. Things weren't going well, and Donna was furious. That night she told Gene the bricklayer had to be replaced. They tried to call him at his house, but he didn't answer.

The next day Gene left for work early and said he would get hold of Bill to fire him and then he would get another bricklayer. Of course, he didn't do either. Bill showed up bright and chipper at seven o'clock as if nothing had happened. Probably because he couldn't remember what had happened. Donna quickly enlightened him. He promised to quit drinking on the job until it was finished if she let him continue. She was too kindhearted to fire him, so they made a deal that he would not bring any more bottles to the job site. She found his bottle in his tool chest and poured it out.

That day went fine, and he finished the chimney. He was doing so well, he started on the inside of the fireplace. He did leave early, but supposedly, he left sober. The next day Donna had to go to a Sister City function. When she returned, he had laid the upright brick across the face of the mantle of the fireplace. The left side was perfectly straight and each brick thereafter began to lean to the west. When he got to the end, the last brick stuck out an inch and a half at the top. She was furious, and the next day she made him take it all out and redo it on his own time.

This time, they had an understanding there would be no more liquor on the farm, he had to arrive sober, and she would stand beside him until he finished. If he went to his truck, he had better get in it and drive away. He finished the job in two days. It was a very trying time for him; he was a nervous wreck and left early every day. At last, the brickwork was finished, and it looked very nice except for a few cover-ups. He had used eighteen bags of cement on a job that should have taken four. They wanted some more brickwork done later, but old Bill died shortly after he finished the house. The family probably saved some money at his funeral as he had already embalmed himself.

During the construction, Gene and Donna slept upstairs in one of the kid's rooms. They lived on cold cuts and sandwiches or they ate out. They could make coffee and have cereal, but they had to eat most of their evening meals at a restaurant or they barbequed.. The construction that was to be completed in October was still in progress in December and far from completed. They lit a fire in the new fireplace on Christmas Day, and it smoked terribly. Bill hadn't extended the chimney above the high point of the house, and Lawrence had to finish it to stop the smoke. He built the new kitchen and made the old kitchen into a large bedroom. By now, Donna and Lawrence had a good working relationship. They should, he had been there forever.

Donna told him she was short and had a problem with standard kitchen cabinets because of her height or lack of it. She wanted her cabinets one inch shorter than standard. Lawrence told her she couldn't have a dishwasher or stove built in because they required a certain height. He would have to build one height for the dishwasher and lower the rest. The stove was in its own brick enclosure and would just be the height it came. Lawrence measured and cut the cabinets, and while Donna was at work, he put them up.

When she returned that night, she examined the cabinets. Lawrence had gotten confused and made them all one inch higher instead of lower. Donna was very flustered. With all the problems she had gone through with all these contractors, this was the last straw.

When Lawrence showed up the next day, she was waiting. After the discussion, it was decided he could cut them back to standard but not lower. He redid them, but they were still a little higher than standard, and they had to put rollers under the dishwasher and stove to make them come up to the cabinet height.

Gene was meeting with the bank where he had arranged his construction loan to get more money. They declined, the bank said they couldn't loan anymore without an appraisal. Donna did what she does best; she talked the contractor into buying the furnace and installing it and traded them some Indian jewelry, including Gene's favorite expensive Zuni bolo tie. That would teach him to get the money arranged next time.

It was April before the linoleum and carpet were installed and the rooms were finally completed. Lawrence had been there so long he retired after he left this job. Gene thought he had partially retired on the job. The neighbors had seen his pickup in the yard for so many months they thought Donna was taking in boarders.

For the ensuing years, all their guests marveled at the beautiful dining room with the fabulous brickwork and complimented Donna on her design and construction. She had designed and supervised it all by herself, and even though there were some setbacks, it was a job well done.

*Exterior of south side after remodel and patio.*

When the construction started, they owed about nine thousand on the mortgage. Gene had told Donna she could spend twenty thousand. When all was done, they now had a new mortgage of over one hundred thousand. It had been a fun trip, and they finally realized their old college dream of getting an old house and remodeling it. However, would they do it again? Gene's answer was a resounding "no."

Then she reminded him the upstairs hadn't been done yet. This sent Gene out on the patio to have a conference with Jack. It was happy hour, and his old buddy Jack Daniels would help him rationalize this one. Jack concluded that since the kids were leaving someday, maybe they wouldn't need the upstairs. Donna overruled him.

The downstairs was now complete, and they were having their second Christmas in the new dining room. It was beautiful with the paneling on the high walls and the green wallpaper on the lower walls. They used the indirect lighting concealed above the windows for dinner lights. Donna had Gene hang her 160 blue Scandinavian plates from Bing and Grondell and Royal Copenhagen on the beams in the dining room ceiling. They added a touch of class to the room. For the first time, they could use the huge dining room table they had bought while antiquing and had been saving for the new room. It had double leaves that pulled out on both ends and would seat twelve people handily.

To celebrate the occasion, Donna had invited her parents, Mac and Gertie, Charlie and Eileen, and several friends. The family and guests were seated at the table. Gene's job was to open the two bottles of champagne they had purchased for the occasion. He sat the bottles and a sparkling soda on the kitchen chopping block and started to remove the cork. There was an open divider between the kitchen and the dining room with just a couple feet of opening at the top. Gene didn't have a corkscrew, so he was removing the cork by twisting and pulling. After a great amount of effort, the cork came out with great force. Apparently, the kids shook the bottles while bringing them in from the outside where they were cooling. When Gene gave the cork a final tug, it came out in a hurry and flew to the ceiling. It hit the ceiling just above the divider and angled down into the dining room. As bad luck would have it, it hit Gertie square in the forehead just above her glasses. She reeled backwards, and Charlie and Mac caught her just in time to keep her from hitting the wall and floor. You cannot possibly even imagine or believe the fallout from this little scene. Dinner was delayed a few minutes while everyone tried to comfort Gertie and convince her Gene hadn›t done this deliberately. She never agreed it was an accident and glowered at him the entire meal. Gene was still smiling inwardly at his accomplishment even though it really was an accident.

Donna was very proud of her new house, and Gene wanted to reward her for a job well done with the remodeling even though she went about $60,000 over budget. She maintained she had to have new furniture and drapes to go with the remodeling. After Gene recovered from the shock, he decided to give her something she had never had since they were married: a birthday party. He secretly arranged with the children and his employees to order the food and decorations. He told Donna they were going to an important dinner at eight that evening on the twentieth, and he wanted to have another couple stop by the house for a drink before dinner, so they must have the house immaculate. Donna had wondered why Gene had spent all afternoon cleaning and setting up his bar, but then he usually did this for the Christmas holidays anyway. Everything proceeded as scheduled. Donna went in the afternoon for a new hairdo and also went and bought a new dress. She wanted Gene to tell her who they were entertaining, but he said it was a surprise, and a surprise it was. They were dressed and ready to leave for dinner when the doorbell rang. In walked a couple employees from the office. Donna said, "What are you doing here? We have to go to a dinner."

Gene told her, "Oh, we can be a little late. Let me fix you a drink before we go." Soon the doorbell rang again, and here came some more friends, then behind them the kids with food trays. Now someone gave it all away by starting to sing "Happy Birthday." The surprise was complete. It was a great success.

Later in the evening, Gene's secretary, Millie, told him to come out to her car with her to carry in Donna's gift. Gene was musing whether to buy Donna some jewelry or what for her birthday. Millie told Gene, "Just give me the company credit card, and I will pick out her gift." When he and Millie went to her car for the gift she opened the trunk and there was this big box for Gene to carry in, he picked it up and began to worry. It was too big to be jewelry and too light to be anything mechanical. As he carried it into the room and presented it to Donna, he saw the label on the box that said, "Harper's Furrier." Now he was really worried. She opened the box and took out the mink stole, a beautiful, shiny brown sable color. Donna was overjoyed and totally surprised. Gene was equally surprised, and all he could think of was, *What the hell did this thing cost?* After opening the fur in front of forty people, there was no way it could be returned. Gene was in as much shock as Donna was. When he wanted to reward Donna, he hadn't considered that big of a reward. Millie simply told him, "She deserves it for having to put up with you all these years." Gene had to agree. It was a beautiful gift, and he would recover from the shock when paying the Visa. Thank you, Millie.

Gene promised himself he would delay the upstairs remodel just as long as possible. He got the refinancing done for the downstairs, the construction loans paid off, and everyone was happy. After the problems with the contractors, he decided he would do the upstairs himself. It was 1997 when they tore up the upstairs and refinished all the rooms including insulation for all the walls and roof.

Remodeling the upstairs happened when Donna and Darlene decided they would like to run a bed-and-breakfast, "Das Bauern Haus en El Valle del Sol." The name was part German and part Spanish and translated to say, "The Farmhouse in the Valley of the Sun,"

This time they had the cash to do it and most of the cost was labor, for which Gene became the laborer, and Donna was the supervisor.

Gene acquired a gas mask, opened all the windows, and got a blower fan and a twenty-gallon shop vacuum cleaner to suck up whatever fell. He started on the west room and removed the window so he could shovel scraps out onto the roof and into a truck. It was a dirty job, and he would do this one alone.

The house was attic type, a slanted ceiling to follow the roofline and a crawl space of about two feet on either side for utilities. There was electric, intercom, and other wires. In addition, there were gas, water, and sewer lines. There was just enough space for a man to crawl down to install the utilities. It was set up well.

He started the demolition by tearing down the asbestos tile ceiling. Dust, dirt, cobwebs, skeletons of mice and birds came down in a fog of sixty-five years of accumulation. Now he discovered there was no insulation in the upstairs wall or ceiling. No wonder the kids said their rooms were always so cold. Now it was ready for the new electrical. Denise was now married to Randy, and it was very timely having an electrician in the family. The upstairs would become an electrician's showcase of indirect lighting courtesy DRB Electric with fans, niches for displaying Donna's Indian pottery with canister lights spotlighting them and indirect lighting. All the upstairs was recarpeted.

The kids could not hold back reminding Donna and Gene that they appreciated it having been fixed after they left home. Being kids, they didn't understand that it was not until he finished getting these "three turkeys" out of college that could he afford to fix the upstairs. With the west side complete, they did the same to the east bedroom, leaving the small north room as a walk-in closet.

It took four long, hard months of working evenings after work and every weekend. Occasional help from friends and relatives were all appreciated. The upstairs rooms and the hall were redecorated with original and print paintings. The shelves and "niches" were filled with selected pieces of Donna's ceramic Indian design pottery, which were spotlighted by canister lights in the ceiling to accent the pottery. Against all odds, the upstairs was finished.

Donna went to town and bought new bed linens to accommodate visits from their growing family. They furnished the rooms with their multitude of antiques left over from their antique business, and they hung paintings they had been accumulating for just such an opportunity to decorate the entire upstairs.

They could now be proud of their upstairs instead of being ashamed of taking anyone up there. A lifelong dream to buy old, modernize, and remodel had become a reality. In the beginning they never realized the time, effort, and cost this would all entail.

When the remodeling was finally complete and after Donna and Darlene had developed all the brochures for the bed-and-breakfast they both developed health conditions that prevented them from ever opening. Maybe someday!

Gene felt he had been conned. He complained he had spent almost six months remodeling the upstairs and refurnishing it to the tune of about twenty-five thousand dollars for this bed-and-breakfast, which never happened. But Donna just smiled because she now had a beautiful upstairs worthy of her family and the many guests and relatives that visited. She had won again.

# The Growing Christmas Tree (1976)

Charlie and Eileen were now living on the farm, and with the encouragement of the kids, it was decided to get a larger tree. Gene, Charlie, and the kids would buy the tree. It was a snowy, windy, and cold winter evening; and they went in the dark after work. Donna cautioned them as they left that it was only an eight-foot ceiling as she was remembering some of the disasters in the heights. Buying trees is like going to a cafeteria to eat, you always end up with more that you intended.

Charlie and Gene decided they had better have a little Jack Daniels before starting out on this venture. They loaded up the kids in the pickup and off to town they went to search the tree lots for just the right tree. Arriving at the tree lot, all three kids took off running to be the first to find the perfect tree.

They found three of them, with each child positive they had found the perfect tree. Now they had to make a decision. Somehow, the colder and darker it got, the smaller the trees appeared. They finally chose a well-rounded beautiful scotch pine. Gene realized it was maybe a little too tall, but he knew from prior experience he could cut a little off the top and bottom and all would be well. In addition, the Jack was wearing off, and he and Charlie were getting cold.

It took the salesman, Gene, and Charlie to load it on the pickup. As they got it loaded, Gene commented he hoped it would fit in his tree stand because now that it was on the truck, the trunk seemed much bigger. He knew he could shave it down and fix it. Home they went with their beautiful tree. It was even more beautiful with the snow now covering the tree. It filled the six-foot bed of the pickup and stuck out a few feet behind the truck. This was not a little balsam as they usually had, but for the first time, a real scotch pine.

Once at home, they unloaded it onto the patio, and Gene got the chain saw and cut a little off the bottom. They opened the French doors, and all helped to get it proudly into the living room. Donna and Eileen immediately saw the problem. An event had occurred that would seem to occur every Christmas. It was a Christmas miracle! The tree had grown on the way home! Donna ordered a ruler and proceeded to measure the tree.

*The cut-off Christmas tree with Donna and* Darrell

Gene and Charlie went to mix another Jack to get warm as they knew what was coming. They would be chastised severely for not measuring the tree before they bought it. Actually, Jack had forgotten their ruler. Gene, Charlie, and the kids all stood at attention while Donna and Eileen lectured on how to measure trees and what kind of idiots would go to buy a tree without a ruler. It probably wouldn't do any good to explain that it was dark and cold and the kids were freezing, so they had to hurry and grab the first tree available. It didn't! Gene finished his drink and realized that sometimes happy hour is a misnomer.

The women finished their measuring and figured out that in order to get the tree in the stand (which Gene had forgotten was over six inches high) and to put the star on the top (which Gene had forgotten was almost a foot high) it would be necessary to cut off at least four and a half feet from the top of the tree or to cut a hole in the ceiling so the last few feet could stick up into the kid's bedroom. The kids were in favor of that solution. Obviously, the only solution was to cut off the tree or return it.

This called for a family conference, and they all sat down to decide what was to happen. Gene remeasured the tree. Surely, she had not measured correctly. Unfortunately, she had. They debated the procedure to follow. They couldn't take the tree back because Gene had sawed some off the bottom. It was too expensive a tree to abandon and buy another one. To take the more than four feet off the bottom would ruin the tree, and they would lose all the beautiful branches that had inspired them to buy the tree in the first place.

Donna and Eileen could see the direction this was taking, and if there were to be a tree up tonight, they would have to take matters into their own hands. They now ordered the top of the tree cut off, and Eileen would use the top part for her tree in her house. Back out on the porch with the tree. Gene got the chain saw and made the cut; it was still almost four inches thick where he cut. How would he mount the star on this stump?

Anyway, it wasn't his problem anymore; Jack was now in charge, and he should take all the blame. Now they tried to affix the bottom of the tree in the tree stand, which was for a six-inch-tree maximum. This tree was over seven inches. Now he would have to take the saw and shave the sides to get it down to six inches. This would be a weird tree.

They called for the troops to open the French doors and help with bringing the tree back in to the living room again. They got the tree in position in the base, and everyone helped sit it up. It cleared the ceiling but not enough to put on the star. Somehow, Jack and Eileen had mismeasured. They would use an old smaller star. Now that the tree had a chance to stretch out, the branches were much longer that at first thought. The tree was too close to the wall, so down it came, and they moved it a few feet farther into the room. That would work. Now they were really in trouble; the branches were now fully unfurled, and there was no place in the room that the tree didn't fill. It was over eight feet across, and it was still growing.

After another family discussion, the conclusion was that they would move the couch and chairs to another room and leave the tree. Charlie thought he and Gene needed to go confer with Jack again, but they were quickly informed that was what got them in trouble in the first place. The women closed the bar. Jack would not be involved in this decision. They got the tree upright, and it still had one problem. It was leaning to one side and too heavy for the stand to correct it. Back to the lumber pile and they made V supports to put under the main branches. This did the job; it was still a little shaky, but it would survive. They got it in place, got out the decorations, and started with the lights from the top down. They were only halfway down and ran out of lights. This was a big tree. It would require a trip back to Walgreens to buy more lights.

Charlie, Gene, and Jack were now denied driving privileges; so Donna and Eileen were off to pick up four more strings of lights. With the women gone, Charlie thought it was safe to confer with Jack again. Adding the lights was another disaster. They had to get a ladder and put Darrell up to the top to wrap the lights around the tree. This worked until someone tripped on the ladder, and Darrell went into the tree.

Once the new lights were installed, the kids proceeded to add balls and decorations. They plugged in the lights and were amazed there were so many bulbs you could actually read by the tree lights. It was like daylight. With the deed done, they mixed a batch of whiskey sours to celebrate the occasion. The bar was reopened, this time at the request of the women. The kids sat on the floor because now they had no furniture in the room. Once again, they had fought the battle of the growing Christmas trees and won.

In 1976, they remodeled the house and built the new dining room, kitchen, and bath. The new addition had a slopping roof being almost thirteen feet at the top and slanting down to seven feet at the outside with beams and roof decking. Finally, they could really have a tall tree by putting it out in the new addition. Off went Gene, Charlie, Jack, and the kids to find a really big tree befitting of a thirteen-foot ceiling. Again, it was a miserable cold evening with a biting wind. Gene and Charlie knew it was a thirteen-foot ceiling, and they were careful to measure this time to get a ten-foot tree. They measured the tree and got Jack to measure again. Just as they were ready to buy, the kids found another tree they liked better then another.

Finally, they shut off the tree looking and said they were going to take this one. This time they got a tree much smaller around, but they might have to cut a little off the top. Christmas was one of the holidays when Jack was invited, but he usually overstayed his welcome and ended up getting everyone in trouble. This year was no exception. Both Charlie and Gene would end up accusing Jack of picking out the tree. On the way home, Gene was now questioning if the tree they finally loaded was the one he had measured?

Another Christmas miracle was about to happen on the way home. The tree grew again. To make it worse, the room shrunk.

A growing tree and a shrinking room can only have one result; the boys were in trouble again. Apparently, the first tree they had measured wasn't the one they ended up loading. The boys hadn't thought about the slopping ceiling, and in the center where the tree was to go, it was only nine feet. In addition, when the tree unfurled, there was no room to sit around the dining room table.

This time the only answer was to cut six feet off the bottom of the tree in order to make it smaller overall. They now had a beautiful eight-foot tree. It was a little weird but still beautiful once it was decorated. There were enough branches left over that Donna and Eileen were able to decorate the fireplaces, above the doors, the patio fence, and the sidewalks leading to the houses. Moreover, they had some nice logs for the fireplace.

This time, Donna had enough; she decided Gene, Charlie, and Jack had created their last Christmas miracle of the growing trees, and they were fired. The day after Christmas, the stores opened at 6:00 a.m. with special sales, and Donna was there. She bought an artificial Christmas tree. Every Christmas, Gene, Charlie, Jack, and the kids expressed their disappointment at not being able to buy a Christmas tree; but the artificial tree was here to stay. Each year as they drove by the Christmas tree sales lots, they looked longingly at the trees and the people happily picking out trees. It was as if one of the most enjoyable parts of Christmas had been taken away from them. Maybe someday?

Christmas Eve finally came, and all went to the early church candlelight service. After church, Gene and the kids placed their farolitos in the lane spaced about four feet apart. They had made up their paper sacks with the sand and candles earlier in the day. They lit the candles, and the magic of Christmas began.

By now, it was after 8:30 and time for a late dinner and some Tom and Jerry (homemade eggnog). As they all sat in the living room admiring the tree and lights while they drank their cocoa and Tom and Jerry's, there came a sound outside. This wasn't surprising as they often had friends drop by on Christmas Eve.

Gene went to the door, opened it partway, stuck his head out, and said, "I don't care who you are, fat man, cut out that ho-ho stuff and get your reindeers off my roof." The kids all ran outside in the snow to look up on the roof. Then they realized they had been duped again. As they passed their father to go to bed, one of them said, "I hope your stocking is empty in the morning." Surely, they weren't serious.

At ten o'clock, they sent the kids to bed. It was time for Santa's helpers to do their work. The kids slept upstairs and had doors to close, so they wouldn't see what was developing. The helpers didn't realize that in that old house the sound traveled upstairs, and you could hear every word if you snuck down to the bottom step on the stairs and sat behind the closed door. It was learned later that is what the kids did every year. It was hard to keep any surprises from enterprising children.

Now the fun began. Gene and Donna had entered the antique business, and someone had come into the shop wanting to sell an electric train, an American Flyer. They bought it for the kids for Christmas. It came in two huge boxes. Now it was time to set up the tracks and have it running when the kids got up in the morning. While Donna and Eileen were busy cooking for the big day, they always cooked a small turkey on Christmas Eve and the large one on Christmas Day; Gene and Charlie set up the train. Each Christmas there was always something to assemble. One year it was the play kitchen and accessories, one year the bumper pool table, and various do-it-yourself projects. This year was the most involved.

The train came with almost one hundred feet of track. Assembled, it went around the tree, around the furniture, formed a figure eight, and had sidetracks and switches. The track absorbed the whole living room. It went through the furniture and tree and under the tables. This was a very good train. American Flyer was the top of the line. It had transformers, switches, side tracks, working green and red stoplights, water towers, crossings, a train station, and a little town. The train had a whistle and headlight controllable from the transformer. There was another train as a bonus, a Lionel freight train. In addition, a repair vehicle ran independently from the trains. With the multiple transformer and the sidetracks, they could keep both trains and the sidecar running at the same time. The two big boys were having a ball. Neither ever had an electric train, and their lifelong dreams were being fulfilled.

By three in the morning, there was track everywhere, and the trains were running. Now Gene and Charlie weren't working but playing. Charlie was sprawled on one side of the room and Gene on the other. The freight train was running and had an open car that Charlie and Gene used to deliver Jack across the room. The glass just fit in the car. They had a ball sounding the whistle upon Jack's arrival. Since Jack was no longer welcome on the tree-buying trip, he was invited to the assembly parties.

The sounds must have been killing the kids with anticipation. This was even more curious than the year they did the bumper pool table and the kids heard the balls dropping until four in the morning. They stumped the kids that time. Gene and Charlie were having a very merry Christmas. That year, about five thirty in the morning, Gene went to feed the horses and animals and got the bright idea to take the Christmas bells and walk up on the roof to ring the bells outside the kids' windows. This brought the children down in a hurry. He never told them it was he ringing the bells, and for a while, at least they really believed it was Santa Claus.

Eventually, six o'clock came, and the kids were in the kitchen and ready to open presents. Gene and Charlie were still lying at their engineer posts but both were sound asleep. Jack was still enjoying his ride in the open flat car. Gene left the big train running when he and Charlie closed their eyes for naps, so it was running when the kids got up. This was a great Christmas. Charlie and Gene had severe headaches and never got to bed, but the train was running. Christmas was always a big time at the Londene house.

There was a sad day coming when Charlie and Eileen were gone, and the kids had their own homes and were raising their own families. There were no more tree and assembly Christmas Eve's on the farm, and Jack had long ago worn out his invitation. Now it was time for the kids to continue the tradition in their own homes with their children, but they would really have to work at it to recreate the wonderful Christmas Eve's on the farm.

# Pool Table, Skiing, and Swimming Pool

Charlie was a great pool player and played competitively. Gene had played pool and snooker all his life. One week the championship touring pool tournament was coming to Albuquerque.

All the big-time players were coming—Minnesota Fats, Boston Shorty, Smitty, and others. They set the tournament tables and bleachers up in the ballroom of the hotel. A manufacturer from Los Angeles brought twenty regular size and four larger professional tables for sale and put them in the hallways. Gene and Charlie went to observe the tournament during the week; and on Saturday night, Donna and Eileen went along to see the finals. The show ended about midnight. On the way out, they looked at the tables. They had discounted the tables, sold the smaller ones, and only three of the professional size remained. The price all week had been $3,600 each. They talked about buying a table. Since this was the final night, they were marked down to $2,400. The company didn't want to have to transport these tables again.

Gene and Charlie haggled the price but to no avail. Eileen crawled under the table to see how it was constructed. Everyone laughed at this rather large busty woman crawling under the table in the middle of the hall of the motel, but she didn't care. She wanted to see if it really was Italian slate marble. She pounded on the bottom of the table, crawled from underneath, and said, "Yep, that is a real table."The salesman thought they were so much fun he discounted the table; however, he held firm at his final price of $1,800.

As they were leaving, Gene took out one of his business cards and wrote a price on it. He handed it to the salesman and said, "Here is my offer, if you get down to this, call me."

At two-thirty in the morning the phone rang, it was the sales representative. He told Gene he could have the table for the price offered, and they had to be there to pick it up by 7:00 AM. They would have it all disassembled so he could load it and to bring cash. Gene had offered $900. He didn't have $900! He called Charlie, and Eileen answered. Eileen would go to the bank in the morning and withdraw $900 while Gene, Charlie, and Donna went to load the table in the two station wagons. They got them loaded, and Eileen showed up with the cash. They now owned a pool table. The sales representative then said, "Well, you got the table at a steal, you might as well have the balls that go with it," and he gave them the balls. Gene said, "What about the sticks." Everyone laughed, but he didn't get the sticks.

On the farm was a metal-covered building used as a horse foaling barn. They had been renovating it for Donna and the girls to use for an arts and crafts building. They had run a cement floor and insulated the walls and roof. Now it appeared this was the only building big enough with a solid floor to hold a pool table. Donna lost her building, and it became a poolroom. Most holidays and weekends included a session in the poolroom. Eventually, all the family played pool. The pool table became in winter what the swimming pool was in the summer, the main attraction.

When they weren't playing pool, they found other distractions. Gene had a new client who managed all the condominium rental associations at Purgatory Ski Resort north of Durango, Colorado. In early December, the family went with him to the annual meeting where Gene presented the accounting results. Before Gene and Donna went to the meeting in the morning, they took the kids over to the ski building, rented skis, and bought them lessons for the morning session. Gene hadn't been on skis since he tried it unsuccessfully in Garmish, Germany, in 1953; now he was forty-five, people retire from skiing at forty-five! After lunch, Gene rented skis, poles, and put on what warm clothes he had, which was a pair of jeans, a sweatshirt, cotton gloves, and off to the top of the mountain they went. Gary had told him in order to turn he should push on his downhill ski. It wasn't working. The third time the kids and Gary passed him, they stopped to help. Now Gary told him the downhill ski is really the uphill ski before you turn, and it is downhill after the turn. Now it worked better. He and the kids were hooked on skiing. When they returned to Albuquerque, they all bought skis, poles, jackets, hats, and sunglasses, even Donna. The next trip, Gene and Donna took lessons for half a day; and they were off on a life of skiing. Donna only went at the insistence of the family, it initially wasn't something she wanted to do, but she eventually went to the top of the mountain and skied several years.

A director of the association from Hesperus, Colorado, hired Gene to do his taxes. A year later, after Gene completed his personal and his ranch tax returns, he owed Gene twenty-five hundred dollars. He asked Gene if he would like to own one of the rental units in the ski lodge, Angelhaus at Purgatory. He offered to sell Gene one for a good price but to reduce what Gene owed him by the amount of Gene's outstanding bills. Gene made the exchange and assumed his mortgage of twenty-two thousand five hundred. They now owned a unit. The family went to Purgatory every year between Christmas and New Years and a couple other weekends for years.

The first day on the mountain, Darrell decided he was a skier. On the practice course, another young skier challenged him to race to the bottom of the bunny slope. They raced. Suddenly, he realized he was in front because the other boy slowed to stop as they were approaching a snow fence straight ahead and that was why he was winning. Now Darrell discovered he had learned to ski, but no one had taught him how to stop. It took the ski patrol thirty minutes while they located a pair of wire cutters to cut him out of the tangled mess he made of the snow fence. He had wrapped himself up like a Christmas present.

The second trip, everyone skied all day. Donna had a bad day because she had failed to make a turn and ended up in a fir tree with her feet and skis straight up in the tree and her lying on her back under the branches. It was very awkward. Gene wouldn't help her out until he took pictures. On the way down, she got to the last steep hill and sat down. Gene went past her and tried to talk her down the hill. Finally, she took off her skis and threw them at him. They came down the hill like rockets. This was before the days of safety stops on skis. She walked down the hill. The runs were very narrow in the early days of Purgatory and were difficult for beginners to navigate. She swore to never ski again, but she did.

The next day went better. They all put Band-Aids on the worn raw parts and blisters. It snowed half a foot, and the trails were easier. The snow was so good they opened the racecourse. Gene and Darrell raced and Darrell got a ribbon. Gene decided he didn't need to do that twice. He almost made it to the finish line. When they got to the bottom, they all stopped at the Pub for hot cider. They waited on Darrell, but he never showed up. Now it was starting to get dark and no Darrell. The girls went to the condominium to see if he had gone home. He wasn't there. There were only two possibilities; he was still on the mountain, or he had been hauled down on a sled. They went to the first aid building. There sat Darrell getting his sling adjusted. He had raced and crashed. They brought him down on a sled and patched him up. They put the left arm in a sling and said if it was broken it would swell up tomorrow, and they should take him to town to the hospital. The next day he was back on the mountain.

The valley had no swimming pool. The kids had to be hauled the fourteen-mile round trip to the Elks Club to swim. The first venture was to buy a steel ten-foot animal stock tank. Gene filled it with water from the irrigation well since they didn't yet have city water. Donna had purchased some chlorine to purify the water. She put it in the pool, and within minutes, the water turned a solid brown color. The well water had too many chemicals that reacted with the chlorine, and bromine hadn't been invented yet. The kids had to swim in an unpurified pool, but since the water didn't cost them anything, they could just change the water more often.

A trip to Sears resulted in the purchase of a fifteen-by-thirty-foot pool with four-foot high sides that held ten thousand gallons of water. The price was about $2,200, and Donna and Eileen decided to split the cost. Little did they know when they elected to erect the pool themselves, how many small parts there were, and how much work it would be for the whole family. They came home and informed Gene and Charlie that the truck would deliver the parts tomorrow, and it was their job to assemble it. The women fixed chips and dips, and everyone had a pool party. They had no pool yet, but they had a pool party. They liked to party, any excuse worked. They sat in the yard eating chips and dips and discussed the location. While they were talking, the pony ate the chips. Charlie thought he better call the county agent for advice before starting the project. Donna thought she better call the vet. Gene just had another drink and said, "Let's get it on." They chose a spot with plenty of sunshine. Gene got out the Farmall tractor and leveled the ground. This was before the age of lasers, so to see if it was level, they built a small dam ridge around it and flooded it to see where the water stood.

Now the fun began, Charlie did what he was best at, reading the instructions, over and over. Gene did his normal thing and just started unwrapping parts and started assembling the underpinning that goes under the pool. Periodically, they would stop to consult with Jack and look at the pictures in the instructions. The kids were unpacking parts—and an orderly control of what came next and what packet of screws went with it—was lost. This was a zoo in progress. Each night required a conference over the next step. It should have been obvious that when Gene and Charlie attached the uprights, they should have been installed with the correct side up. Maybe that was why those funny little letters were on the one end. Now, Donna and Eileen figured out they spelled *up*. They only lost one evening making this correction. Definitely got Jack involved on this one or maybe he was the cause of the problem. It had been a struggle, accompanied by some short tempers, but it was finished and ready to put up the rails and attach the platform. Installing the liner and cap was at least a six-person job. The instructions for the pool said, "Four days for two people." Their people must have had eight arms each.

Now the big day was here. City water had now come to the farm, and Gene attached the hose. The kids had their swimming suits on and were in the pool waiting for the water to rise. They had a ball from the first inch of water. It was still late April and cool, but the sun in the pool made it bearable. By the next morning, the pool was filled to the top, and the fun began. The pool had been completed at a cost of $2,200 for the pool, $300 for the filter system and cleaning vacuum, $200 for food, $200 for Jack and Oso Negro consultations, and $100 for chips and dips to keep the workers on the job. Now it was time for another $400 for floaters, volleyball net, umbrellas, floor nonslip pads, new swimming suits, beach towels, gravel around the pool, and flagstone for sidewalks. Of course, next they had to have lounge chairs to lie on while they dried in the sun, and of course, a barbeque table and benches next to the pool for the chips and dips parties after the swim, and then the radio for the pool area and on and on and on. As usual, the total cost was twice the estimate.

In reality, this was probably the best investment ever made on the farm. The kids stayed home, had many friends in to swim, and they all grew up with no drugs, no smoking, and very little drinking. The pool lasted for over thirty-five years, through three kids, eight grandkids, several little league and soccer teams, Sister City guests, and many parties. The pool became the main social function of the farm with daily usage from April to October. Donna was happy because she could just look out the window and see all her kids at home having a good time.

The weekends now had a different agenda. Everyone got up early to work in the yard, mow grass and weed. At eleven o'clock, the work stopped, and everyone jumped in the pool for a few games of hotly contested volleyball. The pool became the social life of the farm for kids and grown-ups alike. It was amazing how many new friends the kids had. They no longer complained about lack of friends from being isolated on the farm. Gene would start around the table and ask, "Are you a Londene? Yes, eat!" or "Are you a Londene? No, go home." Sometimes they were convinced they were a family of fourteen. Donna just cooked for whatever number might show up at the table. She thought at times she was running a commune.

This pool had a ten-year guarantee. They put it up in 1974, replaced the liner four times, and it finally rusted out on the bottom in 2007 and had to be replaced. Gene mused maybe they got their money's worth. He was already bemoaning the fact he might have to this every thirty-three years.

# Winter of 1971

Christmas had been warm and beautiful. Eileen helped Donna do turkey and all the trimmings. Gene, Charlie, and the kids were out in the poolroom playing pool. After dinner, Gene and the kids played football and basketball with the new balls from Santa Claus. It was so warm they just wore T-shirts. New Year was almost as warm. They sat outside for the first time ever and made homemade ice cream for New Year's Day. It was unusually warm even for New Mexico.

The next day, since they didn't really use the old front door, they decided to close it and make the south French doors the front door. It would give them more room and wall space in the living room. They took two-by-four studs and blocked in the old doorway. They nailed up some insulation and put a temporary piece of plywood over the opening on the inside. They would put up wallboard and finished it the next day.

It was late afternoon, and the wind had come up and it was turning cold. Huge, low-hanging, ominous clouds had come in a hurry, and already it was threatening snow. They got a piece of outside wallboard and nailed over the hole left by the door removal. Suddenly, a very strong wind came. The temperature dropped from a mild sixty degrees to thirty in less than an hour.

By the time Gene went to feed the animals, it was freezing and started to snow. They had been so busy, no one had turned on the TV in two or three days, and they had no idea the weatherman had been forecasting this huge storm. Normally before a cold spell, Gene drained all the water hoses so they wouldn't freeze, so he could water the animals and he and the kids brought in extra wood. This one caught them totally unprepared.

By morning, there was six inches of snow, and the temperature was down to ten degrees. Gene got a comforter blanket and hung it over the open door as the wind was coming in through the unfinished cracks. He nailed more covering on the outside of the house. That night it was down to zero degrees, and they brought in more wood and kept a nice fire in the fireplace. It snowed another foot. In the morning, they arose to a cold house. Gene checked the furnace and turned it up. The only heat in the downstairs came from a floor furnace in the living room. There was no heat in the kitchen or bedroom except what migrated from the living room. The furnace was on but not giving out much heat. Apparently, the gas supply was low. They went into the kitchen to look out the window; it was frozen solid with ice on the inside. Something was wrong. They turned on the TV. The weatherman was explaining what had happened. A huge cold front had come down from Alaska with lightning speed, and the air stream had gone south further than ever before.

The temperature, outside at the airport where they measured, was a record ten below zero. This was unheard of in Albuquerque. The old record was minus five in the 1920s. All the businesses in New Mexico were closed, and the busses weren't running. Albuquerque was at a complete standstill. The highways were closed coming in and out of New Mexico and mostly closed from California to East Texas. Gene got the fireplace going, and they had coffee. Now he had to go out and feed the animals. He trudged through over a foot of snow and got the horses, cow, pig. and chickens fed. He got a sledgehammer and broke the ice in the water tanks. It was cold, and the ice was already thick.

He checked his thermometer. It was seventeen below zero. It was always seven to ten degrees colder in the valley than at the official weather station at the airport on the hill. They didn't go to work that day as the roads were icy and snow covered.

That night, Gene had to carry water from the house to the animals as all his hoses and water faucets had frozen solid. It had turned even colder. They kept a roaring fire in the fireplace all day, and at bedtime, Gene put on a two-foot log that would burn for a few hours. It was a big fireplace. Upstairs there was a gas wall heater in the wall between the west bedroom and the hall. The east rooms had to rely on the heat traveling to their room. Everyone got bundled up in their nice warm beds and settled in for the night.

It was two in the morning when Gene and Donna woke to the patter of little feet coming to get in bed with them. The kids were cold. There was no longer any heat upstairs. The kids said the heater had blown out, which happens sometimes. Gene got up and went up to light the furnace. It wouldn't light! He smelled the gas outlet, and there was no gas. Now what was he to do? He went downstairs to check the furnace since the downstairs was equally as cold. There was no light in that furnace. They had no gas anywhere. He knew this was big trouble.

He got a flashlight, scraped the ice off the window and looked out to see the thermometer. It was twenty-four below zero. Impossible! He went to the bathroom and flushed the stool, no water. The lines were all frozen solid. Even the water in the stool was frozen. Finally, he tried the bathtub. The cold water worked, but the hot water was frozen. The hot water heater was still on the outside of the house. The only water available on the whole farm was the cold water in the bathtub, and that was temporary.

They turned on the TV. All the stations were covering only the storm. The temperature in Gallup, a hundred and thirty-five miles to the west, was fifty-six below zero. Wow. Now the bad news, half of Albuquerque was without gas. The line coming in from Farmington had somehow frozen. The entire valley, which included downtown and the entire business district, was without gas. The heights, the housing area up next to the mountain, had some gas, which was never explained.

Donna helped the kids bring their blankets and pillows off their beds downstairs. They made up their beds on the living room floor and couches in front of the fireplace. They closed up the upstairs. Gene brought in more wood for the fireplace and got a good blazing fire going. Even with the fireplace going, the house was very cold. The windows were old and wouldn't close tight. The cold wind was coming right through the doors and windows. Donna got some masking tape and put on the bad places. Gene got a hammer and nails and drove the nails in over the windows and doors to make hangers for blankets. They brought more blankets from upstairs and hung them over the windows and doors. The room was getting warmer. There was no door between the kitchen and living room; they left that open so the food wouldn't freeze. Gene turned on the little electric heater in the bathroom. It didn't work.

Now it was time to make coffee. Gene ran some water from the bathtub, and they could at least have coffee. Donna made the kids some cocoa with marshmallows. They didn't own any electric heaters. Guess they never had any use for them. Thank goodness they had an electric stove instead of gas. They thought about going out to sleep in the camping trailer where they had butane for heat, but they realized it would only last a couple days. The kids went back to sleep in their new warm beds, and Gene and Donna drank coffee and stared at the fire.

One of the great privileges of having a fireplace was getting up early and just sitting in front of the fireplace watching the flames flicker with the only light being the fireplace. It was hypnotic and soul satisfying, especially on the Christmas holidays. Donna was busy rolling up towels and rugs and placing them in front of the doors. Gene or Donna was taking turns staying up to keep the fireplace going. With all the blankets nailed over the doors and windows, it was like living in a dungeon.

Gene was already sitting there thinking about going out in the cold and feeding animals and how he was going to water them. Soon it was daylight, and a look outside at the snow and ice was discouraging. There was over two foot of snow. Gene put on his long johns and the rest of his ski clothes. He wrapped his head with a scarf and put his felt cowboy hat on top. He didn't really have any warm gloves. He took a pair of cotton gloves and put an extra large pair of leather gloves over them. He dug out his Mickey Mouse insulated snow boots and a heavy jacket, and he was ready for the cold cruel world.

Getting water to the animals was a big problem. He tried a faucet, no water. He tried to break the ice on the tanks, but they were frozen solid. He got buckets and began carrying water from the house.

The chickens were inside the building, but their water holders were frozen solid. The old sow had a litter of pigs in November, and they were about sixteen to eighteen pounds now. When Gene got to the pigs, they were in the little house. He checked them out and found some dead ones. They had frozen. He went to the house for more water and told Donna about the frozen pigs. She dressed and came out to check out her little darlings. When they got in the little barn, they found that all the little pigs were dead. They were all frozen solid. They laid them outside the fence to bury them when it thawed out. It was another sad farming day. Donna was brokenhearted over the loss of her little darlings.

That day it snowed some more. For the next several days, they used the little frozen pigs as stepping stones to get in and out of the pigpen to take water. They took some horse feed and spread it in the machine and hay sheds for the roadrunners, peacocks, and wild pheasants that had moved in from the cold looking for shelter and food. They fed the cats that lived in the hay barn. Everyone was now full and watered at least. Doing chores took up most of their day. Just to top things off, now they had no telephone.

The third day the water finally froze up in the bathtub. Now to get water to the animals, Gene got the old iron tub they used to dip the turkeys in and lit a fire under it. He carried snow and ice to the tub and melted it. The lifesaver was that the only place that had water still running was the toilet. This was very important. They fixed the electric heater in the bathroom, which was giving out just enough heat to keep the toilet from freezing. They had gone down into the well house and put blankets over the well and pressure tank to keep it pumping water.

The next day it warmed up, clear up to five degrees in the daytime, but back down to minus fifteen at night. The third day, they were out of milk, bread, and necessities. He tried in vain to start the car or the pickup. He tried the tractor. The tractor wouldn't start. The kids were home because the school was closed and frozen. The school wouldn't open for a long time due to repairs on water lines.

He remembered the heat lamp they had used for the foaling barn and got long electric cords to run to the car. He put the heater under the car and a blanket over it. Eventually, it should get warm enough to start. He planned to start the car and then take the heat lamp into the bathroom. Hours later, he went out to check the car. The lamp had burned out, and the car was still cold. There would be no milk; they would eat ice cream and fried eggs. Gene and Donna knew from their college days how to survive on eggs.

The chickens got so cold they refused to lay an egg. If they did lay eggs, they were frozen almost immediately.

A salesman from Dixon Paper called to see how they were doing. The roads were now clear enough to drive although still icy and treacherous. He had a four-wheel drive jeep and was kind enough to drive down to the farm and bring some milk and bread.

He used jumper wires, and eventually, Gene's car started. It had warmed up into the teens that day and things were getting better, but they were still frozen solid. At least now, the wind had stopped coming in the house because there was so much ice on the windows. Five days later, as suddenly as it had left, the gas returned. Gene lit the furnaces, and all was well. He got to town, found an electric heater, thawed out the water heater line, and relit the water heater. Now there was more bad news; the water lines outside the house had frozen and broken, including the water heater. The water lines to the animals were frozen and broken. It would take a month to get everything fixed. He managed to get some water hoses that ran directly from the pump to water the animals, and they carried water to the house.

The coldest storm in New Mexico history was gone, but it would certainly not be forgotten.

# Wine Making

The Viola Farm offered many new experiences and exploits. There was a grape arbor with twenty-four vines on the farm. The first year they got a ladder and picked some grapes for jelly. That fall they cut down the trees and trimmed the grapes to four feet high. They restrung the wires and replaced the broken posts. That spring the grapes blossomed out beautifully and all the vines made grapes.

Donna and Eileen made juice, jelly, and pancake syrup. They ate grapes and gave away grapes, but there were still three wheelbarrows of grapes left over. Gene decided to learn to make wine. The Ellis family left all the equipment for making wine and apple cider in the basement. There were barrels, ten-gallon porcelain crocks, bottles, crusher, and all the necessary items for apple cider, wine, or beer. They explained the only way they had to preserve the juice in the days before refrigeration was to make the apple cider and wine and let the alcohol protect it. What a wonderful and convenient excuse. Of course, they had to have their daily juice for the vitamins and other health reasons.

Gene went to town to the Grape Arbor, a wine store to buy supplies. He followed instructions to the letter, added the sugar, tannin, acid, sulfur tablets, some elderberry concentrate, some other items, some leaves from the vine, and a few pieces of actual vine as instructed. He added the warm water and brought the temperature up to just the ideal degree. He let it sit for another twenty-four hours, tested and adjusted the acid, and then added the yeast starter he had made the day before. He covered the crocks with black trash bags and put a big rubber band around the crocks to keep the fruit flies out. Fruit flies are what turn the wine to vinegar.

Next morning there were bubbles and the next day the yeast foam cap on top of the wine was three inches thick and a beautiful pink color. Everyone was fascinated by the way it fermented and worked. He stirred the wine twice a day to submerge the entire cap, and on the seventh day, it was finished. Gene tasted the wine, and it was terrible. He now understood what aging does for wine. Until the yeast and sulfur works out of the wine, it has a terrible bitter taste.

Gene referred to his wine as, "44 Wine." This came about because he jokingly told people he held a forty-four pistol on his friends while they drank, and they held it on him while he drank. The basement was perfect for making wine. The temperature stayed fairly constant, and it was dark. After one year, the wine was ready to drink and bottle. Of course, they had already used up a couple gallons from sampling.

It was time for bottling wine. Gene carefully washed the bottles and corks in sulfur water. The kids helped pour the wine in bottles, then capped and stored for drinking later. Preferably, it would be a few years later for the red wine and one year maximum for the white. To Gene's surprise, his first batch of wine was acceptable and as the years went by he got better and made some premium wines, every now and again.

In 1993, Gene had two years of wine ready. He kept a list and called those who had volunteered to help bottle. His new son-in-law, Randy, along with several others, was to be christened into wine making that night. Gene washed and sterilized the bottles, boiled the corks in sulfur water, and put them in a sterilized bag. When they arrived, they set up an assembly line. Gene supervised siphoning the wine from the large container thorough a cloth sieve and metal strainer into the round crock where the campden tablets and sweetener were added. Of course everyone had to taste it until they got it right, not too sweet, not too dry. It took a lot of tasting, and there were several crocks of wine. He made simple syrup for the sweetener. Once the taste was approved, the bottling commenced. One was in charge of rinsing the bottle in a sulfur solution to keep the wine from spoiling. Then to another who poured the wine in each bottle using a funnel but leaving enough room for the cork. After the bottle was filled, it went to another who took a clean sterilized cork, put it in the corker and positioned it over the bottle. It was Randy's job to make sure there was enough room for the cork and to take the rubber mallet to drive the cork into the bottle. Then another helper labeled them and put the bottles in the rack.

It seemed like a good crew, and they proceeded to bottle over eighty bottles of wine. As they worked, they sampled. Soon one had sampled so much wine that he was getting a little careless and filling the bottles too full. If the bottle was filled too high, Randy solved the problem by drinking it down until it was the required two inches. Gene always brewed his wine to the maximum to make sure it didn't spoil. When wine reaches 17 percent, the alcohol kills the yeast and fermentation stops. Usually, his wine was close to maximum, and it was not uncommon for his helpers to call Gene's wine lighter fluid. Everyone was feeling merry and having a good time. Of course the efficiency of the crew deteriorated.

Gene kept a little TV in the basement so they could watch the football game as they worked. The noise of laughing and telling jokes traveled through the floor to the upstairs and told the women the boys were having a very good time.

The basement had low ceilings and sewer lines running through it with only about six-foot clearance. Randy was six foot five. They all had trouble navigating the basement without hitting their heads. Being six-foot, Gene knew the problem well; many times he came out of the basement rubbing his head. Randy's position in the assembly line was right under a sewer line. Soon he started standing up every so often to reach for bottles. Occasionally, they heard a "clunk," and there was Randy holding his head and making loud comments about someone's son. By the time they got to the last bottle, no one in the basement was feeling any pain except Randy. His head hurt, and he had several lumps on his bald head. Donna and the women upstairs wondered if anything was being accomplished. Finally, they were finished, and at about midnight, everyone started home. Gene was the lucky one since he just had to walk upstairs. One left and drove as far as the shopping center where he pulled in and slept until daylight.

Randy had a two-hundred-yard walk home. At one-thirty in the morning, Randy's wife Denise called to the big house; Randy hadn't gotten home yet. It was only a short walk, and it took him an hour and a half. They never did find out where Randy had been, he wouldn't say. Denise wasn't sure if his head hurt because of too much wine or if he had a concussion from continually banging his head on the sewer line. Either way she was not happy.

The next year when it came bottling time, no one showed up. They had all found out what happens with too much sampling. Denise wouldn't let Randy help bottle wine again for years. Everyone still joked about the "bottling party," but some never came back. Now the granddaughters were getting boyfriends. Next year he would have a new crew to break in.

Regardless of the success or lack of success, wine making was an enjoyable hobby. Gene continued to make wine, but often he made it and sampled it alone. He had learned to hold the forty-four pistol on himself.

# Rabbits

Memories from the farm come from great enjoyable experiences, and sometimes from totally unexpected, impulsive sources. The best memories in life are those that bring a smile to your lips whenever you think of them.

Upon moving to the farm, they raised about everything the family could think of that the kids, Donna, or Gene wanted. Each one had his or her own pets: horses, cows, sheep, pigs, chickens, turkeys, ducks, dogs, guinea pigs, birds, and unintentionally, skunks, mice, rats, gophers, and snakes. One of the first ventures into reproduction and raising their own food was rabbits.

Gene began raising rabbits as a 4-H project when he was ten years old. In addition, Donna had her black-and-white rabbit, Liberace, while living in Manhattan. The whole family liked fried rabbit with mashed potatoes and white gravy and until they had their own supply she had been buying them for the local grocery store who got them from rabbit farms in the valley.

They acquired rabbit hutches, and each kid each picked out a rabbit, two big white does and a buck. It was Saturday, so Gene was home for the day. The kids spent the morning outside as usual, and at noon, Donna called them to lunch. They didn't arrive. She yelled out the back door in a manner that may have brought in the kids from the whole neighborhood. She only needed to say one word in that manner and voice, "Kids!"

Here they came through the back door marching to the bathroom sink to wash. Denise was first since she was the oldest at eight; Darlene was second at five; and Darrell, the three-year-old, came in last. This stair step convoy was the standard arrival. As they walked in the house single file, Donna asked, "Where have you been?" Sometimes you are really not prepared for the answer you get. When the answer is totally out of context, you have to respond accordingly and in a nice parenting way. Today would test the parenting skills. As the kids proceeded to the bathroom, Darrell nonchalantly responded, "Oh, we have been out in the rabbit pen watching the rabbits screwing."

There was a deafening silence from the kitchen. No parenting experience provides one with the ability to respond to this. Donna gave Gene a horrified stare; meanwhile, he was fighting desperately to suppress the hilarious laughter that was building up and spontaneously wanted to explode from within him. He knew he had better not laugh, or Donna would be after him. Finally, Donna gave him a look that said, "I can't speak. You handle this."

Darrell was standing in the bathroom door waiting his turn to wash, so he expounded on his enlightening experience, much to the dismay of his mother. He said, "The papa rabbit gets on the back of the mama rabbit and shakes for a while and then shuts his eyes and goes to sleep and falls over backwards." When everyone thought he was finished, he said, "Then in a little bit he wakes up and he does it again."

Now thoughts were running through both Gene and Donna's mind. How do we, or do we, reprimand for this? How do you explain to children that what they have seen is a normal farm happening, and on the other hand tell them sex has happened for eternity, but they weren't allowed to talk about it. How do you tell them there is a moral Puritanism about grown-ups that makes sex a dirty word? Gene took the easiest cop out and just dismissed it by saying, "We'll talk about it later," which means drop the subject until they could think about how to handle this. Donna could have a talk with the girls, and Gene was supposed to talk to Darrell. Sure, have a birds and bees talk with a three-year-old? That would work? Gene finally made the comment, "That is just the way rabbits have babies," and everyone was content.

While they were eating lunch, Gene was thinking, *How do I explain all this without getting in trouble with Big Mama?* Unfortunately, Darrell was also thinking. Everyone was quietly eating his or her grilled cheese sandwich when the inevitable happened. Darrell put down his sandwich on his plate, looked at his father, and shook the family foundation again. He said, "Dad." It was obvious when Darrell is coming out with a question by the way he says Dad, by making it a two-syllable word with the emphasis on the second syllable, like Day-ed. "If the dog screws the rabbit, will we get rabbits or dogs?" It was another no-answer situation and another pause to regroup.

Who had the kids been talking with to come up with these questions? Gene was tempted to add a little more humor to the situation and say, "No, you get rabbits that bark or maybe dogs that hop." However, one look at Donna, and he decided against that. This time it was impossible to withhold the laughter, and Gene came unglued. His only comment was that discussion was over until lunch was finished. Gene would later explain to Donna, Charlie, and Eileen that rabbits do pass out from excessive exertion with sex. The kids were not admonished for this action. They would be enlightened on the need for where babies come from on the farm and the need for sex. They were all getting a farm education quickly. Years of Donna's protection of monitoring the kid's exposure to the wrong movies were being blown away by real life situations.

After this event, the papa rabbit was put in a separate cage. Approximately twenty-one days later, the kids came in panicked and said the mama rabbit is trying to kill herself because she was pulling out all her hair and scratching herself to death. This required another lesson that the mama rabbit knows that she will have little rabbits today and is making a nest of her own hair to keep them warm. She lives in a wire cage and had no place to find nesting material other than her own body. The babies are born as small pink little creatures with no hair. The warm nest of hair would help their survival.

Just before dark, the kids went out to check the rabbit to see if she was a mother yet. The babies had not arrived, but for some reason, the kids decided the papa rabbit should be with the mama when the event happened, and they put him back in her cage. There would be a sad lesson learned here. The next morning the kids were out early to check the rabbits. Again, they came running back to the house in panic. There were little dead rabbits all over the cage floor; some of them were partially eaten by the papa rabbit who was being mean to the mama rabbit.

Of course, Donna's first reaction was to call the vet. Gene assured her it was not necessary and went out and removed the papa from the pen. He gathered up the dead rabbits. It was time for another lesson, and Gene had to explain that papa rabbits sometimes kill all the young, and the mama rabbit will eat the imperfect rabbits. She will also eat them if she has too many. She will only let live the number that can nurse at the same time. It is simply their nature. That is why they separate the mama and papa before the birth. Later they would go through the breeding and birthing process with a little more supervision, and this time they had six beautiful little baby rabbits.

It takes about ten days for the little rabbits to get hair and get their eyes open. After that, the kids lived with the little fluff balls. Darrell was smuggling one up to his bedroom to sleep with him at night. He was agreeable to ending this venture when he found out a rabbit's bathroom is wherever it happens to be at the time.

They had their first fried rabbit meal, which everyone enjoyed. The kids were unhappy at first, but eventually looked forward to a good meal of fried rabbit. Soon they actually preferred rabbit to chicken. Eventually, the day came when the charm of raising rabbits would fade and the animals were disposed of. It was a sad day.

Years later, the grandkids would raise rabbits but only for pets. They didn't raise any more rabbits to eat because they couldn't bring themselves to kill them. This is another testament to a generation of people who have never been hungry.

# Horses

Gene and Donna had never been to a pari-mutuel horse race before 1959 when they went to the annual New Mexico State Fair and wandered into the grandstand to see their first horse race. They made a $2 show bet on a big gray mare from Pratt, Kansas, named Brief Dream. She paid $3.20 for the $2 ticket. That was all they needed to get hooked on horse racing for the rest of their lives. Both were already big horse lovers, and now they fell in love with horseracing. The excitement, the horses, and the crowds were great entertainment. An afternoon at the horses was cheaper than going out for an expensive dinner and sometimes much more profitable.

They didn't have to bet; they just enjoyed being there. It was not uncommon for them to get up at seven in the morning to go to the track and watch the horses work out and to be among the horse people. So it was only natural that one of their first investments at the farm was a pregnant quarter horse mare. A year later, a filly was born.

When a foal was anticipated, the family, neighbors, and friends gathered for a foaling party. They sat in the kitchen drinking coffee waiting for the big event. Since normal foaling time is early March, it is usually quite cold, and it can be snowing. When it was very cold, they prepared the foaling barn with fresh straw for the birth. When it was warm, all the mares foaled outside.

Everyone drank coffee, ate cake, or had a little schnapps until the event happened, or they gave up and went home. It was always a big event for the kids. Sometimes they gave up and went to bed only to wake in the morning and see a foal already running in the corral. Usually it was desirable to stay up until the foal arrived in order to lock them in the barn to protect them from dogs and to see the mare did not have any problems.

In 1970, the kids were all up for watching the foal being born the first time. In addition to the quarter horse and thoroughbred foaling mares and foals, they had five ponies for everyone to ride on weekends. Horses had taken over their lives.

*Donna riding her quarter horse, 1969*

Gene, Donna, and the three kids would all saddle up. They rode the irrigation ditches and side roads. As the kids left home, the riding ponies left, and Gene and Donna concentrated on raising racehorses. They never won a big race but had several second and thirds in the New Mexico breeders' races.

They eventually had almost two dozen win pictures hanging on the bedroom wall, which Gene affectionately refers as the only

$300,000 bedroom in town. He was referring of course to the cost of acquiring those pictures. Some people buy million-dollar houses, some $75,000 cars, but Gene and Donna own racehorses and many memories.

When Mr. and Mrs. W moved, they left a thoroughbred gelding that had raced but came home hurt. Gene decided he would ride him. He was soon to find out the difference between ponies and high-strung thoroughbred racehorses. It was Sunday evening. and they had partied with martinis and barbeque. After dinner, Gene told Donna if she would hold the horse; he would get on it and see what happened. He bragged he could ride the wind if they could get a saddle on it. They went into the corral, and Gene put on a halter and handed the shank to Donna to hold the horse. He got on bareback on the seventeen-hand tall gelding. They were facing the barn about six feet away. Gene no sooner got straddle the horse when it gave one big buck, and he hit the side of the barn fully stretched out with his head down and feet up, and he slowly slid to the ground on his head. He was seeing stars for a while but finally got up and walked. He didn't break anything but his pride. It took him a few months, but he finally rode the horse.

*Gene riding race horse 1972*

The first foal they had was a quarter horse filly. They couldn't afford to send it to the track and pay the $18 per day for the trainer. Gene formed a partnership and convinced twenty-two of his friends and fellow employees to invest. It is a status symbol to tell your friends you own a part of a racehorse. She ran several times in a row, but she never won a race.

Two years later, they bought a thoroughbred mare, and they had their first colt named Musical Outlaw. He was in the money many times, was a winner and a big crowd favorite. It was the beginning of a forty-year racing career. One year they almost broke even but never had a profit until 2006 when two of their horses had some seconds in big purse races and in 2009 and 2010 when their partnership horse Call the Vet won several races.

There were many experiences with the horses. Horses are the most loving and loveable animals even more than cats and dogs. A cat will scratch you, a dog will bite you, but a horse will bite, kick, throw you off, step on you and run over you, and then love you while you are on the ground.

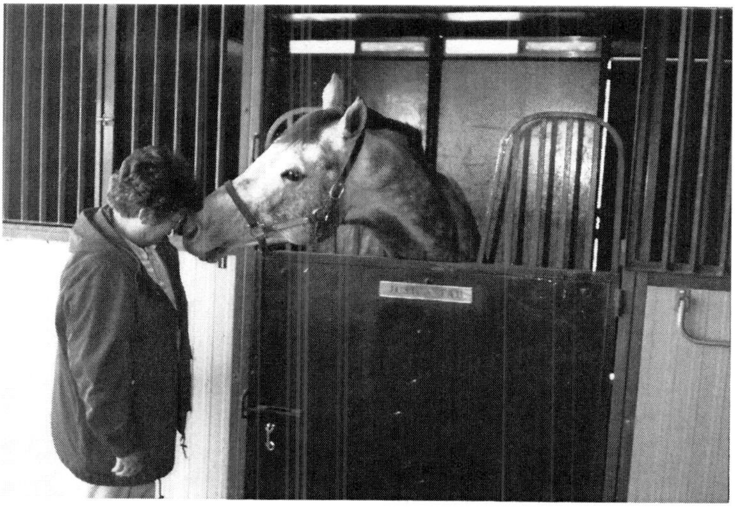

*Donna talking to the animals*

If someone told you your horse had beans, you might think this is some problem with the throat, nose, or ears. One day, the sorrel pony was having a problem. He would stretch out as if he was in pain and stand for some time. He seemed very tender around his stomach area. Naturally, it was time to call the vet. Dr. A said, "No problem, he must have beans." He asked if Gene would be home about noon to help, and he would come over and they would take care of it. Donna said sure he was due in by then. By now, she should have known better. It would not work that way. The vet showed up; Gene didn't.

Donna would have to be the helper. No problem, she liked working with Dr. A in spite of his taking advantage of her city girl lack of farm knowledge and finding humor in her attempts. Dr. A had her get a bucket of warm soapy water to get rid of the beans. No problem with that. Next, he asked her if she wanted to clean the beans away to learn how, and she said sure she would try.

The minute he said pull back the sheath, she hesitated. She was wondering to what sheath he was referring. Now she figured out what end these beans would be found on. You got it. She grabbed the shank and told him she would hold the head still, but she wasn't working on that other end and had no intention of touching that thing. Dr. A would never let her forget this venture. Of course, Dr. A had to tell everyone in the clinic about Donna's "Beans" and probably everyone at the next veterinary conference.

Most of their experiences with horses were enjoyable, but some were drastic. The first winner they had, Musical Outlaw, was a great runner, but he had small frail legs. He had raced admirably for nine races. This year he was entered in the big race at the state fair, the New Mexico Breeders Derby. Shortly before the race, he had a little soreness in the right front ankle. The trainer treated it with an ointment and wrapping, and by race day, he said it was fine. The day of the big race, Donna and Gene went to the barn before the races. The trainer had him clean and shiny. They had varnished his hooves so they glistened. His girl assistant had braided his mane into little ponytails and put red ribbons on each to match the colors he wore. She curled his mane over his eyes and wrapped them with little ribbons. She had made a special nose guard the same color as his tack and bridle.

He would look beautiful for his picture in the winner's circle. Gene, Donna, and Denise were in the front of the grandstand when the horses were brought up for the race. He was one of the favorites. He was feisty and ready to run. He was beautiful. He had been first, second, or third in all of his last nine races. He was now the third favorite on the betting line. It would be a great race. They anticipated a victory, and they had already admired the trophy and anticipated their share of that $40,000 purse. Musical Outlaw was a huge crowd favorite whenever he ran, and many of the family friends were there to see the race, to bet on him, and get in the winners circle for the picture.

The race was a mile and one-sixteenth, started just before the grandstand, and went all the way around. The bell sounded, and they left in a group. He ran with the front group all the way around, and when they rounded the turn and headed for home, he was in sixth place. The jockey guided him to the outside to take advantage of his finishing speed. With a few hundred yards to go, he was third and making a strong move on the outside. He appeared to have the speed to go on and win.

When they bring the gates on the track for the start of the race, they quickly pull them out of the way into the center of the track after the horses leave. The gate wheels leave a small rut where they go in and out. As the horses came to the finishing line, they have to pass over this track left by the gate. Musical Outlaw was running strong on the outside and was second and overtaking the leader, and then it happened, the occurrence that makes a horse owner's heart plunge to their feet. Musical Outlaw stumbled as he stepped on the rut made by the tire track. His head went down as they do when they have a leg problem. He recovered and kept running, but his right front leg was not hitting the ground.

Donna, Gene, and Denise were standing on the rail just behind where he stumbled, a hundred feet from the finish line. He showed the tremendous racing heart he had; he continued running and crossed the finish line fourth on just three legs. The jockey pulled him up just past the finish line in front of the grandstand. It was a terrible sight for all as his right leg was completely broken just below the knee and was flopping around as he ran. Donna, Gene, and Denise were in shock; they were heartbroken, and the women were crying uncontrollably. Gene was dumbfounded. They watched as they loaded him up in the trailer and took him down to the testing barn. They knew the routine. They walked to the car in silence except for the crying.

It is a terrible feeling to have a horse that the family raised from birth come to such a horrible end. They went down to the barn where he was stalled. Everyone else was down at the test barn with the horse. Gene and family didn't go to the test barn. They knew what was happening there. Soon the Mexican handlers returned slowly to the stall with their heads down. As they passed, Gene said simply, "No Mas?"

They answered, "No Mas," which in Spanish means no more. They drove home in silence. It was difficult returning to the farm that night and feeding the other horses.

Gene and Donna felt at fault for letting him race that day. They suspected the trainer had given the horse Novocain to lessen the pain in the leg, and without it, he would never have raced at all that day. They came to realize during the next forty years of racing that this was just an unfortunate part of racing. However, it was still the saddest day of racing for them.

Over the years, they experienced many difficulties with horses. They were bucked off, kicked, bitten, and stomped on. But they still had a loving time with the horses. They had some stillbirths, some that were born with faults and had to be put away, and some that died. Darlene had a tall black gelding for her first horse. She loved that horse. It was a terrible day when she walked to the corral, and he was dead. Denise had a gray pony that loved to throw her off headfirst and bury her head in the sand, glasses and all. Darrell rode when he was young but just never developed an interest in horses.

*Lauren talking to the animals just like Donna*

After the kids got older, they got down to just one pony. Danny was a very likeable gelding that anyone could ride, and he was allowed to graze around the house while the other horses were in the pasture. He thought he was a person, and as some predecessors before him, he would join the family at lunches and chip and dip parties in the yard. He liked Fritos and red chili.

One day Donna was cleaning the house, and she left the back door open so she could go in and out to hang clothes on the wash line. As she started out the door with the next load, she made the turn from the kitchen into the hallway and came face-to-face with Danny and let out a scream. The horse had followed her up the steps. He was halfway down the hall into the kitchen. There was no way to turn the horse around in a three-foot-wide hallway. The kids came to the rescue and convinced Danny he should back out of the house just the way he came in. From this point on, they closed the screen door. Danny was happy just to stand and look in the window waiting on his apple or carrot.

In spite of the problems, there were many high points, and it was always a pleasure to just walk out and pet and talk to the horses. There are great memories of foaling times and a horse's first race. They did get into the winners circle quite a few times. The horses were the highlights of farm living.

As normal, Gene seemed to leave town just before every tragedy and leave Donna with the problem and solution. One Saturday, a new foal had been born. The vet came and gave the shots and all was fine. Things were in good shape for Gene to leave town. On Monday morning, Donna took him to airport to fly to Chicago. He wished her luck, and he was already anticipating the phone call when he got to Chicago.

At noon, Donna was doing dishes and looked out the kitchen window to see the new baby. It wasn't around, and the mare was throwing a fit. She hurried to the pen, and there was the baby stuck part way under the chain-link fence. She could see were it had threshed wildly to get out but now lay still with its eyes shut. She feared the worst. The mare was the worst one they had, and no one could handle her but Gene. The son-in-laws and the vet referred to her as the "Bitch" as she was well known in the valley. The first few days after a foal was born, she would bite and kick and no one could go in with her.

Now Donna was thinking how could she go in the pen and do this. She had the answer, so she called the vet. He wasn't in, and he wouldn't be available for a few hours. She ran to the house and screamed for help. A neighbor heard her from half a block away and came running to help. He had some prior experience and he was afraid of the mare, so Donna finally got up the nerve to go in the pen with the mare. She told him to get on the outside of the fence and push, and she would pull. She told him as soon as the foal was free he should pull her out instantly.

She hesitantly crawled in the pen and carefully approached the foal. Usually, an animal will not hurt you if you are shorter than the animal. While the neighbor pushed, she pulled the baby out from under the pipe and fence where he was caught. The mare was throwing a fit and appeared ready to remove Donna, but she must have known Donna was there to help. Donna got out of the pen quickly. She had been very brave. Soon the foal began to move and tried to stand up. He was going to be okay, but it took several cups of coffee to get Donna back to normal.

With the farm, they also inherited a seventeen-hand high gelding named Fire Marshall. He had bowed a leg on his last race and couldn't race anymore. Gene started riding him as a pony. He got so gentle they felt Donna could ride him. They used a ladder to get her up into the saddle. She rode him around the yard and stopped by some bushes at the side of the yard. He had his head down eating grass. Donna relaxed in the saddle. Suddenly, the horse reared and headed around the house. A horse fly had bitten him. Donna was crossways in the saddle and was under his neck holding on when he finally stopped. She was screaming bloody murder for Gene to stop this thing. She was too frightened to fall and wasn't about to leave that horse. Gene helped her unwind herself, and she fell to the ground. Donna never rode him again.

In the early 1990s tragedy struck again. It had been a warm nice weekend, and the Baker and Capshaw families came to barbeque dinner on the patio. They had a few drinks, a chip and dip party, and went in the swimming pool for a while for some water volleyball games. It had been a good Sunday.

About six o'clock everyone got ready to go home. It was Denise and Randy's first anniversary, and they were getting ready to go to dinner to celebrate. Gene had been doctoring a colt all week that had been injured, and he had to give him a shot each evening. As they were leaving, Gene asked who wanted to help him give the colt the shot. The colt was getting tired of the shots and was giving him a little problem, and he thought he needed some help.

Everyone ignored his question and went home. Donna would have to assist him.

They went to the corral, and Gene went into the pen to put the halter on the horse. He didn't want to cooperate and ran into the barn. To keep him in the barn, Gene took a steel twenty-foot, three-inch oil pipe and laid it across the door supported on two rails of the fence, and he went into the barn to get the halter on. Donna remembers Gene asking her to steady the pipe so it wouldn't roll off. The colt was wide eyed, and Gene knew this was going to be difficult. As he walked in the barn and reached for the horse's head, it bolted. It went out the door on a dead run and all thousand pounds of him ran right through the steel pipe knocking it halfway across the pen.

Just as the horse left the barn, Gene looked out and saw Donna in the pen leaning over the pipe looking at the horse. She didn't have time to move only time to bring her arms up to protect her face. The horse ran through the pipe and it caught her across the arm and chest and carried her almost twenty feet into the corral, dumping her facedown in the dry manure. Gene ran to her, but she wasn't moving. He thought she was dead.

The oldest daughter of Randy Baker was sitting on the far fence watching the proceeding. Gene yelled at her to go to Denise and call 911. Soon two ambulances and police cars came. They loaded her onto a flat carrying board stretcher and strapped her down with her head in a holding vice. The ambulance left for the hospital with Gene in the back with her. They started transfusions and were running tests. Donna had regained consciousness but wasn't very coherent; she was in shock. The ambulance attendants were discussing how to get her shirt off to see if there was damage and how to clean up the horse manure, which was in her eyes, nose, hair, and everywhere. Donna finally told them to take scissors and cut off her blouse and bra.

At the hospital, they took her to ER and tried to clean her up. She was given a shot for shock. They waited for what seemed forever for a doctor who finally stopped by just long enough to order x-rays and tests. She was down in x-ray a long time and spent two hours back in the room waiting for a doctor. It was eleven o'clock before the doctor came to talk to them and said she had a broken wrist, broken ribs, and many bruises. They taped her up and gave her a sling. Finally, at one o'clock in the morning, they said she could go home and to report to the bone doctor at eight in the morning to get her wrist set and cast.

Looking back, the family realized Donna should have been hospitalized that night considering she had a broken and dislocated shoulder, broken wrist, two broken ribs, two badly damaged knees, which required surgery and multiple internal adhesions. She suffered for a long time. Months later, they operated on her shoulder; and during the operation, the surgeon failed to notice her bicep muscle that controlled the lifting of the arm had become unattached. By the time it was discovered later by another doctor, it had atrophied, or shrunk, and was no longer usable. The first doctor also missed the three fractures in the shoulder bone. She had three surgeries on her shoulder, and later had both knees operated on. She wore a shoulder cast for months.

When she first came home, she had her right shoulder in a body cast, her left arm in a cast where the wrist was broken, and it was almost impossible to take a bath or do anything for herself. She was in a pitiful condition and was black-and-blue all over. She looked like she had been in a train wreck. She had never had a broken bone before.

They sent her home in a hospital gown. That night Denise and Darlene decided she could never get any regular clothes on with the casts. Her right arm was taped down firmly. Her left arm was in a cast. They came early the next morning with a mumu-type dress that looked like a tent. It worked.

The girls came to finish cleaning her up. Donna was sitting on the side of the bed facing her dresser mirror. She kept staring at the mirror and finally said, "What is that?" She saw two big black basketballs on her chest. The girls told her that was her boobs. They were swollen to twice their size or more and were both black-and-blue. To this day, Donna can still recall the first sight of staring in that mirror. Gene wanted to take a picture, but she wouldn't let him.

The doctors couldn›t believe her chest wasn't crushed. Donna credits this to her singing exercises pushing a baby grand piano around and stacking encyclopedias on her chest while singing. That had developed tremendous muscles and chest structure. A meeker person would never have survived, but this was one tough sixty-year-old broad.

Shortly after she was up and around, Darrell was getting married in Augsburg, Germany. Donna was bound and determined she was attending. She went to Germany, casts and all. Darrell took them to Munich to the Octoberfest where they serve these one-liter beers. Donna couldn't lift her beer and asked the waitress for a straw. The waitress indignantly informed her, "In Germany you vill not trink beer mit a straw." Donna looked at the size of this woman and accepted her decision. Darrell found her a coke in a smaller glass.

They attended the wedding in Augsburg, and Donna suffered through two weeks of pain and healing. It had been a terrible summer, but she was glad she came.

Horses had really hurt her this time, and she would be afraid of them for many years, but she still loved them.

# Chickens and Ducks and Turkeys

As a young girl on the McCoy farm, Donna developed a fear of chickens and hated anything with feathers. The chickens and rooster would chase the children and attack them. In the 1940s everyone, including the McCoys, raised chickens for eggs to use and sell, or they bought them from their neighbor.

Donna's brother, Bob, had a banty rooster, mean as a fighting cock. Once when Donna and her sister, Dee, went to gather eggs, the rooster jumped on Dee's face with wings flapping and covered her face and head with scratches. The girls were hysterical, threw the rooster to the ground, and ran to the house. That was the last time either of them gathered eggs. Bob loved to tease Donna by chasing her down with a chicken and throwing it at her just to see her run.

While Gene and Donna were living in Salina, they ~~were~~ invited her to a barn dance. She was not prepared for it to actually be in a barn and got dressed in her city square dance outfit and shoes. They drove south of Abilene and pulled into a farmer's yard, parked next to a pen of cows, and just past the pig pen. Donna stepped out of the car and said, "What is that horrible smell? Can't you find another place to park?"

Gene just smiled and said, "No, this whole place just smells like money." In order to get up to the haymow, she had to climb a wooden vertical ladder with steps about a foot apart. Arriving inside the barn, Donna said she wasn't going up that ladder to the haymow where the dance was to be held. The group decided Donna needed a couple drinks to build up enough nerve to climb the ladder. The cocktails worked, and she made it up into the haymow. They danced until about midnight and then it was time to come down. With Gene's help, Donna was negotiating her way down the ladder. Just as she got to the last step, someone had picked up a chicken from where it was roosting for the night. He threw the chicken into the group, and of course, it came to rest right at Donna's feet. They couldn't have gotten enough drinks down her to prepare her for this. She came unglued and ran screaming into the house cussing Gene's brother-in-law and friends all the way. She ran to hide in the bathroom. Thirty minutes later, she finally stopped shaking and recovered her speech. They should have left before she got her speech back because when she did she made it very clear that she did not appreciate how the party ended and where they could put their damn chickens. They never went to another barn dance.

Shortly after getting settled at the Viola home, the talk came around to whether they should have any chickens.

They set up the incubators, bought fertile eggs from the feed store, and put them in the incubator to hatch in twenty-one days.

Finally, on the third try, they had some baby chicks. The kids spent hours holding the newly hatched chicks while they cuddled against their neck and went to sleep. Gene remembered it was a great feeling. Donna didn't have any such recollection and didn't want any. The only thing she wanted from these chicks was for them to grow up and lay eggs and leave her alone.

After going through the experience of hatching their own chicks they realized it was much cheaper to buy one-day-old chicks and decided they may as well throw in some turkeys. Gene agreed to the turkeys as long as she didn't get any ducks or geese, which he hated. But Donna, having agreed to raise chickens, decided she wanted a couple of ducks, and so at the feed store she snuck two baby ducks in the box of chicks.

Gene got the flat box of chicks out of the trunk and took it to the chicken house to put them in the brooder, followed by a train of women and kids.

The baby chicks would have to be taken from the box individually and placed under the brooder, and everyone wanted to help. Gene carefully sat the box on the floor and removed the lid. Immediately, two heads came up above the rest and went "Quack."

Gene said, "What the heck are we doing with two damn ducks? These things will crap all over the newspapers you feed the chicks on and dump the feeders and water cans." The kids held the ducks, and once again, Gene was overruled. The ducks would stay, but Gene insisted when they were three months old, they would eat them or let the German Shepherds have them for pets. Donna told him, "Just live with it."

*Donna's hatch of ducks 1969*

The chickens and turkeys were kept in a pen that had wire across the top to keep them in and to keep the birds out. When the ducks were grown, they were turned loose outside to make it on their own. Surprisingly, even the dogs wanted nothing to do with ducks. At three months, the roosters were separated and were ready to eat. It was up to Gene and Charlie to butcher the roosters. Charlie had a scientific method, but Gene used the axe and a wood stump. It was the same result for the chicken; he was just going to lose his head over the matter. That night was young fried chicken, mashed potatoes, and gravy. Well worth the trouble.

It was now up to the pullets, or young female chickens, now hens, to start laying eggs. All went well until the hens got older and decided to stay on the nest and become setting hens. They had reached the age they wanted to become mothers and hatch out a brood of chicks. Donna sometimes needed eggs during the day when everyone was at work or in school. She got brave, got an iron rod for protection, and ventured into the chicken pen. She waved her iron rod to keep the chickens away and managed to get to the nests and pick up the eggs. Sometimes, she would take some table scraps and throw in the pen at the opposite side of the nests, and when the chickens ran to the food, she snuck in and got some eggs. She backed out of the pen and breathed a sigh of relief. One day, it was rather dark out, and she needed eggs. She ventured to the pen, threw in the potato peelings, ran to the nests, and reached in for some eggs. Unfortunately, there was a setting hen still on the nest who didn't look kindly on Donna stealing her eggs. It let out a squawk, pecked her on the hand, and flapped its wings. Donna went into orbit.

Gene was in the tractor shed when he saw Donna screaming and waving her hands while she ran to the house. She had thrown her egg bucket halfway across the yard. Gene ran to the house thinking she had been bitten by a snake or something. After she quieted down, he and the kids went out and started catching chickens as she had left the gate to the pen wide open. She seldom went in the pen again.

She went to the feed store, which now rated as a sounding board right up there with the vet and the firemen. She explained that egg production was down. He asked what she was doing differently, had she switched feed? She explained that when "I or the kids needed eggs we went into the pen, but the hens didn't want to get off the nests. We took an iron rod and poked the hens until they finally got mad and left the nest so they could gather eggs."

The feed store owner told her, "Hell, lady, if you poked me with an iron bar I would quit laying eggs too." He told her to have Gene lock up the setting hens and in two weeks they would be back to laying eggs but to put the iron rod away.

Donna wouldn't come outside when they killed the first roosters. She waited until they were dipped in hot scalding water, the feathers plucked and the feet and head cut off. Then they were ready for the women to clean them. She insisted, "I won't touch your feet, and I sure won't touch a chicken foot."

Now it was Thanksgiving, and they were ready for their first turkey. They were big birds.

Gene came home from work early, got his axe and wood stump, and put in two bigger nails than he used for the chickens. Gene was to hold the turkey by the feet and put its head between the nails, then, with one swoop of the axe, chop off the head. The turkey had other ideas. Charlie was out of town, and Gene tried it alone. Trying to hold the turkey and swing the axe was impossible. Donna and the kids hid in the house. The kids had read their story about the Pilgrims shooting and eating their first Christmas turkeys. They had never realized it happened in real life, and you really had to kill something. Gene told them, "This is farm life, not fantasy land."

Donna called the vet, and Dr. A suggested the method of getting a gunnysack and cutting a hole in one end large enough for the turkeys head to stick out. This method allowed you to hold the turkey so it would not bruise the meat. It seemed great and a reasonable way to try.

Donna would have to either hold the bag with the turkey in it or swing the axe. Gene caught the turkey, put it in the sack, and laid it on the block. Now all that was left was to put the head between the nails. No matter what Gene tried, the turkey would not poke its head out the hole. The turkey had a premonition that something bad was coming. After a long period of trying, Donna came to the rescue. She had always talked to her turkeys. She wouldn't touch them, but she would talk to them. Now she had an idea, she knelt down beside the stump in front of the turkey and starting chanting, "Here turkey lurkey. Here turkey lurkey." Gene thought she had lost her marbles, but about the fourth time she chanted, the turkey stretched his head out of the sack to listen to her. It had worked.

Gene grabbed the head and put it between the nails. Now someone had to swing the axe, as it was all Gene could do to hold the turkey since it was no longer cooperative. Donna took the axe and made a clean hit and off went the head. She had done it. She screamed, threw the axe, and immediately headed for the house to change clothes. Gene noted the accuracy of the axe swing and vowed to never to let her near an axe when she was mad at him. The turkey had no bruises; the gunnysack procedure was a success. Dr. A had come through again.

Donna used her mother's recipe and made dressing. She tried stuffing it in the turkey to cook but abandoned that. She used the giblets and neck and made the dressing in bowls. One regular and one with fresh oysters like her mother did. Gene and Charlie loved the oyster dressing, but Gene had to cut up the oysters because Donna wouldn't touch them; she couldn't put up with the slimy feeling. The only good thing Gene ever said about Gertie was, "Thanks for the oyster dressing recipe."

Before Christmas, all the turkeys, except the largest, were prepared and sold to friends. It was a huge 25 pound bird and would be on the table at the farm. They killed twelve turkeys, and Donna talked each one out of the sack and on to turkey heaven. She had a marvelous way of speaking to animals and turkeys. She should have been an animal trainer.

Donna liked ducks, and Donna bought the ducks. They were hers. As luck would have it, Donna had acquired only two ducks, but naturally, they turned out to be a mama duck and a papa duck. That meant there would be more ducks. How fortunate, the mama was now sitting on eggs. Donna called the vet and asked how many she would hatch out of the twenty-one eggs she was sitting on. Dr. A thought maybe eight or ten. Dr. A was a very good large animal vet, but she quickly found out what he didn't know about ducks. You guessed it, twenty-one baby ducks. This was a very prolific pair of ducks.

Ducks normally have one setting a year. To Donna's great fortune, in October, the duck hatched another setting of nineteen ducks. Unheard of, Donna must have been out talking to the ducks this time. Gene wondered what she was telling them. They had apparently developed some kind of verbal communication, as at daylight, they would all congregate below Gene and Donna's bedroom window and all quack at once. What an alarm clock. In addition, there were duck droppings everywhere. Now Gene was furious and stated either the ducks go or he goes.

Donna had named the papa duck Charlie. Charlie, a real *Beau Brummell*, was a completely oversexed duck. The chickens and new puppies were considered fair game. He even jumped up on the horse's tail. He was embarrassing, and he had to go. Donna tried to give him to Dr. A, but he had ducks before and said no thanks. Darrell had started school, and his little lady friend lived up the street. Her family had some female ducks.

Charlie the duck was caught and delivered to his new home. They never heard back from this woman, but in a couple years, she had over one hundred ducks. Ducks were everywhere. Dr. A called one day and said this woman up the street had a duck chasing her cats and dogs, and she had over a hundred ducks and didn't know how to stop them. He asked Donna what she did with her duck. They never found out if she ever forgave Donna or not, but Darrell had to get a new girlfriend.

The remaining ducks were to be butchered and eaten. The cavity in ducks is so small Donna couldn't get her hand in to clean them out. She hurt and bruised her hands. The next time they did ducks, they took them to a duck farmer who had a cleaning business.

Charlie, with the help of the county agent, had come up with the knowledge the best way to fix ducks was to put them on a spit on your barbeque. The procedure called for making a tinfoil tray about four inches wide the length of the spit to catch drippings and build a bank of coals on both sides of the foil. They put three ducks on the spit, which turned the ducks about six inches above the coals. They made a sauce of orange marmalade, crushed pineapple, maraschino cherries, peach and apricot schnapps, brandy, and homemade red wine. The ducks took four hours to cook and were basted with this sauce every twenty minutes. The fire was kept low so as not to burn the sauce. Charlie and Gene thought they were great eating. Donna and kids were not so enthusiastic. It had been a lot of work, and there was lots of leftover duck.

They did it again several times until all the ducks were gone. Gene knew he had to eat them quickly, or in the spring, there would be more eggs. He wanted to eat all the drakes first, but sometimes he couldn't tell the difference, so they ate them all. That was the first and last venture into the duck business. Another farm lesson learned.

When the ducks had their hatch, one of the ducks was a runt and much smaller than the rest. Darrell took the little duck as his and tried to nurse it back to health. One morning Donna went to wake Darrell to go to school and saw something moving in his long blond hair. A little head came up and went "Quack." He had been sleeping with the duck. Darrell was instructed to take the duck back outside to its mama. However, by this time, the duck thought Darrell was his mama and wanted back in the house.

Later Donna returned from work. She went to the kitchen and there was the little duck swimming in her kitchen sink where Darrell was trying to teach it to swim. That was the last straw, and the duck was evicted. Darrell was crushed, but it came down to the duck leaving or both leaving. And that is the way it had to be! Big Mama had spoken. Even Donna never asked for ducks again. It was becoming a pattern on the farm; they had to raise something once to see why they wouldn't do it again.

# Goats

Eileen liked goats and goat milk while Gene hated goats. Gene told Donna she couldn't have a milk cow because he knew he would end up milking it. When he left the farm when he was young, he swore he would never milk another cow. Donna sided with Eileen, and they decided to buy a milk goat—a female milk-giving goat that needed to be milked twice a day. Gene said, "Good luck. You are on your own." Charlie went to the county agent to get a book on raising and milking goats. He got another book on how to build a milking stanchion. Charlie was now on a personal basis with the county agent similar to Donna's reliance on the vet, Dr. A.

Reluctantly, Gene helped Charlie build a milking stanchion. A stanchion was a wooden stand with a ramp to walk up and a platform for the goat to stand on while you milked it, so you weren't down on the ground. A goat wasn't very tall. At the far end of the platform was the stanchion or a headlock to keep the goat in place. Now they were ready. Donna called the vet to find out who would sell them a milk goat.

Off went the girls to get their goat from Dr. A's friend who raised goats. They bought a Swiss-Toggenburg milking goat. Gene was upset because they paid more for a damn goat than he could get for his horses. The girls insisted it was worth the price because it came from a prize-winning line. Gene replied, "So what does that do for the milk?"

They got the goat home, and all was fine until 5:00 p.m.came, and it was milking time. Now they asked the question. Who was going to milk the goat? Charlie copped out quickly because all of a sudden the arthritis in his hands got worse. When work came up, Charlie had a hard time getting his hands out of his overall pockets. He usually pretended he didn't hear because he walked around the farm with his radio plugs in his ears. Gene had stated long ago that he would not milk a damn goat. He repeated his position—you bought it, you milk it. Most thoroughbred horse ranchers kept a goat for company for their troublesome mares. Not this horse farm; Gene's horses could just be lonely.

Donna didn't know how, so it came down to Eileen to milk her goat. They got the goat up on the platform, and it lay down. Now she needed help to get it to stand up so she could milk it. Charlie realized he had to raise the feed tray higher so the goat couldn't lie down and eat. There was a slight delay for remodeling. Eileen sat down with her pail under the goat and proceeded to expertly fill the pail with long firm squeezes, which reflected her younger day's experience milking cows. Unfortunately, she had one more lesson to learn; when you milk a goat, and you let the pail sit there on the platform, eventually the goat will tire of this adventure and her back foot will send the pail flying. The goat threw a fit and milk went everywhere, and Eileen ended up sitting on the dirt with the pail upside down on her lap. Gene sent the kids to the house to get the camera. There would be no goat milk for dinner that night.

The kids learned something about goats and also learned a few new words for their vocabulary that Eileen expressed to the goat. The next milking, they read Charlie's book, and Eileen taught Donna to milk. This time they held the pail with one hand and milked with the other. It took longer but had better results. After a few days, they were both expert goat milkers. Gene wouldn't drink the milk. Any respectable former cattle rancher wouldn't be caught dead with a goat. Donna didn't like the taste or smell, so Eileen drank or used the milk.

It wasn't too long before Eileen and Donna tired of fighting and milking this mean goat. She was not cooperative. About half the time, the milk was spilled. Both women had bruises acquired from goat kicks and goat fits. Sometimes the goat would lie down and refuse to get up. Now when they went to pasture to get it to milk, she showed her dislike by walking toward them on her back legs with her front legs six feet up in the air in battle position. This Toggenburg goat got very big and mean. As cold weather approached, Eileen decided she didn't like goat milk after all. Donna found out she couldn't milk the goat because of the arthritis in her hands, and Eileen was having the same problem. The goat was allowed to dry up. Now they had to find how to get rid of her. The problem solved itself.

One day the goat got out of its pen and into the alfalfa field. Sheep can't eat fresh green alfalfa as they develop tremendous gas and bloat or blow up and die. Goats are not supposed to bloat. This one did. Blew up like a toad. Gene found her on her back with her feet in the air. Dr. A said she must have eaten some poison weed. Charlie and Gene dug a hole and buried the goat. The kids built a cross with dandelion flowers. The women didn't come to the funeral. They had a total lack of interest. The goat's popularity rating was less than that of Scrooge at Christmastime.

Donna and Eileen always harbored the suspicion that Gene or Charlie had turned the goat out into the alfalfa. If they did, they never admitted it. Secretly, Donna and Eileen were probably thankful. This was another farm lesson learned by all. The goat experience was over, and there wouldn't be another one on the farm. Gene and Charlie wanted very badly to say, "I told you so." However, they knew better; they were hungry and wanted to eat dinner that night.

# Pigs

Early Monday morning Gene did the chores and fed the horses, the steer, the pigs, and all. He came in from feeding to shower and leave on his monthly trip to the bank at Grants, New Mexico, for three days. As he woofed down his breakfast, he told Donna that one of the young pigs had developed a hernia in the rear end, and she should call the vet. Off to the bank he went, leaving Donna in charge of the farm and pigs as usual. She got the kids off to school and made her call to the veterinary clinic requesting help to look at her pig.

About midmorning, Dr. A drove in the driveway, had a short talk with Donna to see what humorous event had transpired since his last visit and went to look at the pig. It was a young pig at about sixty-five pounds. Dr. A and his new assistant, Donna, gave the pig a tranquilizer and proceeded to sew up the hernia. He told Donna to hold the back feet while he sewed. The next day, Donna went out to look at the pig, and it had herniated again. She called the vet, and he showed up and sewed it up again, this time with more laces.

Donna and the kids fed the animals and went to check the pig, and sure enough, it had herniated again, only worse. Dr. A explained that there was no way they could sew up the pig the third time as the skin was too weakened to hold the threads. He explained the best thing too do was to eat it. Donna thanked him and asked him how to proceed. He explained he was sure that

Gene knew something about butchering a pig. He suggested they wait until Gene got home to see if he could handle it.

He explained that the best thing to do with a young pig was to build a pit and barbeque it. They should gut it, leave the skin on and cut it in two halves, lay both sides on the barbeque with the skin side up, and cook it slowly for about ten hours. He explained very carefully, step by step, how to build the barbeque. They should build an above-ground pit by laying two rows of standard eight-inch concrete building blocks. It should be solid on three sides with a two-foot opening on the downwind side. It should be about four by five feet. After the blocks were in place, they were to lay two metal fence posts across the long way and then cut a piece of chain-link fence four by six feet and lay it on top to hold the pig. Then, according to Donna's relay of the instructions, they should build a wood fire all the way around the outside of the pit and use the charcoals to cook the pig. Everything seemed easy enough.

Gene returned from Grants about five in the evening, and he received the news that this evening would be a butchering party. Charlie and Eileen came to help. While the women and kids were in the house, Gene and Charlie took the trusty Stevens .22 caliber semiautomatic rifle and went to the pigpen to do the dirty deed. It was a small pig, and one clean shot was all that was required. The next step was to take a ladder, tie his back feet to the upper rungs, and raise it to an upright position. Gene had helped his folks butcher many pigs and steers. He proceeded with the cut from the neck to the rear and removed the internal organs.

Donna said, "Save her the tenderloin because Dad had always had the tenderloin for supper whenever he butchered." She was waiting there eagerly anticipating fried tenderloin for dinner.

Now it just so happened that about that time Gene was removing the pancreas from the pig. It was about six inches across and an inch or so thick. He just couldn't resist adding a little humor to the situation. He cut the pancreas loose from the pig, smiled, and handed it to Donna saying, "Here's your tenderloin." Donna was so proud. She held it between her hands and patted it while Gene finished dressing out the pig. They finished, cut the pig in two halves, washed the pig down, and washed Donna's tenderloin.

They hung the pig in the shed where it would hang and cure out for a couple days before barbequing. Then they all went in to the house to wash up and eat dinner. Donna was in the kitchen, had the skillet and the flour ready to dip the tenderloin in, and she was ready to fry the tenderloin. She asked Gene to cut it into strips like her daddy did. At this point, Gene decided it was time to end the masquerade before he got in worse trouble. He told her that tenderloin came from the back strap area and had to be cut from the back, and that what she was holding was the pancreas. Everyone had a good laugh—except Donna wasn't laughing. She was fuming and turning red. The spot on the middle of her forehead that got red when she was sick or irritated and formed a V was beginning to light up like Rudolph the red-nosed reindeer.

Now Donna is from a mixture of Irish-Scotch and German-Russian, and she had inherited the worst of instant temper and reaction from each of these. When she was born, they should have tattooed *warning* across her forehead! Maybe that is what that red V spot is trying to spell. Gene should have looked to see if she was still holding the pancreas when he was talking to her. It was too late. He noticed her starting to wind up, and he just turned away when he was hit in the back of the head by a flying pancreas. That ninety-mile-an-hour fastball would have made Dizzy Dean proud. It made a loud wop, and his hat and glasses went flying. The verbal barrage was of equal intensity.

Not only would there not be any tenderloin tonight, there wouldn't be any dinner prepared tonight either. The kids and Gene made do with the various leftovers in the refrigerator. Charlie and Eileen went home. Hopefully, Donna would be speaking to Gene tomorrow. Somehow, he seemed to learn very slowly that his sense of humor was sometimes wasted and would constantly get him in trouble. This was no exception.

He was already in trouble from the night before. They were watching TV, and they saw these huge fat women in bathing suits. Donna asked Gene if her butt looked that big and fat in her bathing suit. Without thinking about the consequences, Gene replied that he didn't think so, but he would get a ruler to measure. It definitely wasn't the thing to say. It was a good thing they had already had supper that night. Donna and Gene always had a sometimes-stormy marriage, usually Gene's fault. Again, it was always so nice to make up.

Later in life, Gene would continue to let his mouth overload his butt. Donna had started to gain some midlife weight, and she was very conscious about it. One evening, Gene answered the phone; it was Donna's sister who asked if Donna was around. Without knowing that Donna had picked up the other phone, Gene responded, "Oh yes, she is round and getting rounder." He didn't even ask; he just fixed himself a peanut butter and jelly sandwich for supper. He would never learn.

The next step was the barbeque on Saturday. Gene and Charlie built the pit from the concrete blocks, and while they were at work on Saturday morning, Donna and Eileen gathered some branches and wood and laid it around the pit to get ready to cook. When Gene and Charlie returned at noon, they inquired about this wood all around the outside of the pit and were assured this is exactly how Dr. A said to do it—to build the fire around the pit, and then as it made charcoal, to shovel the hot coals into the pit to cook the pig. Strange, but who were Charlie and Gene to argue with the two women and the vet? At four in the morning, they brought the pig from the shed, laid the two halves open side down on the wire, and lit the fire. They had a roaring fire on the outside of the pit, and very little cooking going on. Donna had put a purchased bag of charcoal inside the pit. They did shovel the hot coals into the pit and the cooking started. They soon lost interest with the fire all around the pit and concentrated on one side. They didn't see how the fire outside was doing any cooking, and it was too hot to get near. To settle the discussion, about seven o'clock, Donna called the vet. Dr. A came by on his way to the clinic, had a coffee, a good laugh, and his humor for the day. He explained that he had not said to build the fire all around the outside of the pit but that they were to build a fire on the outside of the pit, some distance from the opening, and then shovel the coals in as they became charcoal. This made more sense, and they were on their way. Gene muttered to Charlie his first exclamation that would follow Donna and daughter Denise the rest of their lives; he described the girls' advice as "a mass of miss-information."

The pig finished cooking about four o'clock in the afternoon, and they proceeded to remove the charred skin and cut up the meat. By leaving the skin on, the fat in the skin keeps the meat from burning. It doesn't burn underneath as you might suspect, and you end up with a well-cooked pig still very succulent and juicy. Most of the fat had gone into the fire. It was delicious. When they finished dinner, they put the rest of the bones that hadn't been cleaned yet in the roaster and sat the roaster out on the screened-in porch on top of the clothes washer so they could cool. They would clean them up in the morning.

They forgot that Donna's new German shepherd, Ginger, was not only large, she was very smart. German shepherds are the smartest dogs Donna and Gene have ever owned. Sometime during the night, the dog discovered that a screen door handle can be pulled down and the door will open. Ginger had apparently been watching people open the door. The screen door handle is flat, and when pulled down a quarter turn, the door opens. Ginger took the handle in her mouth and simply turned her head, and she and the four other shepherds were in. They feasted big time. By morning, there was no need to clean up the bones. They were sparkling clean and scattered around the yard. The ham bones with a lot of meat still on them were gone! Fortunately, the ham they sliced off the bones was in the refrigerator. It was another learning experience on the farm. They installed a screen door hook on the door.

Now that they were experts in cooking pigs, Donna wanted to get in the pig breeding and raising business. Pigs had been her favorite animals since childhood. She called the vet, and he gave her the name of a local pig farmer, a Mr. Wilson who lived a short distance away. Mr. Wilson was a tall black gentleman with a white beard and overalls who raised registered pigs.

Donna told Gene she wanted to buy two little pigs and raise her own meat. He said, "Okay, you can go buy two, but make sure the pigs are taken care of." Referring of course that they were no longer papa pig potential, and he left for work. Apparently, all Donna heard of this comment was the okay. She arrived at the pig farm, and sure enough, Mr. Wilson had many pigs of all sizes and colors. She finally got across to him that she wanted two small pigs that she could raise. She told him that her husband had told her to make sure they were taken care of. Mr. Wilson assured her that all his pigs were well taken care of. This was good enough for her. Mr. Wilson put the two pigs in a gunnysack, tied the end with wire, and put the bag in a box in the trunk of her car. The pigs weighed about ten pounds each. Donna got home with the little pigs. She called for Gene to come look at her new possessions.

Gene opened up the box and took out the bag while it was still in the trunk. He examined the pigs and got upset because they were still boar pigs and were not taken care of. He told Donna he specifically told her that if she got a male pig he wanted it taken care of. Donna retorted, "Mr. Wilson said he always takes care of all his pigs." Gene was too exasperated at this point to argue. He wrapped the wire back around the opening of the gunnysack, shut the trunk lid, and told her to call the vet.

He said, "Take these male pigs to the vet to be taken care of." Now he had to explain to her that taken care of meant castration. Then he had to explain what castration was. Donna reacted instantly, and said, "That's cruel, and you are not going to do that to my pigs." She also refused to use that nasty word and requested Gene did not use that kind of language in front of her pigs.

Gene was about to become unglued. He finally explained to her that it was a common and necessary procedure to raising pigs for food, and they had to be castrated for the meat to be tender. He told her to take the pig to the vet, and he would handle everything.

Donna drove off headed for the vet. As she drove down the street, the car began to sway as if something was running from side to side. Suddenly, she realized that Gene had not tied the bag properly or had not put the bag in the box, and the pigs were loose in her trunk. She arrived at the vet clinic, Dr. A came out to the car and she explained she needed her pigs taken care of, and they were loose in the trunk. Now, Dr. A was not going to let her get away with just saying taken care of. He asked her again what she wanted. She still would not say the word.

Dr. A asked her, "Why do you want it taken care of? Is it sick? Why are you bringing it?" Finally, Dr. A said, "If you want your pig castrated, you have to tell me." She was very embarrassed. Dr. A had a pretty good sense of humor, and he wouldn't let her get past this situation without saying the word *castration*. Doc said, "What does it need?"

Donna said, "It needs cut on."

Doc said, "Say it."

Finally, Donna quietly said, "Yes, I want my pigs castrated." Then Doc told her she could bring in her pigs. As they walked into the clinic, Doc said in a loud voice where everyone could hear, "Donna wants her pigs castrated." She could have crawled in the toilet stool and flushed herself down. She had made another milestone. She was learning to talk farm language.

Dr. A went with back to the car with her to get the little pigs from the trunk. They opened the trunk, and there was the gunnysack, empty. The box was empty. Where were the pigs? Dr. A was too big to get in the trunk. His son was also over six-foot tall, and he didn't fit in the trunk either. The stupid pigs were behind the spare tire. Guess who was going to get the pigs out from behind the spare tire? Donna reluctantly got into the trunk. One pig had gotten under the backseat where he was caught up in the springs.

They had a struggle getting the pigs out and had to pull the backseat, but finally had one back in the bag and in the box. Donna located the other pig and dragged it out of the springs squealing like a banshee. They took them into the operating room, and Dr. A told Donna maybe she should wait outside in the lobby. Donna immediately said, "Good idea." She sat out in the outer office. Soon she heard the screams of the little pigs and knew something terrible was happening. She wanted her piggies back, and she was going to take them back home so they wouldn't have to be hurt. It was too late. The little pigs were no longer future papa pigs. Dr. A brought them out in a box, and Donna took her two little pigs and went home. She was feeling very sorry for her poor little darlings. Next time she would know what to ask for, and she wouldn't have to go through all this misery.

Back home, the little pigs were returned to the pen. When they were about two hundred pounds, they would send them to market for butchering.

Next, Donna wanted a sow so she could have her own little pigs. They bought a female pig, a big sow. It was now time to send the sow to meet a papa pig. Gene helped her load the sow into the truck, and they delivered it to Mr. Wilson for breeding. Two weeks later, they noticed the sow was in heat again, and apparently, she was not pregnant. Back in the pickup and back to Mr. Wilson. The third time, when Gene went to feed in the morning, he noticed the sow was gone. Mr. Wilson called, and said, "Your sow is in my yard trying to get back into the pen." Now Donna had to go get the sow home. With the help of Mr. Wilson, they got it back to its pen. They had to reinforce the pen to keep her home. This time the sow was carrying little pigs and had nine cute little piglets. She started having them about five o'clock in the evening and had one about every half hour. Dr. A had said they might save about five of them.

It was a very cold and snowy night. They had made a nice straw bed in the little A-frame pig house, and the sow was lying there having her pigs. As each one was born, Donna and kids took it into the house to dry it off and get it warm. Then they took that one back to feed and brought in the next one. They finished about ten o'clock, and all nine little pigs were back in the pen feeding. The kids had a ball holding the warm little piglets. With all the pigs happy, the family went to bed with another farm experience under their belt.

As the pigs grew, some were sold, the herniated one was butchered and two were put in a special pen for fattening to butcher later. Donna became very good friends with the two pigs. She named them Hubert and Lyndon. They were very appropriately named. Hubert lay around and accomplished nothing. Lyndon had a habit of getting out of the pen and coming to the house for a handout. He took up residence under Donna's window. In the morning, Donna would stick out her hand, and he would follow her anywhere. She took him back to his pen for feeding time. Soon he was over three hundred pounds. He was so fat he lost his ambition to get out of his pen. As with all big fat pigs, he was destined to be butchered. The day came when they were to load him and take him to Schwartzman's to butcher, but he wouldn't go in the truck. Gene and Charlie worked and worked. Finally, Donna came out and talked to her pig. She informed him he should get in the truck. She walked up the ramp into the truck and the pig followed her. Gene and Charlie shut the tailgate and shook their heads in disbelief. Donna had an unbelievable association with her pigs. They loved her voice. Maybe they did understand her.

In May of 1971, Gene had grown tired of his job at the mortgage company where he was financial vice president. Actually, he liked his job but was tired of getting a promotion in title every year and very little money to go with it. He was sitting in his office one morning with his feet up on his desk reading the newest magazine. In it was an article entitled, "How to retire at age 35?" It went on to say, "You may already have, and don't realize it." Gene continued to read the article, and it hit him right between the eyes. Here he was, thirty-eight years old, had already gone as far as he could with this company, and was just floating with the tide with nothing more challenging than making coffee break. He was third in line after the president and administrative vice president, and they were almost as young as he was. He was dead-ending.

He researched the job market with no positive results. He arranged a one-year management contract with a local printing firm owned by a company in Narraganset and would use that as a stepping stone for his own practice. He had his CPA and decided to go out on his own. He typed up his resignation letter and presented it to the president. He was offered more money, but he declined and gave a two-week notice. About that time Donna called and said, "Let's meet for lunch over at the restaurant on Monte Vista. I have something important to tell you." She sounded distraught.

Gene said, "Okay." He also had something to tell her.

They met and looked at each other for a while, each deciding how to tell the other. Gene realized she was really stressed and had been crying. Finally, Donna said to Gene, "What is your news? You go first." Gene dragged out his resignation letter and told her his news. He said, "Look what I did today. I am now unemployed." She was devastated. She was thinking, *How do I tell him I will have a hysterectomy today and can't do any work for three months?* Many thoughts were running through her mind like do we still have insurance if Gene quit and how would they pay the medical bills without her working.

Now Donna told Gene she had just left Dr. F's office where he told her she had to have hysterectomy surgery immediately. She had been bleeding for sixty-five days. She had been driving the tractor leveling to build an area for the kids' swimming pool. Maedean, a neighbor, was there watching her. As Donna was moving the tractor forward, she fainted and collapsed on the tractor. The tractor continued heading for Maedean's house. Maedean jumped the fence, ran after the tractor, jumped up behind, and pushed in the switch to stop it. Donna went in the house and Maedean said, "You are going to call your doctor right now." She rested a little and made the call. He said, "Get in here right now, hon." Donna got in the car and drove herself directly to Dr. F's office. He took one quick look and told her, "Hon, you have lost too much blood, and you are going directly to the hospital. We will operate and give you transfusions today. Call Gene and tell him to go get your clothes and meet us at the hospital." Of course, she didn't go direct, and she went to meet Gene for lunch first.

Gene left the restaurant to get her clothes and pick up her personal items. He took Maedean with him to drive Donna's car home. Donna drove herself to the hospital. Upon admittance, they bathed her and put on Betadine without asking her about allergies. She immediately turned red and blistered horribly. She was allergic to Betadine. Dr. F came in and said they had to postpone the surgery, and she had to sit in a sitz bath all day until it cleared up. They gave her a transfusion and postponed the surgery a day.

Dr. F was a Southern Louisiana boy. He had very casual bedside manners, and he talked so slow Donna asked him if he could finish the operation in time for her to survive. He had delivered all three of their children. Dr. Farris sat down beside her and said in his slow southern draw, "My god, girl, don't you ever have Betadine on your skin again. You are deathly allergic to it."

Donna told him, "Why don't you tell me something I don't know?"

A week after the surgery, Donna went in for a checkup. Dr F told her, "I don›t want you on the tractor for six months, and you aren›t going back to work." He gave her a lecture and a half.

After the operation and recovery, Donna went home, and the following Sunday she got on the tractor to finish the pool for the kids. This big black Cadillac came swishing into the driveway. Out jumped Dr. F yelling to Gene to get her off that tractor. He went immediately to Donna and told her, "Get off that damn tractor and get in the house. I am going to check you over." He told her she was lucky that nothing had separated or jarred any stitches loose. He sat on the bed and lectured for fifteen minutes. By the time she saw who was driving in, she knew she was in big trouble. He was mad, and she had never seen him mad. He said he wanted her in his office first thing the next morning.

Donna reluctantly went to his office and knew she was going to get another lecture. Instead, he just looked at her and said, "I am sending two men out to fix up your pens and then I will send out fourteen little pigs by the end of the week. I will furnish all the feed, and I want you to feed them out for my restaurant for Christmas. You can keep two for your work. I hope this will keep you busy and off the tractor."

*Donna talking to her pigs for bath time*

They built two pens, one for the pigs and one where they could be moved to dry out after their baths. Donna went to the pen every day in her rubber boots and washed her pigs with a toilet brush and a bucket of water. She scrubbed every pig, and soon each would line up for his or her turn. The pigs loved their bath so much they would sit around her in a little circle waiting their turn. As each was washed, it was put into the other pen. Once, as the pigs got bigger, they got so excited to be first that they ran between Donna's legs, and she ended up sitting in the dirty and muddy pig pen. If the kids had knocked her over she would have been furious, but with her little piggies, it was okay. She loved her piglets. When they were about 120 pounds, they went to market. The truck didn't have a chute to load the pigs. The truck was so big the driver couldn't get into the yard so Donna had him back it down the lane. She cut a hole in the fence for the pigs to get into the lane. The driver was going to use his electric prod to load the pigs. Donna said no, so she got her brush and rubber boots and pail and crawled through the hole in the fence, and she led her pigs into the truck. They thought they were going to get a bath. The truck driver stood there scratching his head and couldn't believe what he had just seen. The butcher told Donna she raised the best pigs he had ever seen. She didn't know how he knew they were the best pigs unless he snitched some of the meat. Dr. A told her he could tell by the size of the ham bones.

Donna didn't raise any more pigs until the granddaughter got pigs for a 4-H project, but she would always hold her "piggies" close to her heart.

# Cats

By now, Donna and Dr. A, the vet, were almost on a daily speaking basis. Sometimes, it appeared he might drop by to check the animals just to get his daily dose of humor listening to Donna's latest venture. On particular day, he came by to see if the horse was recovering from some cuts. They were administering antibiotics for a week to clear up the infection in his legs. While he was there, Donna asked him to look at the stitches in Darrell's foot that had been put in by the hospital emergency a few days before. He had dropped a milk bottle on his foot that broke and almost cut his foot off. Donna explained she had to take him back in to have the stitches removed today. Dr. A said no point in doing that; he would just take them out. He pulled out his little scissors, and out they came. It saved a trip to the hospital and twenty-five dollars. It was a close contest to see if they went to the emergency at the hospital more than to the emergency at the vets.

Dr. A asked Donna if she wanted a cat. Someone had left a large tame calico cat at the clinic to reattach its tail. They wouldn't pick it up because they didn›t want to pay the vet bill. It had an almost severed tail, and Dr. A had reattached it. Doc wanted someone to keep the cat to see if his reattachment would be a success. A horse bit off the tail. The only problem was the tail tipped to one side as it had no cartilage where it had been reattached and no hair. At the farm, a cat was always welcome because they ate mice. Gene and Donna always had cats but out in the sheds. They were usually wild, but sometimes the kids would catch them very young, and they became pets.

The cat came to the farm to live, and everything was fine, and it came with free vet service for the rest of his life. He was a nice cat as long as he stayed outside. He must have previously been a house cat because he stayed up on the porch and ran in the house at every opportunity. He was quickly ejected. There wasn't going to be any cat in this house.

It was May, and Gene was setting up the evaporative cooler on the east side of the house. All of the big swamp coolers have a rotary fan inside. Gene put new pads in the sides of the cooler and closed it up. Then he went inside and turned the electricity back on to the pump and flipped the switch. There was a noise like you have never heard coming from the cooler, and it sounded like a mountain lion with a toothache. Plus, the cooler fan was going *wop, wop*, and Gene thought the fan was broken. He shut off the cooler and opened the side. Out came the cat like a rifle shot. He had apparently crawled in the cooler, and he was inside the rotary fan when Gene turned on the fan. There was cat hair everywhere, and a little blood, but the cat survived. They tried to catch the cat to take it to the vet, but it was gone. It eventually returned and lived a long life, just not in air coolers.

The Londene farm was becoming a home to any of their friends' animals they didn't want anymore. There were always baby chickens after Easter and cats, rabbits, gerbils, and puppies in a box left by the front gate, thinking Mrs. W still lived here. The gerbils and puppies weren't welcome. Their friends would call up and ask if they wanted baby Easter chicks or they would just drive out and leave them. They replenished their chickens every year just from Easter. Gene wanted to run an AD at Easter saying, "Baby chick donations accepted."

A cat arrived at the farm by way of Denise. A family friend gave her a cat, which didn't get along with her cat, Shiloh. Denise decided the cat was too mean so she brought him to the farm. Her friends name was Steinberg, and the name was given to the cat. Steinberg was about three years old and had been treated roughly by the children. He was getting mean. For a long time, no one could even touch him without him turning and trying to bite or scratch.

After a few years, when Gene sat down on the porch to rest and have a beer, the cat warmed up to him and surprised him by jumping up on his lap. Gene had always maintained he hated cats, but Steinberg still got to lie on his lap. There was no explanation for this; maybe the old man was getting soft. When Gene sat down in the porch swing, the cat would jump up and lie right beside him. Sometimes it would dig its claws into his leg, and there was a quick departure with some favorite names by Gene. As the cat lay on the swing, Gene would talk to it and tell it how stupid a cat he was and didn't he realize no one wanted him. The cat would then crawl up in his lap. As the next twenty years went by and the cat was about twenty-three, Donna called the vet and said how long do cats live. He said depending on health, maybe twenty years. The vet showed up to worm horses, and Donna asked him to check out the cat since he was over twenty-three years old by then. Much to Donna's dismay, the vet said the heart was great and there were no other problems. He thought he might live another five years.

Every time the kids called home, they asked about Steinberg. Gene wanted to have a mercy killing, but the kids would have mercy killed him. Within a year, the cat was too old to get off the porch, almost blind, and so thin you could count his ribs. He decided his bathroom was anywhere he wanted. He was afraid of the dogs and never left the porch. He was getting hairless, and he was dragging his back legs. Everyone that came to the farm got the same question, "Would you like to take this cat home with you?" The answer was always no. All of Gene's tax clients came to the house every year, and they all would ask if the cat was still around if he wasn't sleeping in front of the door. It was obviously time for a mercy killing, but no one could do it. The kids all said the cat had to stay; he was part of the farm. Of course, they had all left the farm, and Gene was the one cleaning the porch every day. He had decided it had to be time for the cat to go to kitty heaven. Gene and Donna decided they didn't want to see Steinberg suffer that way, and it was time to go. It was a blessing that the next day they went to the porch, and the cat had died in his sleep. Steinberg must have known his time was up, and he elected to go to cat heaven. Never was there another cat on the farm that gained this status. Steinberg was around so long he actually was part of the farm. He was the only cat to have the privilege of living on the porch. Maybe someday there would be another Steinberg, but for now, the new cat lived in the hay shed where he had mice to eat.

# Dogs

With the history and experience of Bompsa and Nipsy under her belt, Donna was now ready to try dog breeding. Both she and Gene had no use for shorthaired dogs, and Gene wouldn't let her have a bulldog like the one she had as a child. He hated bulldogs, and they were dangerous. They both loved German shepherds. They hadn't really decided to get into the breeding business but did so accidentally.

Donna went to the clinic to pick up some antibiotics for the horses. While she was there, Dr. A asked her if she would like to have a free German shepherd. He had someone come into the clinic with this big female German shepherd. He had treated it, but they were moving to Michigan and didn't want to take the dog with them. It was a large tan-and-black registered shepherd. He didn't want to put it down and wanted to find it a good home. Of course, she would consider taking the dog. Donna went to the pens in the clinic to see the dog; she was the biggest German shepherd she had ever seen. She was a high bred with papers from the prize-winning black-and-tan Yonomoto line. When Donna walked to the pen and started speaking softly to the dog, the dog responded to her name Ginger and came immediately to the fence. Dogs are like people and horses; you can look into their eyes and most of the time you can judge their temperament. Donna and Ginger were easily comfortable with each other.

Like Gene, that soft sexy voice and big green eyes had taken in another animal.

Dr. A delivered the dog. When Ginger arrived, she and Donna made friends immediately. Donna put her on the screened-in back porch to keep her away from the other dogs for a while. When Gene came home from work, he usually parked in back and came in the through the porch entrance. He had come home early that evening, and Donna hadn't told him yet about the dog. When he started to open the screen door, the dog awakened from a sleep, made a lunge at the door, and barked furiously. Gene froze. He thought he was dead. This was the biggest German shepherd he had ever seen, and her bark would have scared away any burglar. She must have weighed over one hundred fifty pounds. Donna yelled at the dog from the kitchen door, and Ginger stopped just short of sending Gene to the Promised Land. This was scary, and Donna told him he should have called before he walked in. Donna tried to introduce Ginger to Gene, but she would have nothing to do with him.

Apparently, a man had mistreated her. Gene used the other entrance to get in the house. It was a few days before Ginger allowed him to be near her, and he wouldn't attempt it without Donna present. Donna went on the porch in front of Gene. She took his hand and reached out for Ginger to smell. Next, she put her hands on Gene, took his hand, and placed it on Ginger. Now Ginger accepted Gene as a friend. Finally, she decided maybe he was all right to be around, and they became friends; but there was no question, she was Donna's dog.

*Ginger, the German shepherd watching TV*

Donna and Ginger talked to each other. Donna would speak to her, and she would cock her head and make some whining sounds. She seemed to understand. Donna had been letting her in the house to lie down beside the fireplace next to her. Donna got sick and had to go the hospital for an extended time. After a few days, Ginger became lethargic and hunted the farm over for Donna. She sat at the screen door, moped, and whined. Finally, Gene let her in the house; she went straight to the bedroom, and no one was there, so she made a tour of the house and went outside to lie down. She was satisfied now that Donna wasn't there. Gene recognized the problem now, that she was really missing Donna. Donna said, "Bring me a tape recorder to the hospital," and talked into the recorder the way she does at home. Donna recorded a message, "Okay, Ginger, everything is okay, and I'll be home shortly. You lie down and be a good girl." Gene took the recording home and played it for Ginger who immediately stopped whining, laid down under a tree, and relaxed. She was happy. Several times a day, Ginger came to the screen door and someone played the recording.

When Donna came home, she was still confined to bed. Gene let Ginger in the house, and she went right to Donna's bed, lay at her feet, and made that strange moaning sound while her jaws moved as if she was talking. When she was put outside, she slept under Donna's window, and she wouldn't move except to eat or drink.

After a few days, Donna was able to come into the living room and sit in her chair to watch the morning soap opera TV series, *As the World Turns*. Ginger came in, laid in front of the fireplace, and watched the TV. There was a girl named Kim on the show whose voice sounded a lot like Donna. Everyday at eleven o'clock Ginger came to the screen door and had to be allowed in the house to see the show. She watched it intently without moving and made funny sounds every time Kim spoke. When the show was over, she went to the screen door and wanted out. It was a daily affair. It is amazing that dogs have such a high degree of intelligence and excellent memories. Of all the dogs that came and went on the farm, Ginger was the only one ever allowed in the house for any extended time.

Shortly after her arrival, Dr. A came by to treat a horse and checked out Ginger's recovery. He listened to her heart and got a smile on his face. He looked at Donna and told her she was going to be a mother again. What a bargain, a two for one. Now they had to prepare a pen suitable for new puppies. A month later, Ginger had two puppies. Only one survived and Ginger was not bred again as she was too old. She lived on the farm until she died years later. She was a wonderful friend for Donna and was great with the kids and horses. She was buried on the farm where she had found a good life, and as other shepherds came and went, Ginger would always remain the favorite memory.

Having watchdogs on the farm was considered a necessity. They had a lot of equipment and tools to protect. After Ginger, they acquired some registered German shepherds. They had several litters of puppies and sold most of them to the FBI and the Albuquerque

Police Canine Squad. They had a pup win the show in Denver, one in Kansas City, and some placed well in other shows. As the bitches got old, they started to be nonproductive, suffered hip displacement, and they quit breeding. An epidemic of Parvo disease put them out of business. They always kept two for watchdogsDonna had never been on good terms with Gertie but was okay with Gertie's dog, Maggie. She was a small Boston bulldog type that barked constantly. Gene disliked this dog and thought it had no real function in life except to waddle around and make gas. Mac and Gertie lived in a mobile home, and the home smelled like dog constantly. Gene would do anything to avoid going over there and sitting in the house with that gassing dog. They must have fed her green chili and garlic. The only thing to the dog's credit is that it rated higher on the scale than Gene or Donna did. The dog came first and lived to a ripe old age. One day, Gertie called Donna and told her that the vet had operated on Maggie. Dr. A had called Gertie back and said the dog didn't survive the operation, and Gertie requested he have it cremated. Dr. A arranged the cremation, and in a week or so, he called Donna and said Gertie wanted her to come pick up the dog. Donna reluctantly drove over to the clinic to pick her up. Evelyn handed her this nice little box, and Donna said what is in there. She didn't want to touch the box with dead dog ashes in it. She had Dr. A carry it to the car for her. She opened the trunk so it wouldn't be up front with her. About the time he put the box in the trunk, a big gust of wind came up and blew the lid off the box, and most of the ashes went down the street. Dr. A quickly closed the lid, and they went back into the clinic. Evelyn said she guessed they could use a smaller box now and got a small empty Christmas candy box. She put the remaining ashes in a box and sealed it. Donna went home with the box and delivered it to Gertie who looked at the box and said, "Is that all there is to Maggie?"

Donna said, "Yes, because she was just a little dog."

Gertie kept it on a shelf where she could see it and even took it to Russell, Kansas, when she entered a home there.

# Cows

Donna had no experience handling cows. Sure, she had been born on a farm, but she was too young to milk or work the cows, and she left the farm at three years old. Donna's neighbor on Viola always purchased a young calf or two each year, and he raised them to slaughter for beef. Donna and Gene thought this was a good idea since they had the three acres of pasture that could be used for the calves to graze. A quick call to Dr. A revealed they could go to the dairy and get on the list for a calf.

Off they went to the dairy. The dairy sold the calves at about two weeks old. You could purchase these by getting on the list, and when your turn came up, you could pick them up for $125. Many Valley residents purchased the calves, fed them for a year or two, and filled their freezer with fresh homegrown meat. Sounded like a great idea.

Donna went to the dairy and got on the waiting list for two calves, one for Eileen and Charlie. Normally, the cows calve in the spring. Sometimes it can happen other times during the year. Gene's dad had always maintained, when talking about newlyweds, that the first one can come anytime, and after that, it takes nine months. The same situation for young heifer cows.

Finally, the two calves were ready to be picked up. Arriving at the dairy, they saw a sea of hundreds of black-and-white Holstein cows. Donna went to the office and paid for her calves while Gene backed his pickup up to the loading ramp.

In the pen were about twenty baby Holstein calves. The kids were already at the fence picking out which ones would be theirs. Donna said, "I've already fallen in love with the one with the big black eyes and long eyelashes."

Gene muttered, "What a beautiful way to pick beef cattle!" An understanding was in order that not everyone was getting a calf, there would be only two. Again, the problem was self-solving. Donna said to the yardman, "I want the one with the long eyelashes." He nodded his head, listened intently, and then proceeded to load the two closest to the truck. It was a logical solution. Turned out the yardman was a Mexican who spoke no English and had no idea what she was saying to him. He had learned the universal language of how to handle women, say yes to everything, and then do what you wanted to and suffer the consequences. As their future son-in-law, Randy Baker often stated, "It is a lot easier to ask forgiveness than to ask permission."

Off to the farm they went with their new proud possessions. Darrell wanted to ride in the back of the truck. It turned out to be a good decision to ride in the front of the truck. When cattle get nervous, such as being moved or hauled, they express their uneasiness with total diarrhea.

By the time they drove the few miles home, the calves had painted the whole truck bed and the rails a sickening yellow, green, and brown. The kids and Donna got out of the truck, moved as far away as possible, while Gene got the garden hose and proceeded to hose down truck, calves, and all. Gene backed the pickup up to the unloading ramp, and the kids got in the truck to bring them out. The calves were put in a pen; it was obvious they were going to be family pets, and getting them to the dinner plate was going to be difficult. That would happen in about a year and a half when they were over eleven hundred pounds.

It was Monday morning, and Gene was headed to Chicago for four days. By now, it was assumed that whatever was to go wrong, would happen shortly after Gene left town.

The next morning Gene left the motel and went to the Savings and Loan in Chicago to work. The call had come in before he got there. Upon returning the call, he was greeted with the usual panic voice and pleading for help. What would it be this time? Help! During the night, a pack of dogs had gotten into the calf pen and chewed them up terribly. There was blood and hair everywhere. Gene imagined the worst. What did she think he could do half a country away? The only response that Gene could give since he was eight hundred miles away was "Call the vet." Dr. A and his son arrived at the farm as soon as possible to treat the calves. They were still alive but chewed up pretty badly. Dr. A said they didn't need stitches, but he applied a dressing and left some to be put on daily. They would survive. He locked them in a horse stall where they stayed until Gene returned.

Donna told the kids, "I will get rid of the dogs." That night while Gene was gone, Donna got Darrel's pellet gun, backed the pickup up the pasture gate, and crawled in the back with the gun. She had been complaining to the county officials for months to get rid of the packs of dogs. Soon two Rottweiler dogs came trotting up the lane between the pens. She aimed and shot, and the dogs left in a hurry. Next was a pack with a big Doberman. The next night the same thing happened with two new dogs. Two days later, Dr. A came by to treat a horse. He told Donna he didn't get much sleep because he was up all night taking pellets out of dogs. Donna didn't say a word. The dogs didn't come back.

When Gene got home, he didn't know about Donna's shootings, so he and Darrell arranged a stakeout. The boys stood inside the barn door that night with shotguns, and waited on the dogs. They locked up their own dogs so they wouldn't shoot the wrong ones. At dark, they went down to stand inside the barn and wait. Gene had a 12-gauge shotgun and Darrell had a 410-gauge. They took their positions and waited. Nothing came, so at midnight they went to bed. The next night it was the same thing. Gene couldn't imagine why the dogs didn't come back. They continued to lock the calves in the barn at night for a few weeks. The calves recovered and the dogs never returned, apparently, someone else took care of the dogs or the owners decided to lock them up as they were required to do. It wasn't until much later Gene and Dr. A learned about Donna shooting the dogs.

Eventually it was time to send the steers to the slaughterhouse. They weighed between 1,100 and 1,250 pounds and had been on a fat diet for ninety days. They were big! Donna and Gene waited until the kids had gone to school, loaded up the steers, and set out for Swartsmans for butchering. The kids were not in favor of sending them, but they had the new babies, and these two were two big to be pets anymore.

They were in beef heaven. Forgotten were the days when it was a total luxury to strain the budget to buy a T-bone steak.

By the time the next steers were ready for market, the kids had hardened to farm life. They were out in the pen with the steers with a permanent marker pen making their claim on which portion was theirs.

Donna had always wanted a Hereford cow instead of the lanky Holsteins. Herefords, the red cows with the white blaze face were bred to be beef cattle.Monday morning, Gene was off to Grants to work for three days, so he told Donna she could go to the sale barn and buy her Hereford if she wanted one. She wouldn't go alone, so naturally she called the vet to inquire where to get a good Hereford. He recommended she call a farmer on the Isleta Indian Reservation who was one of his clients and had Herefords. She called him, and he invited her to the reservation to see his cattle. Now, being from Kansas, Dorothy Country, she was a little nervous about going to an Indian reservation by herself, not being sure what she was getting into. She had been to the Jemez Pueblo but never into an Indian house. She hadn't done business with a real Indian. Now she wondered what if he wanted her to eat something. She wondered what if he was unfriendly. Would he speak English? Her total exposure to Indians was the ladies from Jemez that had come to clean her house, and they spoke very little English and didn't talk unless spoken to. She had only seen the Indians in movies with John Wayne, and most of the time they weren't too friendly to John Wayne! She got Eileen to go with her. Off they went to the Isleta reservation five miles south of the farm. When they arrived, they were surprised to find neat little farms with normal little houses like the rest of the valley. Not like the expected pueblo style. The farmer, a full-blooded Isleta Indian and a governor of the Isleta Tribe, was there to greet them. It developed in conversation he was an Ivy League college graduate. He showed them the cows and picked one out for Donna. He told her this cow would never get pregnant but would make a good beef cow. He was going to take her to market. He was a very nice polite older gentleman and offered to deliver the cow. He was very helpful in helping them pick out a cow of their choice. He must have been one great salesman. When Gene returned home, standing in his pasture with a mean scowl and one-foot horns, was this huge old Hereford cow. This wasn't anything edible. One look at her horns, feet, and sway back told him immediately she was at least twelve years old. It was definitely not a butchering or eating candidate. When Gene drove in, Donna, Eileen, Charlie, and kids were all at the rail to the pen admiring their purchase. Gene was a little critical of their "beef cow" and asked if she came with an assignment of her Social Security and Medicare and if they really planned to eat that thing.

*Mama cow eating off BBQ table*

Donna quickly decided that the best thing was to fatten up this cow and send her to be butchered. Donna started to feed her three buckets of corn a day. This would surely fatten her up and make some tender meat for the table. Normally, they fed heavy grain sixty days or more.

One lesson to be learned when you come to this country is that when dealing with the Indians you should never assume you are at the advantage in the negotiations. Quite often, it is just the opposite. Anyway, he had happy customers. They were enamored with their purchase. They had one problem; no one had the nerve to go in the pen. Gene started to enter the pen and quickly retreated when the cow came toward him with horns in ready position. She was very upset about being separated from her yearling calf and being moved to a new location. Gene got some grain and finally coaxed her into a horse pen to give her some time to adjust to the new surroundings. Within days, Donna had her eating out of her hand. Donna called her "Mama," and that became her name. Donna sat down beside her feed trough and talked women talk to her in her enticing low voice that all the horses, dogs, and other animals loved. She could always calm a nervous animal by just talking to it. The cow quickly responded to the name Mama, and she soon thought of Donna as her best friend. It was a while before Gene ventured into a pen with her or into the pasture when she was out there. He had a great respect for cows with long horns and had the scars to justify his fears from early days on the Kansas farm. He only got caught once and was butted over a wooden fence. That was enough. He had a cracked rib and a broken dignity but survived. He developed a lifelong fear and respect for bulls with horns.

Eventually everyone became comfortable with big Mama. She responded to the new home with TLC and extra feeding. She blossomed into a beautiful friendly cow, and they let her out of her pen to eat grass around the house. After the kids got out of the swimming pool, everyone sat on the wooden tables and had a dip and chip party. Mama came to the table and ate her share of potato chips with hot salsa. She was delighted when they had roasting ears and she got all the cornhusks. She became one of the family. Every time Donna came out of the house, she would look up from her feeding and give a soft moo in recognition. She recognized her name, and when Donna called, "Come on, Mama," she would raise her head up and flop her ears. She mooed and came running. Of all the animals on the farm over the years, "Mama" would always be Donna's favorite memory.

About thirty days later, Donna looked out the window, and the cow was already getting fat and huge; she thought she was bloating. She called the vet, and Dr. A came right over. They went out to the pen, and he got out this big knife and stuck her belly to let out the bloat gas. There was no gas! The smell was atrocious. He looked at Donna and asked if she was sure this cow wasn't pregnant. She said no, the Indian guaranteed it. Dr. A said the belly should have gone down a lot more. He got out his big long plastic glove and proceeded to do a pregnancy test on the cow. Sure enough, he turned to Donna and said she was going to have a calf in a few months. Now Donna decided she couldn't eat this cow. When Gene got home, she told him Mama was going to have a calf. Dr. A recommended Donna cancel the three buckets of corn a day or she was going to kill her from being too fat. He gave her some advice on how to feed her. Mama was going to be around for a while.

One day the time came without warning. Donna called Gene at the office with much excitement and said the familiar phrase, "Shall I call the vet? The cow had a baby calf out in the pasture, and the horses might kill it." Gene assured her this was not the first rodeo for that cow, and she would handle her own problems. The calf would be fine until he got home. There was not a horse in the pasture dumb enough to challenge those horns. Returning home, Gene put the cow and calf in the first pen where everyone could have access. She was immediately the total object of attention. The cow would not let anyone near the calf. They are very protective until they get comfortable with company. Having a calf born on the farm was another chapter in the excitement and wonder of farm life. They had become accustomed to delivering foals from the horses, but a calf was something else again. New baby calves are so loving. They have big soft eyes and no fear of anything. They love to lick you and suck on your fingers, and the kids had a ball with the new baby. Within hours, Donna had Mama calmed down, and the new arrival was immediately the new family pet. Occasionally, Mama would use her horns and strength and remove the fence that kept her from getting to her friend. The fences around the farm weren't in the best shape. She could also open the latch on the gate with her horns. She wandered around the farm eating the prime yard grass until she got Donna's attention. It often created some excitement to wake up in the morning, look out the window, and see a half-ton cow looking back at you. Then Donna had to go to the cow, hold out her hand so she could wrap her tongue around Donna's arm, and hand in tongue, they would walk back to the pen. The relationship between Donna and Mama was akin to a cowboy and his horse. Finally, the day would come that Mama was no longer able to have calves. They tried artificial insemination, but it wouldn't take. Donna called the vet, and he came and tried to get her inseminated. It didn't work; she was too old.

Since Mama was no longer productive, Gene said she was just too expensive to feed for just a pet. Her pen was needed for younger steers or a board horse. It took a while for Donna to conclude that the cow had to go. On the day the truck came to haul her to the sale barn; Gene was at work. The trucker had difficulty convincing the cow to walk up the ramp to the truck. Donna told him to stand aside and get out of the pen. She went in with the cow and calmly explained to her that she needed to get in the truck and go bye-bye. She held out her hand to the cow who promptly nuzzled her hand and followed her up the ramp and into the truck. The trucker closed the door, still mumbling that he had never seen anything like that in his life. The truck left for the sale barn, and Donna followed to do the bill of sale. She was heartbroken, but she knew it was necessary. When she got to the sale barn, they tagged Mama and put her in the pen with a maze of cows. Donna went home. She wouldn't stay for the sale. Shortly after Donna got home, the phone rang. They called from the sale barn and told her, "Mrs. Londene, come and get this cow and take her home. She doesn't have a brand, and we can't sell her. The inspector will be here shortly, and if he finds her without a brand, he will take her and you will get nothing for her." He suggested she take the cow to Schwartzman's, and he would buy or butcher her. She jumped in the car, went to Webb's Trailer Rentals, and rented a trailer to take her to the barn. Two cowboys got a lasso and went to get Mama out of the crowd. They wanted to know what number she was, and they would find her. Donna said, "Hold your horses. I can get her myself. All I have to do is call her."

The cowboys laughed and said, "That woman is crazy. This we have to see." They opened the trailer and lowered the ramp. Donna stood on the back of the trailer and called, "Come on,

Mama, hurry up. Come on, Mama." Up came the head with the horns and ears at attention. She wound herself through four pens of cows, and when she finally got to the chute, she was on a full gallop. She was coming home to Donna, and she came up into the trailer. The laughing had stopped among the cowboys; they just watched and shook their heads. Donna drove her over to Schwartzman's. He knew Donna quite well by now. Donna was in tears; she explained about the brand, and she didn't know what to do. He told Donna not to worry, he would buy her, and he did. Donna still cried all the way home. Mama was gone.

The next year they acquired the usual calf to raise for beef. This one was an Angus cross. Over the years, there were many beef cows that came and went. However, there would never be another Mama.

The next calf they had to use a different butcher. This time their meat came home substantially underweight from what they expected. They also had a fattened pig, which they sent to market. It came back with two sizes of pork chops. One side was four-inch chops and the other was six-inch chops. Donna was furious; a pig can't be two different sizes. In addition, they got back very little meat from a two-hundred-eighty-pound pig.

During the college days, Donna had worked in a meat market. She knew the cuts, and she knew what to expect. The next steer that went to the butcher, she arranged to be there with the butcher when it was cut up, and she helped package and label the meat. From then on, they did much better.

Cows on the farm never achieved the same status as horses, but to Donna, they were much more her favorites.

One beautiful New Mexico spring morning the Orkin Bug man came to do his monthly spraying around the house. He was down in the basement finishing up. While he was down there, Donna's 1,300-pound steer Jeremiah opened up his pen and came to the house to get Donna to come play with him. He had learned to lift the iron hooks on his gate and go for a walk. The first night he got out, he came up the bedroom window at two in the morning, pressed his face against the screen, and let out a loud, "Moo." The screen was on Donna's bedroom window, which was open, and the head of the bed was just a couple feet from the screen. Donna came straight up out of the bed, and Gene went for his shotgun. When she recovered, and got off the ceiling, she got the nerve to go back into the bedroom. There stood Jeremiah with his big brown eyes waiting with his ears flopping. He had his mouth slightly open as if he was smiling. He wanted to play and wanted Donna to come run with him. Donna said to him, "Get back in your beddi-bye right now." Surprisingly, he went.

The Orkin man finished in the basement and came up the outside stairs. As he turned the corner of the house, he came face-to-face with what looked like a 1,300-pound fighting bull ready to charge. Jeremiah was standing in front of the Orkin man with his head down, pawing the ground and doing his dance. He did this little dance, shuffling back and forth, and rotated his ears like antenna as if he was tuning in to see where Donna was. He pawed the ground and threw his butt around as if he was ready for a bullfight. This was his way of getting Donna to walk and play with him. It had been a fun game when he was little, but now he was huge. His body had grown but not his mind.

The Orkin man froze in his tracks and yelled to Donna, "Oh, Mrs. Londene, there is a big bull attacking me." He was so petrified he couldn't move. Donna yelled out the back screen porch to Jeremiah, "Get back to your beddi-bye." She went out with her apron flopping and told the Orkin man to step inside the door on the screened porch, and she would take care of the steer. Donna walked up to the steer and stuck out her arm, Jeremiah wrapped his tongue around her arm, and they walked back to the pen together. The Orkin man recovered and asked if the steer really knew what beddi-bye meant. Donna said, "Of course he does, he went to the pen, didn't he?" From that time on, the Orkin man called in advance to make sure the animals were locked up.

The time came to send Jeremiah to market. The kids had already taken chalk and marked out their steaks. The man with the truck came to pick him up; he was too big for Gene's pickup. The driver was very upset because they still didn't have a chute for loading the steer. He put out the ramp to the truck and got out his electric prod to force the steer to get into the trailer. Donna said, "Put that away and let me handle it." She walked over to the pen and opened the gate. Jeremiah was happy to see her, and she told him, "We are going for a walk." He wrapped his sandpaper-like tongue around her arm, and he was very happy to go for a walk. They walked up the ramp together. She turned him around so she could wave good-bye to him. The man just put down his prod and said he was really impressed. He was still shaking his head and mumbling as he drove off. Donna was always sad to see them go, but she knew she could now start another one tomorrow, and she loved to train them. Gene could have his horses; she had her cows and pigs, and they were often better trained than his horses.

All the animals on the farm knew Donna as their friend. To Gene, they were just another steak on the hoof; but to Donna, they were her family, and she loved all her family.

# Sheep

After the goat experience, there was some discussion about getting some sheep to eat the grass and weeds. Gene had no desire to get close to sheep because they were smelly and oily. Sheep have to be sheared every year in the spring, and Gene remembered the time his father and the landlord had joint ventured one hundred sheep. Gene was about eleven when the men came to shear the sheep for the first time. The procedure was to hang large burlap bags from the rafters in the sheep shed where the shearing was to take place. As each sheep was sheared, the pelts were wrapped in twine to make it into a ball that could be handled. The shearer then climbed the ladder and tossed the pelt into the sack. Someone had to be in the sack to properly stack the pelts and stomp them down so you could get more in the bag. Gene spent the whole day in the bags stomping down and packing the wool.

They threw the pelts in, and sometimes he was under the pelt. He became as oily and stinky as the sheep. Afterwards, he had to shed all his clothes outside, step into the house and directly into the metal bathtub on the porch. It took a lot of hot water, soap and scrubbing to get him clean. Siri put some Clorox in the water. Now he still smelled bad, but it was a different smell. For the rest of the week, Gene was excused from school. After this event, Gene wouldn't eat mutton and never did until Sara Jean came along.

Darrell had joined junior 4-H, and as with all members, he had to have a project. He wanted a sweet little lamb. The 4-H was one of the only social functions for the valley kids in the summer, and all three kids belonged. Darrell had just turned eight and probably weighed about fifty pounds. They got him a lamb, which he named Sara Jean. He played a lot with the lamb, taught her to chase him, and he would chase her. When he caught her, they rolled in the grass together. Darrell chased her down this little hill, and she chased him back up. It was a great game and hilarious to watch. The baby lamb was very sweet and cuddly, and a lot of fun, and was easy for Darrell to work with.

Then something happened. The lamb grew faster than Darrell did, and the game started to get a little rough. Darrell had acquired a military officers' dress helmet liner. To protect himself from the lamb's butts, he wore the helmet for the game with the strap under his chin. Now the game was different; the lamb would catch Darrell not paying attention and ram him from behind and roll him down the hill.

This comedy went on for weeks until one day Darrell had enough, and he marched into the kitchen crying and told Donna, "Mom, I want you to eat Sara Jean." The sheep had gotten too big and too rough, and the game was over. Donna feared she might hurt someone, so arrangements were made to take her to the butchers. Darrell had no remorse as his bruises hadn't yet gone away.

Donna and Eileen planned a meal of lamb chops with mashed potatoes and gravy. They smelled good. Donna told Gene and Charlie, "You are elected, and you will eat the first lamb chop." They were to eat first to set an example. All sat down to the table, and the food was served. Everyone was served a chop because Donna put them directly on the plates. Refusal was not an option. After filling the plates, it was time for the first big bite. All eyes were on Gene and Charlie as they cut their chops and lifted that first bite to their mouths. Without fanfare, they cut another bite and nodded in approval. Donna and Eileen were also now happily chewing. The chops were surprisingly excellent eating, and the platter was soon empty. Sara Jean was a success, and everyone's prejudices were compromised. Even though all praised the lamb chops, this was the last time they would ever be on the menu. Donna told Eileen, "Please take the rest of the lamb." Gene decided he could learn to like lamb if his old dislike wasn't so strong.

From that point on, they were content to drive by the fields of new little lambs, say, "Aren't they cute," and drive on their way.

# Snakes

Snakes were plentiful around the farm, but they were no problem as they were mostly nonpoisonous types, like garter and bull snakes. One day, Donna called the office in desperation. She and the kids were standing out in the yard and afraid to go in the house. She had been cleaning house and organizing, and she and the kids had carried some things to the upstairs porch, which was now an enclosed room.

She didn't have her glasses, and she didn't see too well without them. Donna laid her cowboy hat on the bookcase on top of the plastic snake Darrell had won at the State Fair. To Donna's amazement, the hat rose up and fell to the floor. What magic was this? Maybe the house was haunted, or was it a mechanical snake? Something was wrong; now her books were moving. She panicked. She turned on the light for a better look. Now Darrell's toy snake had company. A huge four-foot snake raised its head and looked her in the eye from the second shelf of the bookcase. She screamed as if she was wounded, and the kids ran to see what the matter was. Whatever they were carrying went into the air, and they were gone. She and the kids probably set a record in getting downstairs; they left the room in a hurry and ran down the north stairway. The kids couldn't believe their mother had beaten them out of the house. They were all outside, and they weren't going back in. The snake had found a place in the sun and had settled in for the winter, and they had disturbed his nap. Now

Donna really came unglued; she was deathly afraid of snakes or anything else that crawled. She wouldn't go near one outside. She rated snakes right alongside of chickens and birds. It was all she could do to put a worm on a fishhook.

Now she had a huge snake in her house upstairs! How did he get in the house? How did he get up on the second floor? He was right next to the kids' bedroom. Maybe he had a wife and kids who had already made it to her bedroom.

Dr. A was out on calls. His wife, Evelyn, said to ignore the snake until Gene got home. Sure! You knew she wouldn't take that advice. She called Gene at his office. She demanded, "You leave your meeting and come home right now before the snake decides to move into our bedroom."

When Gene arrived, everyone was still out in the yard. As he got out of the car, four people all started talking at once. He now had the impression the snake was somewhere between ten and ninety feet long with huge fangs and florescent eyes and had already devoured all the furniture and books on the porch. He went upstairs, and sure enough, there was a huge snake sunning himself. Gene looked at the tail; there was no rattle so it was not a rattlesnake. He looked at the head; it was not a copperhead or a moccasin. Therefore, it must be a big, fat, harmless bull snake wrapped up in a ball enjoying the sun.

Gene went to the garage to build a snake catcher. He took a six-foot two-by-two board and put a circle screw in the end, added a long piece of thin electric fence wire, and fastened one end to the screw head. Then he fed the other end of the wire back through the screw head to form a wire loop that was dropped over the snake's head. When he pulled on the wire, it tightened and made a noose so he could carry the snake downstairs by its head. This was an old Indian rattlesnake-catching snare from Kansas. He caught the snake and carried it downstairs with the snare. Everyone gave him lots of room as he carried it out in the yard. After he had some fun scaring the kids, and everyone had their pictures taken, he put the snake in a box. On his way back to work, he hauled him down the road a few miles and turned him loose in the Bosque. You always saved the bull snakes because they ate mice and rodents.

Gene replaced the rotten screen on the air vent for the furnace in the basement. It had been another exciting day on the farm. For the next few nights, the kids did a thorough examination of the upstairs before they turned out the lights and crawled in bed. They left the bathroom lights on. Someone had taken Darrell's carnival snake and laid it in the bathtub. For weeks, Darrell tortured the girls by crawling up to their beds in the dark and hissing like a snake. Then the screaming brought a parent to the stairway to quiet things down. The kids turned down their covers, turned out the light, and jumped from there into their beds to keep their feet off the floor. For several nights, Donna inspected her bedroom before jumping in bed and made Gene turn off the light. Gene had to make a nightly inspection of looking under the bed and bedroom furniture before she would come in the room. Eventually, snakes were all forgotten.

When they started raising German shepherds, one of them had a passion for catching snakes. He eliminated snakes from the farm and became Donna's hero. He did lose some of his popularity when he brought them up and laid them on the steps to the house and Donna stepped on one in the morning. She used the other door until Gene removed them. Snakes were never popular.

# Bob and Pat

Pat—Donna's best high-school friend in Russell, Kansas—hadn't seen Donna and Gene since their wedding. Several years after their arrival in Albuquerque, Donna, Gene, and family were on the way to Kansas for Fred's birthday. They decided to leave a day early and stop in Russell for the Prairie Fiesta Fall Celebration and stay the night with Pat and Bob. They had a few things in common. They all liked to party, drink, dance, and have a lot of fun, and they usually carried things to extreme. They enjoyed each other, and it became an annual part of their trip to Abilene to spend the first night in Russell. Sometimes they stayed a couple more days and went to the lake to fish in Bob's boat or went pheasant hunting.

Some time later, Bob and Pat came to Albuquerque to visit on their way to El Paso. The group started out innocent enough, going dancing and drinking a little that evening and just visiting at the farm. On Saturday, Bob and Pat were going to El Paso. Gene and Donna had wanted to go to El Paso to go the horse races at Sunland Park. They decided to go with them, and they could all go to the races for a day.

They drove to El Paso and went to the races. After the races, they crossed the border to Mexico to eat at the Florida, a steak house in downtown Juarez.

They decided to go to the dog races. Gene said he knew how to get there and proceeded to drive to where he thought it was.

Soon they were headed up the hill to the residential area. This wasn't right; he had missed a turn. They tried again, and they were still lost. Pat owned a liquor store in Kansas, and Bob knew he could always go in a liquor store to ask directions. The rest were watching from the car. They were poised to observe one of the most humorous international excursions they would encounter. Bob asked the manager of the liquor store how to find the dog track, but the manager spoke no English, and they encountered a language problem. Bob resorted to sign language. By the time he got done, he was in a half crouch with his hands out in front of him trying to look like a greyhound running while he was going, "Varoom, Varoom." Soon the man behind the counter started doing the same thing. There they were, two grown men, looking like they were trying to play grasshopper or something. Even people passing on the street stopped to watch and laugh. The manager was a little fat man with an apparent good sense of humor, and he was enjoying the situation.

Finally, Bob got his point across when he again went through the motions, but this time he started bouncing and barking going, "Bow wow" and "Woof woof." Now the man understood. He also crouched, put his arms out like a dog running, smiled, and repeated, "Bow wow" and pointed the way to the dog track. The man behind the counter and all the bystanders were laughing and having a good time with the show put on by the crazy American. They all applauded as Bob left the store. Bob just smiled, gave a victory sign, and made his way to the car. They finally got to the dog track.

Over the years, Bob and Pat were wonderful, fun-filled friends. However, the escapades of these two couples when they got together was something you can only take occasionally. It may have been fortunate they were seven hundred miles apart. Just another example of the variety of their many fun friends.

# Don and Dana

When they arrived in Albuquerque, Gene and Donna didn't know anyone in town. Gene started his job, and at work, he met another Swede, Don. They were about the same age, and in conversation at lunch, it developed both couples played bridge. They got together for a bridge game, and during the conversation, they found out both couples loved to dance. Then they discovered all of them loved to fish. Don's wife, Dana, was a Norwegian from Canada, and Don was from Montana. They had so much in common; they spent the next few years spending many of their entertainment nights together. They would get together for barbeque early in the evening and then play bridge for a few hours. After nine o'clock, when the kids were gone to bed, they got a babysitter and they went dancing until two in the morning. This became at least a weekly affair.

The first night they went to the Hawaiian nightclub on Nine Mile Hill. It closed at midnight. On the way back into Albuquerque, they passed the Hitching Post, a Western nightclub. It was open until two o'clock so they stopped in. It had a large dance floor, a live Western dance band, twenty-five-cent beer, and no cover charge. They had found their home for the next several years.

Donna and Don were dancing very fast to a jitterbug and somehow he threw her away and their hands didn't connect. Donna went flying across the floor bouncing on her rear end, and she slid clear to the door. Glen Campbell announced over the loud speaker, "Watch the lady do the dribble dance." It was very embarrassing for Donna since this was in the day of miniskirts but not enough to stop her from dancing. At the break, the band came over and congratulated Donna on inventing a new dance. The years with Glen Campbell and his band will always be one of the highlights on their memory list.

Just before they met, Gene and Donna had started going fishing with their neighbors, Harry and Evelyn. When summer came, Don and Dana joined in. They camped out in the mountain lakes and rivers almost every weekend. Again, fishing was an activity that didn't take much money. It required a six-dollar license and the gas to get there. They acquired a tent together and slept on the ground on air mattresses that usually lost their air during the night. Later they splurged on a gas-cooking stove and ice chests. Fortunately, they usually caught enough fish for many meals, so what they saved in groceries paid for the gas.

They went to the Trout Lakes or Nutrias Lakes in Northern New Mexico on Labor Day. They weren't catching any fish. On Saturday, they fished in the upper big lake until dark, and they walked back to camp. As they walked by the little lake where they were camping, Gene still had a worm on his hook so he casually flipped it out in the water. He had two hooks on and caught a fish on both hooks. Now everyone got excited and all six of them started fishing. At midnight, Gene made Donna quit fishing because he was tired of cleaning fish and his hands were freezing. They must have had over a hundred fish. Later they found that fish know when the big winter storm is coming, and they go on a feeding frenzy to last through the winter. Too bad they didn't know that earlier.

The next morning, Donna awakened to find Denise was not in the sleeping bag. She was two years old then, and she was sitting by the door playing with this white stuff. Donna got her back into the sleeping bag, and she was frozen. That white stuff turned out to be two foot of snow. All night they had heard this noise like something on their tent. Now they knew what it was; it was snow sliding off the tent.

They dressed and started to dig out of the snow. They bundled up the kids and put them in the backseat of the car to keep warm. They were nine miles from the highway on terrible roads. They were at 9,300 feet, and the highway was at 6,500; it was a long way down. The roads were bad when it was dry. To make it worse, they had a flat tire on the car. Don changed the tire while Gene packed up. There were five cars leaving, and they had no hope of getting out of there. Soon a miracle came to save them. A couple from Albuquerque named Anderson had been camping at the upper lake. They had a four-wheel drive Jeep station wagon with a winch. They proceeded down the mountain, and he pulled each car through the bad spots. While being pulled through the mud, Don's Oldsmobile picked up a big rock stuck in the A frame, and when they came to the cattle guard, they took out a couple of the crosspieces. Now they had to jack up the car and repair the broken cattle guard to get all the cars across the opening. The men were muddy, wet and cold. They finished off Gene's Jack Daniels at this stop. The caravan didn't get to the highway until four in the afternoon. However, they got all six cars there, muddy, wet, and tired. Now they all gathered at a picnic area on the highway and pooled their food for dinner. They had a big party. When they got ready to leave, Gene gave the Andersons with the jeep two bags of fifteen fish each. They hadn't caught a single fish since they went to bed before the big feeding frenzy started. Limits on fish weren't enforced yet at that time. The whole group had been very fortunate to be pulled off the mountain, and they will never forget the name of the person that saved them, Andy Anderson.

# Charlie and Eileen

Finally the difference in ages between Gene and Donna and Eileen and Charlie started becoming more pronounced. The days of sharing the swimming pool, Jack Daniel parties, and meals had come to an end. Charlie had developed emphysema and had become bedridden requiring Eileen to be a caregiver full time. He was sick for over two years and eventually passed away at home.

It was a devastating time for Eileen .They had been married over forty years. She was lost without Charlie, and her attitude completely changed. She found little to inspire her except for her outings to her church where she met a retired widower.

Soon after, they decided to take to the road and travel. She sold the mobile home she and Charlie lived in to Gene and moved into an apartment, leaving Viola Road, the family compound.

Shortly after moving away, her new male friend reported that while they were traveling in Ireland Eileen had a fall that killed her. Before the trip to Ireland, they reportedly had been married, and she had assigned all her possessions and investments over to him.

To Gene and Donna, this was a very strange sequence of events. In the months after Charlie's death, Eileen became a different person and lost interest in her adopted family. Donna was deeply hurt and never came to understand what had happened to Eileen's state of mind. It seemed that Eileen never fully recovered from the loss of Charlie. They had big questions about the events in her second marriage.

Regardless of the outcome, Charlie and Eileen were as much a part of the farm as the Londene family. They contributed much to the operation and improvements on the farm and were always a part of the social and holiday life. Donna will always feel she lost a sister.

# Edelweiss Am Rio Grande

Gene spent his military time in Bavaria, West Germany, and he loved every minute of it. He loved the German dances and beer, the customs, the Bavarian and Alpine dancers, and the music. When he returned home, all that was gone but not forgottenDonna had danced in Russell all her life in the modern big band era and to the German polka bands. She was a more sophisticated dancer and almost a professional jitterbugger. She did performances with her brother at conventions.

When Gene opened his office in the valley in 1970, a German club downtown required German ancestry to join. When he moved to the new office on San Mateo in 1973, The Edelweiss Am Rio Grande German American club had relocated just up the street. Gene and Donna talked about it, and Donna called the club for membership information. She was told they had to be of German blood and a member had to sponsor them into the club. She qualified for the German part, but they didn't know any members to sponsor them. For the time being, they dropped the subject.

Several years later, Gene acquired a tax client that paid dues to the German club. He inquired about it, and they invited Gene and Donna to come to the club to see if they would like to join. They went by the club and got the applications. They were impressed with the way the members had taken this old retail building and made it into an authentic, traditional German Gasthaus with atmosphere and many decorations. It had a bar and a big dance floor. They went to orientation and joined the club.

The first Saturday night was a fest with the club's Edelweiss German Dancers performing. Gene and Donna got there early and were thrilled with the dancers all in German Bavarian costumes doing traditional folk dances. After the performance, Donna had noted the instructor and dance leader was a Mr. Ulibarri, a teacher at the school Denise had attended. She introduced herself to him and asked about the possibility of joining the dance group. He said come to practice Tuesday evening, and the group will extend an invitation if they decide you can dance. They went to the practice, and they were immediately inducted into the dance group. They acquired the lederhosen, dirndls, hats, shoes, and all the things that made up traditional Bavarian and Alpine costumes. Within two weeks, they were doing their first performance at a function at Sandia Base. For the next ten years, they danced all over the city and New Mexico and even went to Germany on tour.

*Performing at Edelweiss Club*

They practiced weekly with "Rudy's Edelweiss Dancers." This group, combined with "Rudy's University Dancers," were invited to the Kempton Music Festival in Kempton, Germany. They made a three-week tour and danced all over Southern Germany, Austria, and Lichtenstein. It was the highlight of their dancing careers.

On their arrival in Frankfort, Germany, they rented a van and drove to Heidelburg for a short tourist visit and then on to Stuttgart. They spent the first night in a youth hostel, which has open floors with many double bunks. Supposedly, there was one floor for men and one for women, but somehow they got intermixed. When they checked in, the man on the desk asked Donna if she wanted a douche. Donna was shocked. "Why would he ask me such a personal question when he doesn't even know me?" She called for Brigitta, a member of their group who was raised in Germany. Brigitta had a good laugh and told Donna that a bath in Germany is called a douche. He was not being personal. Donna was relieved but wasn't sure she could trust her German to speak it anymore.

Donna went to sleep in a bottom bunk on the women's floor; Gene was downstairs with the men. In the morning, she awoke to voices from the top bunk. She looked to see who was there and saw a pair of man's boots. She was shocked again. What was he doing here? He was talking to his girl friend in the top bunk. He finally left and went back down to the men's floor. She got up and went to the bathroom. As she sat in the stall, she noticed the stall next to her had a pair of man's boots. She heard him speak to a friend next to him, and it was definitely a man. Had she gone to the wrong bathroom? She was confused. She dressed quickly and got out of there. She wanted to shower but decided against that. She just had her first experience with co-ed youth hostels. There would be more.

It was in Germany Donna picked up the nickname of Big Mama. The German host of the group on the trip came to the United States after the trip to Germany. He stayed at the farm with Gene and Donna for the week. He had referred to Donna as Big Mama in German. It is a literal interpretation of the German title for the big boss. It translates to Big Mama in English. He referred to her everywhere as Big Mama, and soon everyone did the same. To this day, Gene also refers to Donna as Big Mama. He and Lewis, the grandson, named a recent filly born on the farm as Foxy Big Mama. She was a beautiful sorrel mare with flying red mane resembling the color of a red fox. She was Donna's horse and won at the track with the same will to win that Donna has.

Donna and Gene had danced together since Salina. Even at Manhattan, where they had no money for entertainment, they went to the Student Union for free dancing. They went to every nightclub in Albuquerque, to the Officers Club, and Sandia Club on base. Big-time bands come to the clubs regularly. Dance contests were popular in the sixties and seventies, and they entered dance contests everywhere they went. In New Mexico they won at the Officers Club on Sandia Base, the Sandia Club, Taos, Angel Fire Lodge, Sandia Inn, Santa Fe, and others. One night they stopped at the Sandia Inn for a few drinks on their way home from a function, and everyone was dancing. They joined in, and to their surprise, they were selected to be in the final four; and they won the dance contest. They had been drinking a little and didn't even know it was a contest. When there is music and a dance floor, their feet automatically join in the dance.Another night they were in Taos, New Mexico, for a bank meeting. As they returned to the motel, they passed a big hall where there was music and dancing. They went in and it was all Spanish, but they didn't care, they liked the music. It turned out it was a wedding reception. They stayed anyway. When the night developed into a dance contest, they won the prize for the polka and waltz portions. They got to waltz with the bride and groom by request. They participated in the custom of pinning money on the dress of the bride. They could fit in anywhere there was music.

They knew that in order to meet people in a club you had to get involved. They were happy just to be members but also their daytime concern was acquiring new clients for their CPA business. Gene volunteered to become membership chairman for the German club. Here he would have direct contact with all six hundred members, and he acquired clients who stayed with him for years. Donna was active on various committees.

The next year Gene was nominated for vice president. He was elected. In the summer, while they were in Germany with the dance group, the president resigned. Gene arrived home to a banner, "Welcome Home, Mr. President." He was now president of the club. He served his term as president but did not run for reelection. It took too much time away from his business. However, they both stayed very active members of the club and participated in the entertainment, the children's Christmas party, and the operation of the club.

Donna headed up "Downtown Saturday Night" and helped the club make a lot of money. The city had a dedicated German night with food, beer, music, and dancers. Both of them helped build floats for the club and the dance group, and they won first place at the State Fair Parade and the Fashing parades. Fasching in English is carnival, and in other parts of the world is called Mardi Gras. It's the period from November 11 until Ash Wednesday preceding Lent celebrated by the Germans with balls, parades, and parties. Gene was chairman of the Fasching Elferat committee or Council of Eleven. In 1984, Donna and Gene were selected the prince and princess of Fasching at the club and reigned over the activities for the year. The club consumed all their social activity for a few years, and they seldom missed a guest dance band. Darrell was head of the youth group and was the junior prince of Fasching one year. Denise danced with the group at times. She was the Funkenmarichian at the club for Fasching one year. This person leads the entrance to the ball for the Fashing group. Everyone at the club thought Gene was German; he never told them he was one hundred percent Swedish.

When they had the dancing and dinner nights at the club to celebrate Fasching season, usually the Edelweiss group performed. They had a Roaring Twenties night, and Gene and Donna were asked to do a surprise performance as Ginger Rogers and Fred Astaire. They rented a tuxedo complete with top hat, cane, and cummerbund. Donna went to her hairdresser and was fitted with a beautiful blond wig. The beauty parlor did her makeup and nails. She wore a long flowing peach gown with a low-cut neck. They performed a dance to their old favorite, "Lisbon Antigua." After a rousing applause by the crowd, they danced to the back and exited behind the curtains. Some figured out it was Gene, but everyone all night was trying to identify the beautiful blond. Donna took off the wig and dress and returned to the club as normal. It cost them over a hundred dollars to rent the tuxedo, top hat, and cane for Gene and the wig and beauty parlor for Donna. They would go to any length to do a performance and have a good time.

*Impersonating Fred and Ginger*

They continued to dance with the Edelweiss Dancers until accidents, health, and old age forced them to retire. Giving up dancing was one of the biggest disappointments of their life. They have always felt sorry for people who don't dance. They were missing so much. They were constantly disappointed their children and grandchildren preferred movies, telephone, and TV instead of making an effort to learn dancing.

# Sister Cities International

When the children were old enough, Donna became a great citizen. She got involved as Girl Scout leader, Little League, director of Mime Theater, Edelweiss Am Rio Grande German American Club, various school and church functions and Sister Cities. She thrived on involvement with people.

Her first venture with Little League was as equipment manager. To save money, she bought new liners for the helmets. She had seen Gene use a new thing on the market called super glue. She had no experience using super glue, and of course, she didn't read the instructions. Gene was in his office when the call came from the kids, and he headed home early. Donna wasn't able to dial the phone. As he walked in the house, there sat Donna with a helmet glued to each hand. She had held the liners in place while they dried. She had been crying and couldn't even pick up a Kleenex to wipe her eyes. It was hot summertime, and she slept in a shorty nightgown. That morning she took off her housecoat and was doing the helmets in her nightgown. Gene couldn't keep from laughing and as usual went for his camera. Donna screamed some objections so he forgot that; he was already in enough trouble for laughing. She had the kids call Dr. A, and he had suggested the fire department. Now the problem was how to dress her; she couldn't get the helmets in any sleeves. Gene finally stopped laughing, got a baby blanket, and pinned it around her. Now she was crying again, and the kids had to go along to wipe her eyes. Off went Gene, Donna, and a string of kids to the fire department with Donna hanging one arm with the helmet attached out the window and the other one in her lap. It must have looked ridiculous walking into the fire building with two helmets dangling at her side. The firemen knew she was coming, and they were all at the door to greet her with their cameras. It was very embarrassing. Everyone had a great laugh as the firefighters used a special solvent to remove Donna from her helmets; it didn't work. Finally, they went to the store for super glue remover. Of course, it now was Gene's fault for not warning her about super glue. The fire department boys never let her forget this one. Of course, news of this event got back to the veterinarians, and she was sure she was mentioned at the next convention.

Donna first joined the Albuquerque Sister Cities in 1983 at the request of Harry Kinney, the mayor of Albuquerque. Harry was a member of the Edelweiss Club, and she had worked with him on other functions. In 1983, the city adopted a new sister city in Helmstedt, Germany. Helmstedt was the gateway to East Germany on the road to Berlin. Donna became president of Albuquerque Sister Cities and worked closely with the mayor. The first time Donna got involved with Harry he called Donna and told her he had a group of German college professors and national sports directors coming to Albuquerque for a professional visit to review the education and sports situation. He said he was trying to find homestays and asked Donna if she could keep one in her house for a few days. She said, "Yes, I enjoy having people on Sister City exchanges."

Harry said, "Fine, meet us at the airport at flight 330 at nine o'clock tonight and pick up your guest. You will host Dirk Albrecht, the Director of Fussball (soccer)." She told Harry she needed one that spoke English. He replied, "No problem. The paperwork says they all speak English."

At nine o'clock, they went to the airport to pick up their guest. She wanted Gene to go along in case they were speaking German, and he could respond. Gene could speak some German, and Donna could understand a lot of German from her childhood because her grandmother only spoke German. When engaged in conversation, Donna would understand what they were saying better than Gene, and Gene could respond. They arrived at the airport and off the plane came these twelve tired men. Four more than expected. Harry had three hosts there to take guests home. He was single at the time, and he was taking three. When everyone picked up their guests and had gone home, all that was left was Harry with his three guests and Donna and her one guest. However, there were still three more Germans just standing there without a host. Harry said he only had beds for three and didn't know what to do with the other three. He and Donna called friends but found no beds. It just so happened that the girls were both gone to college and Darrell was in Houston staying with his cousin, Raymond, going to school to learn German. There was only one solution. She now had as additional guests: Bodo, the Minister of Science; Joakim Brown, the youth administrator; and a congressman.

It was more than a little crowded in the car going home with an additional four big people holding some of their bags on their laps. Fortunately, at that time, Donna still had her big Cadillac. They arrived at the farm about one in the morning. Donna indicated to them they were sleeping upstairs and to bring their bags so she could show them their rooms. They didn›t respond as they appeared to be very tired, and they just followed her upstairs to the rooms. Donna showed them the bathroom and the towels and told them breakfast would be at seven in the morning. She knew how tired they were, and she thought they wanted to go to sleep quickly. She bade them good night, and started down the stairs thinking all was well. She realized something went wrong; they were all following her. Oh no! Now both Donna and Gene realized they didn't understand a word of English, and the guests had no idea what she had told them.

They all arrived back in the kitchen, Gene asked in German the best he could "Do you want something to drink?"

And they all said, "Ya, aine trinken, bitta."

Gene asked in German, "Was trinken zee, wasser, milch, beer, oder schnapps?" They all responded schnapps. Gene served them some whiskey and vodka. They were happy now. They had seconds. Now they got very talkative, but Donna and Gene were not sure what all they were saying. Everyone laughed and nodded as if all understood. Gene and Donna were always amazed at how much German they could understand and speak when they had to. This was especially true after a couple of drinks. Donna was very frustrated and figured the best thing was to get them to bed. Finally, she convinced them to go to their rooms and said good night. She told them, "Breakfast will be served at seven o'clock as we have to be in the mayor's office by eight thirty."

They all stood and looked at her. They made no effort to go to bed, finally she figured out they were hungry and she sat some rolls, bread, cheeses, and meats on the table. They ate heartily and asked for another schnapps. Gene just sat the bottle in front of them and let them pour their own. It was now two in the morning. This was going to be fun and expensive. They were over their bashfulness, and they started talking some English, at least two of them. Gene and Donna had no idea what some of them were saying. At last, they were full and half soused, and with a little explanation and encouragement, they all went to bed. It may have helped when Gene started turning out the lights. Donna told them again breakfast would be at seven as they had to be at the mayor's office by eight. This time they understood as she used more sign language than words. They were learning to communicate by pointing to the watch and simulating eating to get their point across. It worked better.

The next morning Donna got up, cooked pancakes, fried some eggs and some crisp bacon. None of these guys had ever been out of Germany and knew nothing about American food habits. They sat down, and Donna put a big pancake on each of their plates with an egg and a couple pieces of crisp bacon. They stared at the food and at each other. None of them ate. They had never seen a pancake or fried bacon. They didn't eat fried eggs, only boiled. Donna recognized the problem and said, "This is how to put butter and syrup on the pancakes." They tried them but only took a bite or two and left them. They had never heard of a pancake for breakfast. They ate potato pancakes but not for breakfast. They didn't know syrup. They all talked and took their spoons and sampled the syrup. They also thought the bacon was burnt too bad to eat since it was crisp. In Germany, they eat a type of bacon called Shenken, which is actually cold thin sliced ham and not overcooked. They were completely confused.

They would not mix their foods. They ate their egg and two or three pieces of toast each. They had a conversation about the toast because it was so thin. They had never seen a toaster, and they all went to the kitchen to watch it pop up. Then they had to do their own toast. They were like little kids with a new toy. One watched the toast pop up and said, "Disneyland." They loved American thin-sliced white bread for toast with butter. They finally ate the bacon, eggs, and toast but not the pancake. For the rest of the time there were there, they all requested bacon and toast. They were now fascinated with the crisp bacon and the thin white bread toast as they ate a whole loaf. Gene deciphered they were talking about the weak coffee when they called it American tea. He made another pot that almost walked to the table by itself. Now they were happy. Gene thought what a waste; he made the strong coffee as they wanted, so what did they do? They diluted it with an equal amount of milk. He had lived in Germany, and he knew about their strong coffee. It was a very interesting morning.

As is customary, they all brought nice gifts for the hosts. Since Donna now had four guests, she got many gifts of beer mugs, a clock, china, table clothes, chocolates, and German cakes. Gene got a necktie from each. Of course, they were all the same and had the print Saxony on them.

Donna took them to the morning meeting and welcome by the mayor and his staff. After the meeting, they had lunch at a Mexican restaurant. They had never seen hot chili. They had never experienced having all these things served on one plate with the chili juice running all over everything. German food is served each in its own bowl or plate. What was this mess they got with everything on one plate? They thought it had been dropped and put back together. They were probably thinking that old adage, "Is it something to eat or something somebody already ate." It took a lot of conversation for this meal also. Fortunately, at the breakfast were Wolfram and a couple of German speaking hosts. They were not impressed. Gene overheard one saying, "Ist das fur der Swine?" He was implying he thought it was pig slop. They never ate Mexican plates the rest of the trip. However, if each item was served individually, they ate it. They loved burritos. To an American, they were strange people. They undoubtedly were thinking the same about Americans.

After lunch, they came home to relax for the afternoon before going to the evening banquet. It was a sunny warm day for October. They all went up to their rooms and put on some skimpy tiny swimming suits and went outside and sunbathed. The pool was still open, and all the deck chairs and lounges were still in the yard. They seldom see the sun on a warm day in Germany as Helmsted is the same latitude as central Canada. These suits were just a cloth strap. They made a bikini wearer look overdressed. Donna took a tray of snacks out to the swimming pool area to them. She was very embarrassed. They had almost nothing on. She didn't know this was the European style. They ran around the house and farm this way. The neighbor called and asked about her cute nude boyfriends and asked if she was running a nudist colony. Donna prayed no one would drive in while they were sunbathing. It was an experience.

Bodo wanted to see the Grand Canyon. A friend at the German Club loaned him their car for the trip and gave him a map. It is straight down I-40 from Albuquerque to the Grand Canyon road turnoff at Flagstaff, Arizona. You couldn't get lost. He didn't return that night or the next day. Finally, he shows up two days later. He had taken a shortcut across the Navajo Nation and been stuck in the snowstorm and lost for a day. He slept in the car in the snow and below freezing weather. He asked for directions, but no one could understand him. He finally got home, and he had lost his tourism desires.

Another guest, the head of the fussball or soccer association, wanted to fly to San Diego to see his long lost cousin. When he got there, he couldn't speak enough English to get a room; the hotel clerk couldn't understand him so they put him in a fabulous suite on the top floor. He had mistakenly asked for a suite instead of a room. It cost him five hundred dollars for the room. He never found his cousin, and the next night he slept at the airport. When he returned, he would only say, "Nix gut" (not good).

Donna thought it would be nice if she did their laundry. As usual, the washer was set for warm water, which bordered on the hot side. She took the washed clothes out of the washer and put them into the dryer. American dryers are very hot, not like German dryers, which remain cold, if you could find one. She took the dry clothes upstairs and put on a bed. The men all thanked her with great enthusiasm.

In the morning, downstairs came the Germans for breakfast. Each was carrying a pair of socks. They showed them to Donna, and she took one and tried to stretch it out. All the socks were now about five inches long. She didn't realize they wore all wool socks, and everyone shrunk to a third of their normal size and couldn't be stretched back out. It was an embarrassing moment, but soon all were laughing and they all threw the socks in the trash. They asked Donna, "Are there any elfs in the neighborhood to give the socks to?" It was a hilarious start to another fun day, and they were off to meet the city dignitaries.

The days passed quickly, and each night the schnapps loosened everyone up to where they were all having quite a conversation. Donna had stressed to them in German, "Langsam, bitte," which meant please speak slowly. Both he and Donna now understood a lot of the German they spoke. One of the group was a German senator from lower Saxony, and he wanted to meet a US congressional representative. Gene called Pete Domenici's headquarters, and sure enough, Pete was in town. He was speaking at a CPA gathering, so Gene arranged for all of them to meet him.

Rolf, the senator, made the gift presentation to Senator Pete Domenici. After the formal presentation, he went back to Pete, took off his necktie, and held it out to him. Pete was not sure what was happening. Donna made a quick assessment of the situation and told Pete, "He wants to trade ties with you." Surprisingly, Pete took off his tie, and they made the trade. Rolf went back to Germany with the tie, and to this day, it is in a special case in his office with a picture of the presentation. They don't know what Pete did with his.

Every second year a group of about twenty people came from Helmstedt to visit Albuquerque for two weeks, and on the alternate years, a group from Albuquerque went to Helmstedt. The group was composed of many businesspersons and city and county officials. These exchanges were great fun and educational. Donna always hosted at least one couple at the house and took them to all the functions and tours. She was also the cochairman for the Helmstedt group and helped arrange the bus trips for a week of sightseeing. Naturally, Harry relied on Donna a great deal for scheduling the Sister City functions. When they needed a place to have a barbeque for the Sister City International group of over two hundred people, it was at the farm. They had cars and city busses parked as far as two blocks away. Donna arranged all the food and drinks and organized the whole program. Donna and the Helmstedt Chairman, Wolfram, worked close together on all the trips to Germany and the return visits to the United States. Wolfram was from Austria and spoke fluent German, and the two made everything work out. Donna directed in English, and Wolfram translated into German.

Wolfram, the chair, and a city employee came to the farm to pick up the guests and introduced himself to Donna. She joined Sister Cities and Wolfram invited her to be the cochair for Helmstedt. They worked well together and continued to represent Helmstedt for years until Donna became ill.

Donna and Wolfram took the Albuquerque group to Germany. Each visit was for two weeks, and homestays were provided. When Albuquerque hosted, it was a continuous schedule of events, open houses, and parties. When the Albuquerque group made a return trip to Germany, the first few days in Helmstedt were formal as presented by the Burgermeister or mayor, and the second week was a bus trip to various places of interest. There was always a trip to Berlin and a trip to the "wall." Helmstedt is on the edge of the wall, and when you went there, you could see the East German soldiers with the machine guns and the guard dogs. It was scary and weird. Each time they rode the bus to Berlin, it was a little scary as you passed through the East German guards at the checkpoint for inspection. Sometimes it took an hour or two to get through the checkpoints, and occasionally, they went through your bags and purses. They made you wait deliberately. Always there were guards with steely eyes staring through you. In addition, there were the German shepherds walking on a leash and watching. It was a relief to return from Berlin and cross the border again. Back in Helmstedt, they felt safe.

When the Helmstedt group came to Albuquerque, Donna arranged homestays for all by calling Sister City members and others. It was a great big party for a week. For the second week, Donna chartered a coach, and they took a trip. They visited the

Grand Canyon, Bryce Park, Monument Valley, Tucson, Carlsbad Caverns, and White Sands. It was a whirlwind trip of about three thousand miles. Donna and Wolfram prepared sack lunches for everyone so they could travel faster.

On one trip to Carlsbad Caverns, they used city vans instead of a big bus. On the trip were the chief of police of Helmstedt, several city officials, and the photographer for the TV station there. Gene drove one of the vans. They had a luncheon scheduled with the Alamogordo Sister City group and the mayor of Alamogordo. They were late, and Gene put the pedal down. While going through the Valley of Fires near Carrizozo, a siren wailed behind them. The patrol officer walked past the last van and Gene, who was driving the first van, went back to meet him. The patrol officer started to explain that they were doing ninety-five in a fifty-five zone. The TV cameraman from Germany set up his tripod and began filming. All the Germans got out of the vans and flashbulbs were flashing everywhere. They were all talking in German excitedly and pointing to his uniform and guns. The chief of police from Germany came up and showed his badge and hat and proceeded to tell the patrol officer in broken English everything was all right. Then the chief of police offered to trade hats with him and wanted to see his gun.

Now the patrol officer was getting nervous, and he wanted to know why this was all being filmed. Gene explained this was for a TV station documentary, and it would be shown in Germany. The highway patrol officer was getting very frustrated, and he was turning red. Gene looked at the camera and decided to spice it up a little. He held his hands straight out to be handcuffed and looked at the camera with a horrified look. The patrol officer just shook his head and said, "Oh no." The flashbulbs were flashing all at once. The Germans were having a ball laughing and talking loud. Now he was really uneasy. He blushed and made some under the breath comments. The cameraman asked the patrol officer to face the camera for better filming and tried to pose him and Gene so he could get a better picture. Again, the German chief of police offered to exchange hats for the picture. He asked him his name. The patrol officer refused. He didn't understand what was happening here. Everyone in the vans was out on the highway having a ball laughing and filming.

Finally, the patrol officer wrote Gene a ticket but for only $25. Forty miles over the speed limit should have been several hundred dollars. He didn't assess the other van anything. Everyone had so much fun; they passed the hat to pay the ticket. The patrol officer took the money and didn't even write a receipt; he climbed in his patrol car and got out of there while he still had his hat and gun. He was probably wishing he had never made this stop.

That night they stayed at a motel in Alamogordo before going on to Carlsbad.

Wolfram was in Gene and Donna's motel room planning out the trip and making lunch bags for the next day. About eleven o'clock, the phone rang. It was the hotel management asking Donna to get her guests out of the closed swimming pool. They had been to the bar for a couple hours and had climbed the fence to get in the pool and some of them were naked. It was mid-October. Donna sent Wolfram so he could tell them in German to make it clear. The Germans reluctantly went to their rooms to get dressed, went back to the Western music bar, and partied until closing time after two in the morning. The next day they slept on the bus. They were enjoying America.

The next afternoon they went to White Sands. Donna had Wolfram explained to them that they could run through the sand barefoot but not naked. They had to keep clothes on. They all went over the dunes and walked off. The hamburgers were ready and lunch was served. Donna told Wolfram, "Do you see what I see? There are two men coming over the hill with only their G-string swimming suits on and their walking sticks." From a distance, everyone thought the men were nude. They had laid their clothes behind a yucca plant. Again, nudity is a perfectly normal thing to do for Europeans, and these skimpy bathing suits were acceptable. They were just enjoying the hot sun that they seldom saw.

The final night was always the big barbeque at the Londene Farm. To the Germans, this was the highlight of the trip, and each incoming group would already know about the party at the farm and looked forward to it. It was their first experience with a real Western barbeque with a western band, dancing, and lots of beer and food. They didn't do outdoor barbeques in Germany, and this was all new. Gene ran the barbeque and the bar. It was great fun. Donna and Gene went to great lengths to create a farm for entertaining. They had several large picnic tables, a huge patio area, plenty of barbeques, swimming pool, pool table, volleyball, horseshoes, and sometimes a horse to ride. The music was piped to the patio and surrounding area. They could handle crowds over one hundred easily.

On party days, Gene and Donna hung flags of the represented countries the thirty-foot length of the porch. They always flew the American, New Mexico, Swedish, and Sister City flags in addition to the German and Saxony flag for Helmstedt. Gene usually hung his Bavarian flag even though he knew it irritated the northern Saxony Germans. That was like hanging a rebel flag in Boston.

The porch looked like the United Nations. They also flew flags when the kids came home. The flags flew as long as the Sister City guests or the kids were staying there.

When Wolfram and the local TV weatherman got married, these weddings were at the Londene Farm. Denise and Randy had their reception at the farm.

When the Londenes went to Helmstedt, they were treated like royalty. To Helmstedt, Donna was America. When she walked down the street in Helmstedt, everyone knew her from the pictures and articles in the paper. They came out of the stores and said, "Our sunshine is back." It seemed every time Donna went to Helmstedt the sun shown until the day she left. The minute she got on a plane to come home, the rain started again. She doubled as the cochair and as the tour director. The years of Sister City involvement were a lot of work but will always be a highlight in Donna's memories.

Donna had a way of making the Germans guests at ease. On the first trip, they had a mixed group of two different political parties. They didn't speak to each other. When they left in two busses for the Grand Canyon, one political party got in one bus and the other in the other. They sat at separate tables in the restaurants. Donna had enough of this baloney. At the next stop, she called a meeting and read the names of the ones on the first bus and the ones on the second bus. She mixed them up.

When Donna started driving, she noticed they weren't talking to each other. She knew Germans loved to sing. She told them, through one of the ladies who could interpret, that her bus was going to go slower and slower until they all started singing and talking to each other. They looked at each other and probably thought Donna was out of her mind. However, by the time they got to Flagstaff, everyone was singing and having a ball. The stop for some schnapps probably helped. Later, one of the group told Donna he had never in his life spoken to the members of the opposite party, but he found out they were really nice people. They had lived in the same block for forty years and had never spoken. They were very formal people. By the time the group left, they all loved Donna, and they were even talking to each other and using first names.

On another trip, Donna's friend Marty accompanied them with her motor home, and they followed the big bus to the Grand Canyon. When they got to the Painted Desert, after touring the Petrified Forest, it was very hot and everyone wanted a break at the information center for some ice cream. A park ranger came up to Donna and said, "Will you get that lady off the top of your motor home? I think she is nude." Donna told him she didn't think so, but she went quickly to the motor home and crawled up the ladder to the roof. She found her houseguest taking a full sunbath. Donna told her to get dressed; they can't do that in a public park. The ranger was very happy to see them leave.

Life in Germany was so different from in the United States. The Germans had many nude beaches, spas, and parks; and nudity was totally acceptable. They didn't understand why Americans were so prudish.

The first two trips to Helmstedt Donna went alone with the group. Gene went the third trip. Their hosts were exceptionally gracious. They ate breakfast at the kitchen table. Beside their plate was a cloth napkin, which by now Gene had learned went in your lap. After breakfast, Gene and Donna laid their napkins on their plates. The hostess quickly informed them they should fold their napkins and lay them beside their plates because each day only one napkin would be issued, and it was to be used for breakfast, lunch, and dinner. Gene and Donna thought this odd but accepted it. It worked for Germans because the napkin was just a formality; they didn't really used it. They never touched their food and everything, including toast, was cut with a knife. For breakfast, she served a plate of halved-hard boiled eggs with two little smoked fish on top since she had found out that Gene was Swedish. In Sweden, their salads are always served with two little anchovies or herring on top. Gene loved it, but Donna almost lost her breakfast. They served Quark, which is some kind of curdled milk dish, which neither Donna nor Gene could eat. Germans eat it every day, and they can have it.

Each city has a shooting hall. This is like a country club with an inside shooting range. They each took a turn to shoot. When it was over, Gene had won the shooting contest, and Donna came in second. She felt her pattern was really better than Gene's, but it was a "male" thing when they made the awards. Gene noted her accuracy, and he vowed when he got home he was hiding the shotgun.

Her house was filled with souvenirs, memoirs, gifts from guests, and pictures from the German visits. Occasionally, Gene and Donna will sit on the patio in the evening and say to each other, “Do you remember the crazy party when?

# Fishing

Gene and Donna loved to fish. While they were living on Guadalupe Trail in Albuquerque in 1959, their neighbors, Harry and Evelyn, invited them to go to the Jemez River fishing for trout. Neither of them had ever seen a trout, except in pictures. They had to buy two $6 licenses, which emptied their bank account. Harry loaned them two spinning rods equipped for trout fishing.

They got to the Jemez River, and Gene found it humorous they called this a river. In Kansas, they called this a spring or a radiator leak. Harry showed them how to put this little tiny trout hook on a line and put two little red salmon eggs on. Again, Gene thought it was a joke.

Now it was time to fish. Harry and Evelyn fished upstream, Donna fished by the car since she was pregnant, and Gene went downstream. Catching your first trout was a great thrill. They hit hard, jump high, and are very dead set against being your next meal. After the first few bites, now called hits, neither had caught a trout. They always found a way to get off the hook. Gene blamed those damn little hooks. Donna hooked her first fish and realized she was up on a bank, and it was a long ways down to the water. She yelled for help to bring a net. The fish was jumping in the air, and it tangled her line on a tree branch. Gene ran back to where she was fishing. There she was with her line over a tree limb and the fish dangling at the edge of the water in the middle of the pool. She wasn't about to wade out in the deep water so she just stood there until help arrived. Gene wanted to take a picture, but the camera was in the car. Finally, he got a long branch and pulled the line off the tree. Donna reeled in her line, but the fish was gone. Maybe there was more to this than they realized.

At the end of the day, all returned to camp. Harry had his six-fish limit, Evelyn had six, Donna had some, and Gene returned with none. Harry was at the car with his fish cleaned, and he promptly chastised Gene for not being a fisherman. Gene countered by saying he had caught a few but turned them all loose because they were only nine or ten inches long. Harry then showed him his fish, which were all eight to ten inches long and explained that they don't get more than ten inches in the Jemez except in rare circumstances. Gene had thrown away all keepers. Nevertheless, Gene and Donna were now avid trout fishermen. Over the years, the kids were dragged to almost every lake and stream in New Mexico on at least every second weekend in the summer. They started out in sleeping bags on the ground with a tarp under the bags and one on top. Harry introduced them to the "Trout Lakes" or Nutrias Lakes north of Cibola, New Mexico, at about 9,300 feet altitude in the high country. It was always cool and damp there, but the fish were plentiful, and it was a great place for camping and kids. They cooked in campfires. Later, they purchased gas lanterns and a stove. The skunks walked across the top of their sleeping bags while they slept and the wind; rain and cold soon convinced them to buy a tent with a floor and door.

They went fishing often with their friends Don and Dana, and Harry and Evelyn usually joined them. They bought an eight-by-twelve-foot tent with a floor and a door that zipped shut. It took over fifteen years to move up from there to a twenty-one foot camping trailer with heat and refrigerator. What luxury! Gene and Donna hauled that little trailer to every mountain lake and stream in northwest New Mexico.

Gene quit his job 1971 and took a one-year management contract to liquidate a printing company for a big Eastern investor. During the last days of the printing company, a customer wanted some printing. Gene met with him and reminded him he owed a large delinquent bill, and he could not give him any more credit. It was a $2,500 job, and he needed it desperately. He asked Gene if he could advance him the money personally. The customer made him a deal telling him he owned this subdivision and trailer campground in Colorado on the Conejos River, and he would give him a deed on a lot as security. In addition, Gene and the family could go to Colorado that weekend and stay in one of the rental cabins free while they picked out the lot they wanted. They hadn't been fishing in three years since they bought the farm, so they were ready for a short trip.

The family loaded up their fishing gear and food and headed to Colorado in their new 1971 Ford Station Wagon. They arrived at the Ponderosa Campground on the Conejos River and were enthralled with the trees and beautiful river. It was at an elevation of 8,500 feet and in a huge canyon. They spent the weekend and caught many fish. They loved the area.

The family selected lot 7, and Gene borrowed the $2,500 from the bank and loaned it on the lot. He received a deed to the lot to hold as security. Two years later, the customer died without repaying the loan, and they now owned the lot. Every year they went to the Conejos River for summer vacation and dreamed of building the cabin.

Donna and the kids stayed at the campground for weeks at a time, and Gene went up on long weekends as his work permitted. In 1985, they bought the thirty-two-foot Avion camping trailer, which they left in Colorado for the summer. This was a substantial improvement, as five almost grown-ups in a twenty-one-foot trailer was a disaster when it rained for days.

The family always thought of the Conejos as their home away from home. For years, they planned to build a cabin. Often they walked the half mile from the campground down to the lot area and sat in the grass on their lot. They took sticks and marked out where the cabin would go and discussed how to landscape the lot. It was only five-eighth of an acre, but it had huge blue spruce and fir trees on it. The lot was a stone's throw from the river. Finally, in 1975, Gene thought he could finance the cabin, and they drew up the plans. He contacted a builder in Las Vegas, New Mexico, who would put up the frame, roof, and close it in for $15,000. Donna had other plans. This is when they had the vote and decided to remodel the house instead. They started the remodel on the house that year. Once again, the cabin had to wait.

It wasn't until 2002 that son-in-law Randy decided he wanted to help put up the cabin on the lot. Gene and Donna met with Denise and Randy on the building, and they decided to use Gene's original plans of a twenty-four by thirty-two foot cabin with a half loft. Randy and Gene went to Colorado in April, laid out the foundation, and contacted the contractor. Two weeks later, Gene and Donna left for Helmsted, Germany, on a three-week Sister City exchange visit. When they returned, the foundation was poured, the walls and roof were up, but the cabin had grown to thirty-two by forty-eight feet and an extra four-foot high. The cabin grew like the Christmas trees. Randy had been busy; he thought he needed more room. The cabin was finally finished in 2007. The cabin is finally a culmination of forty-five years of dreaming and several years of labor. Thanks to Randy and Denise, Gene and Donna were now looking forward to retirement and summers at the cabin.

# Bridge Playing

As a young couple in Manhattan, Kansas, they were on a limited budget. Gene only got $125 a month from the GI bill to go to college. Recreation at a price was nonexistent for them.

Playing cards was the major indoor recreation for them. Donna was already an accomplished bridge player. She played with her family and in college. She introduced Gene to Bridge. On arriving in Manhattan, they quickly located some bridge players through the student union. They met a couple and played five or six hours on Friday nights.

Gene and Donna became very good as partners. They played with a four-table group of pilots from Kirtland Air Force Base in Albuquerque. The group eventually got tired of Donna and Gene winning the four-table round robins and made them switch partners for the rest of the evenings. They played two- or four-table bridge nights with associates from work. They played with Fred and Sally, a retired naval commander and his wife who were almost professionals. Fred and Gene began playing duplicate bridge at the Sandia Base Officers Club. They did very well, winning a few times and acquiring some master points.

Gene tried playing with a duplicate bridge group a few times, but he didn't like the group. These people were bridge freaks, and they yelled and screamed at their partners when something went wrong. Donna wouldn't play duplicate because of the people being to serious as she normally talked and laughed her way through a bridge evening. Both Gene and Donna liked to discuss the hands and play to learn. With these people, this wasn't allowed. She just wouldn't play if she had to shut up.

For years on the farm, Donna substituted with a group of air force wives. After a year or so, Donna figured out they insisted she come to play bridge just so they could hear the latest disasters on the farm. She loved to tell her stories, and they loved to listen and laugh with her.

In the 1990s they found a couple they enjoyed, Bill and Sue, who lived bridge. They got together for occasional bridge evenings. One day, Sue mentioned they had a two-bedroom timeshare in Mazatlan, Mexico. They invited Donna and Gene to go with them for two weeks to relax and play bridge. They played every day and ate their way through Mazatlan.

One night Bill suggested a restaurant that specialized in coconut shrimp. Gene didn't really care for coconut shrimp, but while reading the menu, he came across quail. He hadn't had quail since bird hunting in Kansas in his youth, and it sounded great. The order came, and everyone else got their coconut shrimp. Gene got a plate of short ribs. He called the waiter over and tried to tell him his order was wrong. The waiter spoke almost no English. Gene repeated he wanted his quail; the waiter pointed to Gene's plate and said, "Si, quail." Gene stood up and began flapping his arms like a bird in flight and going, "Cheep, cheep." He said again, "Quail, bird." The waiter got down as if to get on his hands and knees, looked up, and said, "No, no, oink, oink." It was a riot. Gene was flapping his wings and chirping and the waiter was gesturing and oinking. Soon they both were laughing at each other. Now they all realized that quail in Mexican was pork. Everyone in the restaurant was having a ball watching this fiasco. Gene ate his "quail" while everyone kidded him about his floor show. The waiter was a great sport. He felt so bad about the confusion he said in broken English-Spanish he would fix them a dessert for free. He came to the table with a cart, and in front of their eyes made a wonderful banana flambé complete with the fire and burning tequila sauce. It was a wonderful ending to a strange meal, and Gene tipped him generously. Where was their movie camera when they needed it?

They say every second generation reverses. None of Gene and Donna's children or grandchildren would even consider learning bridge and never played. In fact, they seldom play cards, and they aren't competitive when they do. TV, movies, and texting had become their life, and games to develop their minds are a thing of the past, replaced by a hand held computer game that does your thinking for you. Gene and Donna often express their disappointment at what has happened to the home life of modern-day families. They live someone else's life through the media, cell phones, and computers.

# Hobbies

Early in life, both Gene and Donna were infatuated with the arts. Both were involved with music, singing, and musical instruments. Donna had studied art in college. When they married, Donna brought with her all her books, publications, and supplies for painting. She had some very good sketches and drawings, and she had won contests. Gene couldn't draw, but he had always liked painting.

If raised in another time and situation, both would probably have pursued an art or music career. Gene got his first set of watercolors before starting school, a little tin with ten colors, and he would sit upstairs and paint for hours. He had no method to his painting, just having fun. In high school, he excelled in geometry and drafting. These both contribute to an understanding of shapes and design and the effects of distance created by narrowing the lines. In college, he needed a two-hour elective course to complete his requirements. The only thing left was art appreciation; it was not hands on but quickly became his favorite subject.

Shortly after the first week of the art class, Gene was home alone on Friday night while Donna played bridge. He was now enthused, so he got out Donna's water paints and paper canvas from her college days, and he decided to surprise her and paint her a picture. He did a South Seas island with water and swaying palm trees with the sun coming up over the horizon. He obviously did not have an understanding of the effect of colors on each other or on the use of intensity of colors. His bright yellow sky with orange sun coming up over a bright blue ocean through the bright green trees was impressive. He finished the painting in a couple of hours, and he propped it up on a chair where Donna could see it when she walked in the front door. He was so proud. She came home, closed the door, and upon seeing the painting, was apparently speechless with appreciation. Actually, she was trying to keep from laughing and trying to think of something good to say about the painting. All she could muster was, "Are you serious?" She was tired, and she was not impressed. She said, "Is that what you are learning in class?" His painting was a classic example of what not to do.

She studied the painting again over a cup of coffee and tried to think of something good to say about it. Finally, she gave up, and after a good laugh, she went to bed. This rebuke rated right alongside the praying mantis comment when she saw him in just his shorts on their wedding night. Her harsh reception made Gene determined to paint. He got out Donna's art class book from college on how to paint and proceeded to read and absorb everything in it until four in the morning. He particularly studied the section on the effect of mixing to produce soft and complimentary colors for contrast, and the creation of light and shadow. There apparently was a guideline for this stuff. He experimented with the procedures, and to his surprise, the books were correct. By mixing certain colors, you could change the tone and intensity. Now he was ready for painting number two. This he did with Donna watching over his shoulder and guiding him through the painting. Donna knew her colors from school and doing room decorations and what colors complimented each other. He ended up with a reasonable watercolor painting. He did some more and each got better. He had become a painting monster sometimes until two in the morning, and he absorbed everything from Donna's books. Sometimes on Sundays, Donna painted with him while she lectured on blending and staying away from the harsh colors.

They didn't paint again seriously until 1971. Denise was enrolled in Barcelona Grade School. The University of New Mexico had a program where they came to the schools and taught art to parents for a small fee. Donna and Gene both signed up. This was an oil painting class; it was a new program with a lot of interest. Like any thing good, it was discontinued after a semester for no obvious reason. They both produced some reasonable paintings. The skills learned in that class contributed to their painting for years.

Gene didn't paint seriously again until 1999 when he discovered the world of acrylics. He had quit painting in oil because the smell of the turpentine and paints in the house bothered Donna. Now with acrylics, there was essentially no odor. He could paint in the house again, and he set up his painting upstairs. The necessity of spending more hours in the office again slowed the painting. Bob Ross and other painting instruction shows were now showing up on TV; and the more Gene watched, the more he wanted to paint again. He set up shop out in the new building they had built for Donna's pottery and went back to oil and acrylic painting. By 2005, he had his first art show at the art club he had joined and actually sold his first painting. Donna now concentrated on exhibiting her flower arrangements and brought home many ribbons and awards from the fair.

Donna, Darlene, and Denise had started a company to do arts and crafts manufacture and sales. Darlene was very talented in making small crafts, and Donna and Denise handled the assembly and sales. They named the business L Enterprises.

Donna concentrated her art skills on ceramics. She now had a mold pourer, pouring table, molds, and made all her own pottery. She converted the old chicken house into a pottery pouring room and had a man from Laguna Pueblo come daily and pour the pottery. She had two kilns for firing and several Pueblo Indian artists painted and glazed pottery. Through L Enterprises, Donna sold hand-painted and gold-glazed pottery in New Mexico, Florida, New York, Germany, and Arizona. It was a wholesale business and shipped almost $3,000 a month to trading posts and stores for several years.

She had a woman artist from a Pueblo who supervised the painting and did the glazing and painting herself. She was an exceptional artist and knew all the Indian designs. Donna specialized in contemporary design. They made traditional Indian design hand-painted pottery, ornaments, and glazed pottery with gold accents. Donna helped pour the pottery, cleaned and carved in designs, and glazed. In the late 1990s, the Indian Pueblos reportedly decided their artists would paint only for their own retail stores, and she was no longer able to hire artists. One morning, her regular painter came to work and told Donna she could no longer work for her. They both cried, and she got in her car and disappeared from the farm forever. None of the other Pueblo painters ever showed up again at the farm. Donna closed down the ceramic business.

Donna lost her true friend and artist from the Pueblo. She had worked for Donna at the farm for seven years. Donna had been to her home in the Pueblo. After she left, Donna tried to call her at the Pueblo, but she wouldn't return her call. Maybe she never received it.

A year before she quit, she got married. The wedding was at the Pueblo, and the entire Londene family was invited to the wedding. They were the only nontribal people there. It was a tremendous and rare honor for the whole family to be invited. In a real surprise request, Gene and Randy were asked to film the wedding for the couple. Filming a tribal event inside a church was considered taboo, but they were allowed to film since the bride requested it.

It was a Catholic wedding. Donna had made hundreds of ceramic wedding vases, now she would actually see what these vases were used for in Indian wedding culture and tradition. They weren't just a piece of pottery any longer, now Donna understood their actual use and the sacred significance attached to them. They used a wedding vase Donna had poured, and her friend had painted just for this occasion. They had used all their talent to make this one outstanding. Each of the parties drank from their respective side of the vase. The groom drank from the longer side and the bride from the shorter and smaller. The bride and groom ate something during the ceremony from dishes Donna had made and they had painted.

After a few years, Donna had considered this artist as one of the family. When Donna's daughter, Darlene, got so sick and she was almost terminal, Donna told her the bad news. She and Darlene had painted together in past months. She went home and consulted her medicine man at the Pueblo. A week later, she came to Donna with a little jar of something gray-looking like ashes and asked Donna to take her to see her Darlene in the hospital. Donna asked her where she had been and she replied, "I have spent five days in the kiva with the medicine man and had only water. No food was allowed. I must see Darlene." It was late afternoon when they went to Darlene's room in the hospital. Darlene was barely conscious. She closed the drapes and just she and Darlene were there. She put ashes on Darlene's forehead and chest, and all around the bed. She recited something to Darlene while she spread the ashes. She told Donna to talk to the nurse and make sure no one disturbed Darlene until morning. She closed the drapes and left. As they walked to the car, she said, "Don't worry, the medicine man will take care of her. She is in his hands." She returned to the reservation, and Donna went home scared to death about what they had done. Donna was amazed at the sacrifice she had made for Darlene. She couldn't imagine any of her other friends doing this. Pueblo Indians in New Mexico had very special ways.

The next morning, Donna got up at six o'clock and went to the hospital just as the doctor opened the drapes. The doctor and Donna were both shocked and surprised. Darlene was sitting on the bed, had showered by herself, and put on makeup. Her hair was combed and shiny. The doctor examined her and released her later in the day. Later on Donna asked her what was in that jar. She replied only, "Ashes blessed by the medicine man." To Donna, this was unexplainable. Not to her. She lost several pounds in the ordeal and had sacrificed a week of her life for Darlene. Donna tried to reward her, but she wouldn't take anything.

Donna treasures her tape of the wedding. Her grandchildren will be able to view this film and have some understanding of the tribal tradition. She would forever miss her friend, but even though the pueblo was only a few miles away, she never saw her again. Darlene didn't understand all that had happened, but she and Donna were forever grateful, and they had wonderful memories of Indian tradition and the people. Donna remembered her fear during her first trip to an Indian Pueblo, and now the fear had been replaced by a great feeling of respect for talented, humble, and passionate people. Donna became the Brownie scout leader for the girls and Gene was the Webelo leader, but Donna was the one who got involved with Little League Baseball as vice president and equipment manager. Donna was on the board of directors, and she worked very hard with Little League. The first meeting she set the tone for the meeting. She was the only Anglo women, and all the rest were Mexican Spanish men. The others started speaking in Spanish, and she couldn't understand. When it came her turn, she gave her presentation in German, and none of them could understand. They had a quick understanding that from that point on, the meetings would be conducted in English.

The whole family was involved with 4-H and Mime Theatre. The kids all had 4-H projects and raised something, either crops or animals. With baseball, basketball, soccer, wrestling, and band, there was always somewhere to go. All the children performed in plays put on by the Mime Theatre group.

One day Donna had to drive the pickup to get the kids from school. They went to Old Town to buy gifts. As she drove swiftly around the square, a man ran after her yelling, "Stop, stop." Of course she ignored him. She came to a barricade and was told her pickup was now in the movie being shot. Now they wanted to keep that shot in the movie so they had her go to the casting director and sign up her and the pickup. She signed up with all the kids. They would be paid seventeen dollars a day as extras and twenty-five for the pickup. The series was *Nakia* with Robert Forester and they were in several of the sequences.

At thirteen, Darrell performed with a group of stunt performers, and he was applying for extra parts in movies. In order to get the kids to the movie set, Donna had to go. Darrell got to film with George Maharis of Route 66 fame. The whole family was in the show while they robbed a bank in Los Lunas. Gene did two scenes and decided he had enough of that. He couldn't justify giving up a couple hundred dollars a day for a check of less than twenty dollars. They used Donna and her pickup in several episodes. One scene they had her drive down this sunken road in Corrales at night in her mothers' car. They didn't tell her that the pickup was coming seventy miles an hour and was going to jump over her car. She almost had a heart attack. That one had to be a "take." She wasn't about to do that scene again.

One night the whole family was in a sequence when they simulated burning down a two-hundred year-old church in Corrales. They put fire burners in each of the window openings, and where it came out it looked as if the building was on fire. About eleven at night, while shooting about the third take, everyone was standing around waiting for completion of the scene. Suddenly they realized the roof of the church was actually on fire. There was a lot of panic until they got the fire extinguishers and put it out. The fire department arrived and made it official. They actually used this scene in the movie and there was not a retake. When the movie *Flap* was made in 1971 with Anthony Quinn, one of his offices as mayor of the city was Gene's office in the national building. They rented it for the week.

Some years later, the whole Baker family, daughter Denise, husband Randy, and kids Jennifer, Lindsey, and Kristen got parts as extras in several of the TV series episodes of *Wildfire*, which was a several year running series about racehorses filmed in Albuquerque. Donna and Gene filled in on two days filming at the racetrack and were in one weekly show. After two days of being on set from 4:30 in the morning until late afternoon in thirty-degree temperatures, they decided a movie career was not for old people.

In the summer of 2006, the other daughter Darlene's kids, the Capshaw twins, Sam and Kat, were home from England for the summer. Denise was on the State Movie Board and encouraged her three girls and the Capshaw girls to enter the film festival for the three-minute movie skit. The kids filmed their movie on the farm. The entries were judged for the presentations Saturday night at the banquet. They did a movie about a racehorse called Pokerface, the name of Donna's new colt. Gene had to put a horse down the week before, and they used that as a theme, except in their movie they saved the horse. In the afternoon, the girls were called and requested to be at the banquet. The category they entered had twenty-eight entries from professionals around the country. They were the only ones to use a 38 mm home camera competing against professional camera operators.

When they arrived at the banquet, they took their seats, and they weren't sure why they were all invited to the dinner. They ranged in age from nine to sixteen, and everyone else seemed to be adults. When it came time for the award in their category, they were amazed they had received the first place award. They won a new computer and software for making more movies. Many of those at the banquet said the movie was so wonderful it made them cry. The kids decided that maybe they had the talent to grow up to be movie producers.

Everyone in the family is on the reserve list for movie extras and can be called for being in the background as extras quite often. The kids are still looking for their first speaking role and making the big time. It is always a thrill to watch a TV series or movie and see members of the family even if only as a background in the picture. It is very educational and something everyone should do once.

# Antique Business

Donna and Gene grew up during a time when all furniture was made from natural wood. It wasn't until the 1940s, after the Second World War, that light metal and plastic made their appearance in furniture. The furniture builders weren›t allowed to use metal during the war. In the 1950s, the fad was shiny metal-chrome tables and chairs with a vinyl-type top. They went to yard sales, checked out ads in the paper, and went to used furniture and antique stores. If they could find good a piece at a cheap price that needed refinishing and repairs they bought it. They had a 1,500 sq. ft. house to fill.

As they bought things they liked, they started spending weekends stripping, sanding, and varnishing. Soon they had the house furnished with quality furniture.

In 1961, they went home to Kansas and stopped at as many antique stores on the way they could find. In Abilene, they found a goldmine of antique shops. They also noticed that no one was buying oak, golden or American oak. They rented a sixteen-foot U-Haul trailer and filled it with oak tables, chairs, stands, and rocking chairs for less than $100 dollars. They paid $20 for the solid oak tables and $5 to $8 for big rocking chairs. When they returned to Albuquerque, they had a great time cleaning and refinishing their new pieces. They took the new furniture into their house and ran ads to sell the old stuff they had bought and refinished the first year. They sold all the furniture at a nice profit.

In 1968 when they moved to the Viola farm, they now had a bigger house, and they needed more furniture. Gene borrowed $3,000, and off they went to Kansas to rent a big U-Haul truck. They found by selective buying of pieces not so much in demand, they could fill the twenty-six-foot truck for less than the $3,000, so they rented a sixteen-foot trailer, filled that, and towed it behind the truck. Running out of room on the inside created the necessity of tying rocking chairs to the outside of the truck and trailer. They bought out of antique shops, homes, and anywhere there was used furniture. When they pulled the truck into Blue Rapids to Laura Brakes Antique Shop, everyone knew what they were there for. Soon the townspeople would come around and tell Donna they had some antiques in their garage or barn they would sell.

They were a few years ahead of the big antique rush where the California buyers came in to the Midwest and bought up everything. When Donna and Gene started buying oak, no one else wanted it. There was so much of it from the 1920s and 1930s that it wasn't considered a status symbol to own oak. Donna and Gene recognized the need for young couples to buy oak just as they did.

Initially, they drove to Kansas together, rented a truck, and one drove it home. Sometimes they rented a trailer to pull behind the station wagon. When the inventory got low, Gene caught a plane on Friday night to Denver to Salina, Kansas. They prerented a big U-Haul truck to be waiting for him when he arrived in Salina. He usually flew in to Salina about midnight, got his rental truck, and drove to his folk's house in Abilene for a little sleep. Sometimes he took a bus to Abilene and rented the truck there. At daylight, he headed north to Blue Rapids and Oketa where Laura would have a couple of the town drunks help load furniture all day.

By late afternoon, the truck was loaded, and Gene headed for Dodge City where he finished loading the truck at Racky's. If there was too much at Racky's, he rented a sixteen-foot trailer in

Dodge City and loaded it. About six o'clock in the evening, he was fully loaded and headed for Albuquerque. He drove all night, stopping occasionally for an hours nap, and arrived at the farm in Albuquerque sometime Sunday morning.

They had a standing list of dealers and customers in Albuquerque by then who anticipated his arrival and were at the farm when Gene arrived. They sold many pieces right off the truck. The rest were unloaded onto the porch, chicken house, or hay shed.

In 1970, they rented a commercial building on Coors on the west side. Later they moved to west Central. Donna and her dad, Mac, operated the store the Real McCoy for several years. Gene still made the buying trips, but by 1980, he was having trouble finding inventory. The antique craze had caused too many people to get into the market. Rocking chairs they had paid eight or ten dollars for in 1969 were now costing seventy-five to a hundred if you could find them.

Gene and Donna were known as the Rocking Chair Kings of New Mexico as they had pulled into town many times with rocking chairs hanging all over the outside of the truck and trailer. Most of the rocking chairs were purchased by young people just starting out or by the Indians from the reservations.

One day, Gene pulled in with a load of old furniture he had bought out of a barn in Kansas. They unloaded a couple iceboxes and put them on the screened-in porch, adjacent to their bedroom. That night, Donna woke Gene with a scream. There was a huge black ant on her pillow, and it had crawled across her face. Gene turned on the light and found a couple more on the floor and in the bed. Donna came unglued. She screamed, "This is your fault for bringing me to this damn farm. You know I can't stand crawly bugs." She pulled off her nightgown and threw it at him. These things were huge and black, about three-quarters of an inch long. That night they moved upstairs with the kids. The next day, they started through the new furniture on the porch and finally found the ants. They were in one of the iceboxes, and there were hundreds of them. They spent the day spraying, and a few days later, they moved back into the downstairs bedroom. Donna still made Gene get up first every morning to turn on the lights before she would get out of bed.

It was a zoo on the day the truck came in. Their customary sale price was between two to three times what they paid in Kansas. They had to recover over a thousand dollars of truck rental and gas. They learned quickly that if they came across something they had never seen before, they bought it. They knew they could triple the price because no one knew what it should cost. One trip they found a dealer with over a hundred old "potty boxes" out of an old hotel. These were walnut or cherrywood boxes with a lift up lid and a metal potty bucket inside. They were the bathroom of the old hotels. They bought twenty and brought home. They all sold the first day. Some still exist in attorney›s offices as flower or magazine stands. Many people bought them as nightstands for waterbeds. Donna called back to buy the rest, but they were all gone. They didn't even have one left for themselves. They had purchased them for five dollars each and sold them for fifty.

Gene furnished his office with antiques. Over the years, they furnished their house and some of the kid's houses with quality old furniture. The antique business was one of the most fun things they did in their lives, and they would love to be in the business again. Maybe someday after retirement, they will.

# Denise

Denise, the oldest daughter, born November 2, 1959, was small at six pounds three ounces and nineteen inches long. She stayed small like Gene's mother and eventually ended up about five foot two. She also grew up to add credence to the old saying that dynamite comes in small packages. Denise had inherited her mother's eye problems. She began wearing glasses early after Donna caught her in the basement putting together a child's puzzle upside down. She was feeling the pieces like a blind person and feeling where they fit together. Just before she started school, she was operated on to straighten the eyes. It was mostly successful; her cross-eye problem was cured, and her eyesight greatly improved.

While they were preparing her for the eye surgery, Donna asked the doctor to check her hearing as she wasn't hearing well on one side. The doctor examined her ears and proceeded to remove a two-inch sprouted watermelon seed from the ear. Gene liked to squirt seeds at the kids while they were eating watermelon in the yard, and one must have gone in the ear. For years, the doctor had it preserved in a jar in his office.

When Denise was about two and a half, Donna took her to the Piggly Wiggly grocery store to do the weekly shopping. As they went down this aisle, Denise said in a very mature voice, "Mother, you forgot the coffee."

An elderly man pushing his cart behind them asked, "Oh, she is so pretty. Oh, what a beautiful child. Is she a dwarf?" Donna said no. He asked, "How old is she?"

Donna replied, "Two and a half." He said he had never heard a two-year-old talk so professionally. Donna said, "She came out talking and hasn't quit. She has had lots of practice already."

When Denise was in the first grade, the teacher called Donna and wanted a conference. The teacher asked her, "Is Denise always tidy at home?" Donna told her she guessed she was. The teacher said, "When all the kids went out for recess, Denise stayed and straightened out the teacher's desk, rearranged the coat closet by color coordination, and no one could find their coats when they were ready to go home."

At Barcelona grade school, Denise excelled in her classes and was a straight A student. The principal called Donna about Denise's temper. Donna asked what he meant by that, and he said Denise had slugged a little boy at recess that morning. Donna couldn't believe she had hit another child. The principal had asked her why, but she wouldn't tell him. Donna went to the school and said, "Let's call her in, and I am sure she will tell her mother."

Donna asked her, "Why did you hit that boy?"

She reluctantly replied, "He kissed me, and I didn't like it so I hit him." The principal looked at Donna, and she smiled back at him. Case dismissed with a grin on both sides.

Denise came home from the sixth grade with her hair pulled down over her one eye and half her face covered. Donna said, "You didn't go to school that way, did you?" She brushed Denise's hair aside, and to her horror, she saw she had a black eye.

She asked, "What happened? How did you get this?" Denise finally told her mother that two Hispanic/Chicano kids wanted her lunch money, and she refused to give it to them. The boys threw her up against the vending machine and took her lunch money. She told her mother she was having a lot of trouble with the Chicano group. Denise was very small for her age, and they picked on her. She was still wearing children's six X clothes because Donna couldn't find junior miss clothes small enough.

Donna told her she would take care of it. Donna went to see the principal. She told him what had happened and that it won't happen again, and he was to see it wouldn't happen again. The principal asked her if she was threatening him. Donna said, "No, but if it happens again, I will be over here and mop the hallway floor with your fat little body." Donna left confident she had accomplished her mission. Sure enough, Denise had no more problems that year. The principal accompanied her to class, lunch, and to the bus. Apparently, he took a good look at Donna's coveralls and boots, and he had understood what she said. It's amazing how much authority five foot three and one hundred thirty pounds can generate if presented properly.

She left no doubt she was Donna's child with the philosophy of, "Let's solve the problem now and not fret about it." Denise was difficult but grew up to be a very good mother and friend. Over the bad years with Donna and Darlene's illnesses, she was among the first to help.

Denise was a good student, and after completing the eighth grade at Harrison Middle School, she became a student in the first women's class at Albuquerque Academy. She graduated from the academy, enrolled at the University of New Mexico, and got her degree from Arizona State.

After graduation, she worked in her father's CPA firm for a few years. There she met a client, a David Randall Baker. Randy was six foot five inches at two hundred pounds. Denise was five foot two at one hundred eighteen pounds. Randy was an electrician like his father in Gallup, New Mexico, and had just started his own company in Albuquerque called DRB Electric, Inc. Donna hired him to wire her pottery pouring building. While he was putting up a light fixture and Donna was cleaning a piece of green-ware pottery, he turned to her and said, "I am going to marry your daughter." Donna rose quickly from her chair and instantly squeezed the piece of pottery so hard she crushed it. She had no reason to be prepared for this. Thoughts of horrible happenings with this giant of a man and her poor little daughter ran through her head. Surely, he was jesting. Then she had the chilling thought, could he be serious?

They had a long talk; he was serious. Randy got down from his ladder and pulled up a stool in front of Donna. He proceeded to tell her all the bad things in his life and all the good things. He promised he would give up his wild partying and drinking days and be a good husband. Donna was too much in shock to answer. She told Gene that night that Randy had asked to marry Denise, or rather said he was going to, and Gene expressed concern about support. He had been doing Randy's tax return and knew his income or lack of it. They knew Denise, and they were sure this would blow over.

The next night, Randy called the office about five o'clock and asked if Denise was working late, and Donna told him yes. He said to tell her he was bringing her dinner. A little unusual, and Denise thought weird, but maybe that was okay. She had worked on his monthly books and talked to him when he came in her office, but otherwise, she hardly knew this man. He showed up at the office at promptly six o'clock. He set the table in the kitchen with a fancy tablecloth, china, silverware, and napkins. He brought a bottle of wine with wine glasses and lit a candle. He was ready. He summoned Denise and asked her to sit down to dinner. She was totally embarrassed and flustered. She didn›t know what to think of this. He served her dinner, wine, and dessert. When they finished, he got down on his knee and proposed. What kind of nut was that? She said no; she wouldn't marry him because she hardly knew him.

The wedding was at the church, and the reception at the Londene farm. Down the aisle Gene and Denise they came. When it was time to lift her veil, they realized the veil had never been put over her face and was just sitting on the back of her head.

Other than that, the wedding went off without a hitch except for the weather. Everyone headed to the farm for the reception and outdoor dinner and beverages. The food was catered, and the catering company furnished the food tent and the serving personnel. Randy, the family, and friends had all pitched in to make the farm a beautiful reception area. There were tents with tables and chairs. A band, the Rocking Wranglers, played on a stage built into the hayshed.

A bar was prepared under the awning of the Avion camping trailer, and Randy's friends were bartenders and parking lot attendants. It rained and blew the night before and continued to blow with huge low hanging threatening clouds all day. May 23, 1991, was the coldest May 23 in fifty years. By the time the wedding party arrived, the guests were huddling for what warmth the sun could provide. The sun came out just long enough for the cake cutting ceremony and the dancing. The guests were frequenting the bar more than usual trying to get warm. Nevertheless, the wedding party finally arrived and the cake-cutting ceremony took place on schedule.

Just before departing the reception, Denise came crying to her mother, "I don't want to be a baker. I don't want to go home with that man." Randy and the car were ready to leave. He was patiently waiting on the front porch. She was having second thoughts about giving up her name and independence, and she wasn't going to get in the car. Donna went out to get Randy to talk to Denise to convince her she had to go with him. Randy got her up and out on the patio but had to wait on a special event. Denise wanted one last dance with her father on the patio to the music, "Daddy's Hands." It was very special for both of them.

Randy had reserved a suite in an Albuquerque Hotel, and their best man delivered them there. A new life was starting.

Randy bought the two acres behind the farm at the end of Londene Lane, and the newlyweds moved into the mobile home on the property.

Their first day was interesting, but it may have been their last. Since their property is only a few hundred feet away, Donna heard Denise screaming and feared the worst. She knew she shouldn't have let Denise marry that giant. The newlyweds had their first disagreement, and Randy had picked Denise up and set her on top of the garage roof telling her she could come down when she controlled her temper. They were adapting to married life.

Gene had warned Randy about her temper, and he always told the story that when Denise and Randy were married, instead of sending Randy a congratulations card, he had sent him a sympathy card and a thank-you note. Denise and Randy raised three girls gifted in good grades, sports, and music: Jennifer the future artist, Lindsey the sports star, and Kristen future TV chef. They became a typical successful American family. Well, maybe not so typical.

# Darlene (1962)

Darlene, the second daughter, was born November 21, 1962. Darlene was all Swede with blond hair and fair features.

The doctor discovered that during birth Darlene had suffered a broken collarbone. She couldn't lie in bed without crying. It was many sleepless nights for Donna before she took her back to the doctor, and he discovered the problem.

When Darlene was in the fifth grade, the principal called Donna and suggested they enroll Darlene in the mentally handicapped school. Donna was devastated. The teacher called and explained that Darlene was brilliant one day and could recite things from the encyclopedia that she knew she hadn't read, and they next day she couldn't write her name and flunked every test. She had developed the ability to run a fever of one hundred five in fifteen minutes. Strange as it may sound, she could get rid of it in fifteen minutes. She also developed the ability to dilate her own eyes. Donna took her to the hospital where they ran tests and discovered her brain just went to sleep. Other times, it ran in overtime. The doctors agreed to try Ritalin, an experimental drug not yet on the market. Within weeks, Darlene was a straight A student almost to the point of being a genius. Her teachers were amazed.

Darlene grew up to be a teacher and musician. While a freshman at Rio Grande High School, she returned from school one day to find Donna's aunt Grace and uncle Pete from Michigan, and

Donna's mom and dad at the house. They made the mistake of asking her how school was. Darlene replied they had the first day of sex education, and she was part of the demonstration group. She held out her arms to the side with the forearms pointed down and said, "Look, I am a fallopian tube." Everyone took it good naturedly, but Donna was shocked.

Darlene always had a very matter of fact approach to things. She had always been very religious and leads a life reflecting it. She loved church, went to see Billy Graham, and became an avid reader of the Bible and Bible stories. She sang in the church choir and is a Sunday school teacher.

At Rio Grande High School she was in band, orchestra, and concentrated on music. She could sit down at the piano or pick up any instrument and within a few hours be proficient at it. She told Donna, "I need a saxophone. I want to be in the stage band." Donna rented one on Friday; Darlene went out in the travel trailer and practiced all weekend. On Monday, she tried out for stage band and made first chair.

She came home and announced she was going to play the wedding march at a wedding. Donna told her, "You don't play the piano." She responded, "By Saturday, I will," and she did. She also played all the music for the reception. It seemed her musical talent was never ending. She graduated and received a music scholarship to North Texas State in Denton, Texas, where she graduated.

She married, and after graduation moved to Lake Dallas, Texas, where she taught grade school and music. They had a daughter, Lauren, born June 16, 1986, and had to quit teaching. Her marriage turned out to be a total disappointment, and after a couple years, they divorced. She and the baby moved back to Albuquerque into the mobile home that had been empty since Charlie and Eileen died. She had a really tough time, she wasn't well, but she didn't know at the time she was developing an immune system problem.

She taught school at Los Lunas, New Mexico, until she met Phil Capshaw and married again. He worked for American Armed Forces Exchange Services (AAFES), and he was managing the BX at Kirtland Air Force Base in Albuquerque. Soon it was announced there would be an addition to the family.

Darlene had begun having health problems shortly after the birth of the first daughter, and she was undoubtedly not in good enough health to have another child. The doctor had advised her not to have another, but Phil wanted a child. Then they got the good news that it would be twins. Darlene had to quit work as her health wouldn't permit her to work full time. On June 14, 1989, the twin girls, Samantha and Kathleen, were born. Within thirty days, Darlene realized something was wrong. She was sick, always cold, and needed a lot of rest. She developed a yellowing of the hands, feet, and skin similar to yellow jaundice. She developed black spots under her fingernails and her eyes bled. The doctors blamed it on fatigue. Donna was helping take care of the kids. In July, when it was very hot, Darlene walked up to the house with overshoes and gloves. She was freezing.

Darlene went to the specialists on related blood diseases at the hospital. The resident doctor was on the national six-person board for the type of blood disease for which she had been possibly diagnosed. She continued to get worse. She was told she had a rare immune deficiency disease that was not responding to medical treatment. The disease was destroying her platelets and immune system, and it caused the body to shut down. She was dying. The doctors put her on the national interhospital viewing and monitoring system where doctors specializing in this disease as far away as Houston, UCLA, Mayo's, and Rochester would be viewing and monitoring her illness. One weekend she was flown to Houston. One week, they brought in vials of seventeen shots of an experimental drug from UCLA at a cost of $1,500 each, and the UCLA doctor came to administer them. She went in weekly for blood removal and cleansing on a special recycling machine. She got to where she had no spots left to insert the needles for transfusions, and her veins were collapsing. She was a very sick girl and was very thin. She spent her days just curled up on the couch.

Two days before Thanksgiving, the doctors at the hospital called her in and gave her their final diagnosis. The doctor said they had concluded there was absolutely nothing they could do to stop the progression of this disease and that she should prepare for an early Christmas. This was devastating news for Darlene and Donna. Darlene was so beaten down by now that she didn't care anymore. Donna recovered her composure and encouraged her. They met Gene for lunch, but no one could eat. Darlene had a combination of six separate diseases already and had no immune system left to ward off anymore. She had the most advanced and serious stage of lupus, rheumatoid arthritis, scleroderma, and others. The most serious and untreatable was the internal lupus. She was also developing Graves' disease, which affects the eyes. There are twenty-one different kinds of lupus; she had the worst one, which infected the bloodstream and acted like a form of leukemia.

Thanksgiving was not a happy time. Darlene spent most of her time rolled up on the couch in a blanket with gloves on. Donna recovered herself from a night of crying and cooked Thanksgiving dinner as usual. On Monday, the doctors saw Darlene again and put her on some new medicine to give her some relief. They explained that her disease was similar to HIV, and there was a new medicine that might help her, but they couldn't prescribe it since she didn›t have HIV. The doctor gave her the news they were giving her another very powerful medicine, and if the disease didn't kill her, within six months the medicine would. Her immune system had revolted and was eating up all the platelets as fast as she manufactured them. They had given her transfusions of platelets, but in a few days, they were gone. He said, "Darlene,

I am going to give you some pills. They will kill your lungs, but it will make your dying so much easier."

This was some very hard news to take. Darlene and Donna just sat there stunned and looked at each other. Surely, in this day and age, this couldn't be true. Doctors don't just give up. They had tried everything, but this seemed overly blunt. Darlene took her medicine bottles and went home to die. Donna was beside herself but tried to comfort Darlene and took the kids for the night. Darlene flushed her new pills down the toilet.

Gene's CPA practice had a German-owned client that manufactured and sold homeopathic medicines. The company was one of the largest and leading homeopathic companies in the world and had a major interest in promoting homeopathic healing in the United States. Albuquerque was their home office for the States. On Tuesday after Thanksgiving, Gene had a luncheon with the three officers from Germany to arrange that year's contract for doing their audit and tax work.

After completing their business, one of the doctors asked Gene the usual conversation opener question of, "How's the family?" Since he asked, Gene told him the whole sordid affair about Darlene and the death sentence by the doctors at the hospital. All of them were very distraught and said this situation and solution simply couldn't be true. They said their primary reason for coming to the United States at that time was to demonstrate their new Dermatron machine in analysis of immune system disorders, and they were having a demonstration at the El Dorado Hotel in Santa Fe the next day. He suggested they bring Darlene to the hotel, and their doctors would give her an evaluation on the machine. It was a fortunate coincidental timing. It was worth a try. By now, Darlene was so weak she had to be practically carried to the car and into the hotel. They performed the evaluation. The test has a range of results with a rating of one being totally healthy and a rating of twenty-seven on the other end meaning they were ceasing immune functioning and were near death. Darlene's rating was over twenty-six.

That was terrible! Her immune system had ceased to function. The doctors conferred with some of the fifty specialists at the seminar, the conclusion was that Darlene must be on a plane to a clinic in Reno that could treat her the next morning, and there would be someone at the airport waiting to take her to the clinic. There, they could treat her with some things that were not yet legal in New Mexico but very acceptable in Germany and most of the world. They were beginning to find out how antiquated and behind the times the American medical thinking was. The German doctors called the clinic and made all the arrangements for an emergency arrival.

Early the next morning, Donna and Darlene were on the plane. Darlene had to be assisted to the plane, was sick, and slept almost the whole trip. Donna was worried about what she would do if Darlene didn't make it. She was so nervous she was sick. A week before Darlene had hemorrhaged, and Randy had to come down to her house and carry her to the car to get her to emergency as fast as possible. Would it happen again while flying due to the altitude and change in air pressure? It was a scary situation. Donna was nervous at being shouldered with this responsibility. It seemed like an eternity to get to Reno. She held Darlene and stared out the window, not sure what awaited them at this clinic. It seemed like a desperation move, and she worried about what have they done by going to a completely unfamiliar place. She looked at the huge billowing thunderclouds and remembered how peaceful and fun their life had been just a few months ago. The family was so discouraged with doctors and medicines by now they didn't know if this was a waste of time or if it was the right thing to do. Phil had opposed Darlene going to the clinic, and Gene and Donna had said they would pay the bill and she was going. What if they were wrong and Darlene didn't survive? Many of the terminal people with related diseases had gone to

Mexico for treatment. Darlene wouldn't go there, but she was too sick to object to this trip. Did they dare have hope? At least it was some hope.

They arrived at the airport, and a van with a wheelchair was there waiting on them. The crew came on board the plane and quickly had them in route to the clinic. They immediately took her direct to the treatment room and started several IVs. They took all her medicines she was taking and threw them away. What was happening here? How could she survive at all without the medicines? The doctor was from the Philippines, and they practiced medicine very differently. The doctors and nurses in the clinic worked on Darlene all day, and at night took them to the hotel to rest, to be back at nine in the morning. At the hotel, she slept. She was exhausted, and they gave her something to sleep. Donna couldn't sleep. She checked Darlene and went down to the casino in their hotel for coffee and something to eat. She found a slot machine and played a few coins. Then back to the room to check Darlene. She took Darlene some food, but she wouldn't eat. About ten o'clock, when Donna returned to the room, Darlene was rolled up in a ball and shaking uncontrollably. Donna called the doctor who said to go to the store and buy white vinegar and give her a hot bath in vinegar water. Donna couldn't lift her and called room service and told them of the emergency. The employees of the casino/hotel responded immediately. A practical nurse on duty came to the room and helped Donna get her into the bath and a bellboy ran down the street two blocks and returned with the white vinegar. It was a hectic thirty minutes. It worked, and Darlene quit shaking, became coherent, and warmed enough to sleep. Every time Donna went up to her room, her heart was in her throat. Would Darlene still be alive? She lay so still that Donna couldn't tell if she was breathing. She just lay there in a ball, and it took a while to determine that she was still alive. They had given her something to make her sleep, and it was working. Donna wanted to take one herself, but she decided she better stay up and keep monitoring.

The next morning they came to take Darlene back to the clinic; it was back in the chair with all the bags and IVs doing their drip, drip, and drip for the whole day. After the second day, the doctor sat down and talked to them. She explained that what Darlene was getting was bags of super vitamins, an immune system builder, and that beginning that day she would begin chelation. Chelation is a blood cleanser, which has gold filings suspended in liquid and fed into the body with an IV. Chelation was developed years earlier as a treatment for lead poisoning. It would clean the body of unwanted harmful minerals, toxins, and chemicals and open up the clogged blood vessels. Darlene would spend four hours every morning getting chelation and the afternoons getting the other fluids. Her arms and upper hands looked like pincushions from the IVs and now they were trying to use the feet to find a new place to put a needle for injections. That would continue for at least three weeks and maybe longer, but they should see some positive results in a few days. Chelation was illegal in New Mexico, naturally, and in most of the United States. It could only legally be used on patients with HIV/AIDS or lead poisoning. The insurance company would only pay if you had one of these. Darlene's illness was similar to HIV/AIDS but not defined as such, so it is not covered. The family concluded that American doctors and the American Medical Association did not recommend anything that might help a patient and make them well. Of course, since the doctors didn't approve of this procedure, none of it was covered by insurance. It was expensive.

Each night was the same routine. They went to the room and ordered room service, and Darlene tried to eat; then she would take her sleeping pills and sleep, and Donna would stay up most of the night and worry. The doctor had informed Donna confidentially after the first day she didn't think they could save Darlene.

On the fifth morning, Darlene was sleeping soundly. Donna had gone to bed that night as she was also exhausted and they both slept twelve hours. Donna got up early and went downstairs to get some coffee and a roll. By now the casino employees all knew her situation and came by to comfort her and see how it was coming. About six in the morning, she went back upstairs to wake Darlene to start the day's procedure again. Fearing the worst, she quietly opened the door. She was shocked. There sat Darlene on the edge of the bed. She had just taken a shower, was fixing her hair, and had already put on her makeup. Her first comment was "I am hungry, let's go to breakfast." It was a wonderful day. What kind of miracle was happening here? Donna got her camera and took a picture of Darlene. The bleeding in her eyes and under her nails had stopped. The black spots under her nails were gone, and the yellowing had disappeared. It was unbelievable. For the first time in months, Darlene was almost herself, but she tired very easily. She would never be able to be around perfumes and shaving lotions or anything that was toxic, and she would have to change her lifestyle for the rest of her life.

The treatments continued for three weeks. Donna engaged in conversation with many of the staff and people being treated. She and Darlene talked to people that had come in to this clinic in the same or worse shape as Darlene and were now leading a normal healthy life. It was almost a miracle situation. A woman from Nebraska said she had been brought in a few months before on a stretcher and had been bedfast for four years and her feet were turning black. Now, she was walking, and she drove herself to Reno. If all this was so good and true, why weren't her regular doctors doing this treatment or sending her to the clinic? When they returned to Albuquerque, they would find out.

Before they left, Dr. C asked Donna why she was having trouble walking. Donna told her she had a bone spur on the back of her heel that her Albuquerque doctor said the only treatment was an operation to remove. Dr. C came with a bottle of pink liquid and a cotton swab. She told Donna now this is going to sting a little while she applied this liquid to the spur. The liquid foamed pink bubbly stuff and stung like crazy, and Donna was about to tell her where to put that stuff. Soon she stopped and applied a bandage, saying we will take it off tomorrow. The next morning, when the bandages were removed, the spur went with the bandage. It was gone and never returned. Donna never understood, but it never bothered her again.

After three weeks, they returned home. It wasn't a final cure, and in a few weeks, they would be driving Darlene back to the next treatment. She got very sick again. On this trip, Gene drove them up and both he and Donna took chelation along with Darlene. It was recommended to prevent future heart attacks and strokes. They tried it since they were there anyway. Insurance paid none of the $125 per day. The family concluded the insurance companies were apparently under the influence of the doctors who were opposed to chelation because it cured people. It wasn›t considered an acceptable practice for insurance purposes, and they paid nothing of the several thousand dollars of bills. Donna and Gene had driven Darlene this time and as they started home soon Donna exclaimed, "I can read the signs with my bad eye." She had a dormant eye since childhood and now, after the chelation, she could see shapes and forms. Later she discovered she could now also see some color, but she wasn't able to read. What other miracles did they perform here?

There were several trips to Reno over the next year, and Denise helped by accompanying Darlene on one trip, and Darlene was back functioning in a respectable manner. She would probably never be one hundred percent cured; her eyesight wouldn't fully recover, but eventually she got back to a somewhat normal life. Within a year, she was driving, teaching Sunday school, and homeschooling her children. There were occasional backsets where she had to make a quick trip to Reno.

They were informed in Reno there were some medicines in Europe and Africa that would help her, but the AMA refused to allow the sale in the United States. The family concluded it was probably because a US drug company didn't make them. Donna was thinking how unbelievable it was how the drug companies controlled the medical association. They found a way to obtain these medicines and smuggle them into the United States on an as-needed basis. The shipments cost Gene several thousand dollars, but the cost was not important. One of the medicines was called Wobe-Mugos and was commonly used in Africa for HIV. The other was a worldwide-approved medicine everywhere except the United States called Interferon. Ten years later, it was approved for US distribution in a watered-down version.

They had friends and associates who brought home a few of these medicines each time they traveled to Europe. Travelers can always carry some medicine for their own use. Donna contacted the New Mexico Congressional representatives to help them get a special allowance to bring in a few of these medicines each month. They not only refused, but one of them apparently contacted the FDA to check for illegal interferon coming into Albuquerque. The FDA actually called Donna about the investigation. It appeared the senators and representatives were not about to go up against the big drug companies and lose their generous political contributions from them. The family was shocked that the New Mexico congressional representatives and doctors would do absolutely nothing to help them acquire the medicines. Gene and Donna had always contributed to political campaigns. They have never contributed since.

When they returned from Reno after the second treatment, Darlene kept her appointment with her "death" doctor in Albuquerque. He was amazed at her partial recovery, and he was congratulating himself for his miracle. Instead of being overjoyed that she had found something to help her, and hadn't died as predicted, he threw a tantrum and told her if she wasn't going to take the medicines he had prescribed, she didn't need to come back to see him anymore. Darlene was shocked. This was not the reaction she expected from a nationally accredited physician. Darlene had thought how pleased the doctors would be that she had found a treatment for her disease, and she wanted to share it all with them. Instead, he said, "Darlene, what are you doing here? You should have been dead by now." Darlene was flabbergasted and left his office in tears not intending to return.

She continued to see her blood doctor and soon the hospital called her and asked her to come to a large international seminar they were giving in Albuquerque. The local doctors wanted to do a study on her disease and recovery and present her at the seminar as a case study since they considered they had performed some kind of miracle. Darlene refused to go; they had done nothing after predicting her funeral.

Darlene did not speak at their conference, and they still would not approve of the usefulness of the chelation. The doctors did not believe in it and would not acknowledge it. The whole family lost a lot of faith in the American Medical Association and the doctors who control it. The doctors would not consider that homeopathic and holistic medicines have a place in this world and would never prescribe it or condone it. Her insurance wouldn't pay for any of the immune builder prescriptions she got in Reno because they were homeopathic.

The Londene family had never heard much about homeopathic or holistic medicine even though they would unknowingly buy some over the counter or in health stores. They had never heard about chelation, but they were certainly believers now. The family credits Darlene's recovery wholly to the trip to Reno and the treatments there. They are forever thankful for their friends in Germany. The American doctors still do their best to close down these clinics that use alternative medicines, and reportedly, most have had to move to Mexico to escape the wrath of the AMA. A doctor, who was the physician for the astronauts at Sandia

Base in Albuquerque and had reportedly administrated them chelation while in flight training, retired, and opened a clinic in Albuquerque. New Mexico, had finally given approval to the chelation treatment, apparently, only because it happened as an offshoot to the astronaut program. Donna and Gene took the required twenty treatments, and in later life, both still have clear veins, low blood pressure and no heart trouble. They are believers.

Darlene completed her chelation treatments. She had developed some additional problems, and she was having some occasional bad times. She went to a new doctor in Albuquerque for this new problem, and they made a diagnosis. There had been enough study done that they had come with a name for her disease. It was now called Refractory ITP and was classified in the immune deficiency category. They still couldn't treat it, but now it had a name. Big deal! When she got really sick again, they started last resort steroid treatments. These created some additional problems, like swelling of the face and weight gain, but over the next few years, she functioned pretty well. She knew the steroids were a temporary fix and not a solution.

When the twins were eleven years old, Phil was transferred to Germany and the family went with him. They lived in Germany through two tours in Germany and Bosnia, four years in England and eventually back to the States.

The children all inherited the musical talent and love of music from their mother and grandmother. They could all sing and all learned musical instruments.

Lauren, the oldest, excelled in violin, music, and voice. She graduated from a military high school in Ansbach, Germany, in 2004 and from the University of New Mexico in 2010. She married Derek Morganti in 2011 and works for a hotel chain.

The twins, Kathleen and Samantha, graduated from high school in England and enrolled at the University of New Mexico in 2007. All three of the children are very talented in music and voice. The grandparents are delighted to have their grandchildren back in New Mexico after eleven years.

In 2007, Darlene began having some problems with the steroids. Life was just never going to be easy for her. However, with her strong religious faith, she has demonstrated that she is a survivor. She is forever grateful to the homeopathic medicine she received from the German doctors in Reno, and the timely coincidence of bringing all this together which saved her life. Darlene believes her faith in God is what gave her the strength to get through these issues in her life and today she is devoted to working for God.

# The Funeral Party

In his CPA practice, Gene did a lot of estate executor work and estate liquidation.

Gene and Donna both got a pretty good picture of what a mess it was when someone died and didn't leave a clear will or proper instructions for disposition. Armed with this information, they prepared their will and distribution list and encouraged the kids to do the same. Donna was in shock the evening Gene told her he had written her obituary and wanted her to approve it. She asked, "Are you planning to make it prematurely useful?" She glanced toward the old septic tank lid to see if he had dug it up. Gene had commented previously if she died, he was going to save the funeral money and just drop her in the septic tank. She refused to plan for a funeral and didn't ever want to talk about it. However, they both prepared the obituaries and a will for the reason that when a parent dies; the kids are really burdened to come up with the data at a difficult time. Both Gene and Donna were well acquainted with the problems of dying without preparation. It is difficult on the survivors to write the obituary and make the arrangements. Gene completed the death packages, which were filled with their will and trust, and included a prewritten obituary with funeral and burial instructions. They prepared a list of special things each kid was to receive. Everyone should do the same.

When Darlene was very ill in the nineties, there were times that the doctors had told her this was the final go round. They said they couldn't help her anymore and suggested she prepare for her final days. One day, Donna took her to her treatment at the hospital for the dialysis. As they drove up the street to the hospital, they passed the mortuary, which was conveniently located across from the hospital. Darlene asked Donna to drop her off at the hospital and then go back and pick up a burial package for her at the mortuary.

Darlene wanted to get everything in order. The hospital had asked her the day before to prepare a living will with instructions. Donna delivered her to the hospital and then reluctantly went to the mortuary. It took all the strength she could muster just to walk into that place. She pulled into the parking lot and just sat there a while debating maybe she could call on the phone and they would deliver it to her car. Finally, she got out of the car and walked slowly up the sidewalk. It was a long trip, and her feet didn't seem to want to go. She opened the drape-covered door; even the door looked dead. Her hands were sweating. The room looked dark; maybe she could assume the mortuary was closed and quickly leave. She would just tell Darlene no one was home.

As she walked in, they were playing this grim, melancholy sounding music. It was mortuary music; the lights were dim, and the drapes drawn. Donna made sure there were no caskets in the room and sat down on the couch. There were some flowers sitting around that needed water; maybe they were dead too. An elderly gentleman in a pin-striped suit with a somber face resembling Mr. Gloom entered the room and mechanically and stiffly walked toward her. He had a very soft deep velvety voice and said, "May I help you?" A chill went up Donna's back as he spoke. He clasped his hands crossed in front of him and looked like he may have been a customer himself that had been there too long. Maybe he was trying to work off his funeral bill.

By that time, the atmosphere got to her and the tears began to flow. Donna took a deep breath and said, "I need six packages for arranging funerals." He stepped back and gasped, white as a sheet, and asked if there was an accident. Donna blurted out, "No, I am planning a funeral party."

He looked at Donna as if she were crazy. He hesitated, and then said, "A what?"

She repeated, "A funeral party. We are going to have wine, cheese, dips, and the grandchildren will be in the bedroom watching TV, and we're going to have a party with all our kids and plan everyone's funerals."

Donna realized this was beginning to sound like she was planning a mass murder, or she was just plain crazy. That was too much for the old gentleman to take. He knew she was serious, but he wasn't sure what to do about it. He could just imagine another "Jonestown" occurring in Albuquerque. He stood there as if he couldn't come up with an answer, and without speaking, he abruptly turned and went to the back to get the folders.

Donna waited anxiously, expecting the police to walk in the door anytime, or the little wagon with the men in white shirts and the straight jacket. She had that tingling feeling on the back of her neck like her hair was standing straight out. He was gone an awfully long time, and the music seemed to be getting more melancholy. She knew he must be back there calling the police or the nuthouse, and she debated running away. Finally, he came back up front with the folders looking like he had seen a ghost.

He had recovered a little, and he asked her name. She told him she would write it down and bring it back to him. She didn't want to give him her name because she thought he would call the authorities. She dried her tears and got out as quickly as possible with her six packets. She backed out of the parking lot so he couldn't get her license, picked up Darlene, and got out of there. He was still standing in the doorway watching her drive off.

On the way home, Darlene asked why all the packets. Donna told her they were what she picked up at the mortuary, and they were all going to have a funeral party. Donna thought it would be easier for Darlene to do if everyone was involved together. Donna wasn't sure what the party would be like, but the next evening she got everyone at Darlene's house and sent the kids to the bedroom to watch TV. Darlene and Phil, Denise and Randy, and Donna and Gene were there. Darrell was in Germany and couldn't attend but would be contacted later. They all sat in a circle in the living room, and they elected Darlene to be secretary. Actually, she volunteered as she said she would probably be the first to go. She was very matter of fact while the rest of them were quite anxious as to the proceedings. Darlene had amazingly made her peace with God and accepted the inevitable. Everyone had attended the meeting with a little anticipation of what was happening here. This wasn't the normal family get-together.

Both Donna and Darlene have a way of lightening problems by attacking with something humorous or completely off the map. Darlene had made a list of questions for everyone to answer. She went down the question list, and all raised their hand for yea or nay. When she came to the part about being cremated, all raised their hands except Phil. They asked, "Well, Phil, what do you want to do?"

Phil answered, "I don't want to be cremated, and I am going to be buried next to my mother and dad in Oklahoma."

Donna replied, "Oh, that's too bad, Phil. You are going to miss all the fun! We're all going to be cremated, and we will put the ashes in an urn. Then bury them on the cabin lot at the Conejos and have a tree planted on top of us. At night, we can all go out fishing and have a party. You'll be buried all the way over there in Oklahoma where it is hot and miserable, and you won't have anyone to play with and you will miss all the fun." To this day, no one knows if he changed his mind, but he must have been wondering what kind of nutty family he married into.

Three weeks later, Darrell called from Germany. He had no knowledge of the meeting yet. He must have had some telepathy thing with them. "Mom," he said, "if I die, would you come over to Germany and get me?"

Donna told him, "That depends, are you going to be cremated or be in a box?" Darrell said he was going to be cremated. Donna said, "Then I can carry you back, no problem. What do you want me to do with you?"

Darrell said, "Well, I've been thinking, we had the most fun when we were kids at the Conejos River in Colorado. I want my ashes spread on the lot." No one had talked to Darrell since the party. It was very unusual he was on the same wave of our thoughts. Donna was thinking about this telepathy thing again.

When Donna told him what they had planned at the funeral party, he thought the plan was great. Donna heartily recommends every family have a funeral party. What was anticipated to be a lot of stress on everyone turned out to be a cordial get-together. It was only difficult because of Darlene's immediate situation. Every family needs to sit down and have this type of conversation. Fortunately, it wasn't needed as urgently as they thought, but it was good to have it out of the way. Each person completed their will and funeral instructions and agreed to write their obituaries and have them on file.

Donna is afraid of funerals, and she won't go unless forced. She had told Gene about having nightmares of waking up in a dark-cold box freezing and couldn't get out. It really bothered her. Gene told her it wasn't cold he was worried about. He thought the cremation would just be a warm up for the next place.

Eventually their friends began dying, and Donna had to face reality that someday it would happen to her and Gene. Many of their old friends, bridge, and fishing partners had already gone. Donna was thinking about their friend, Don, still sitting in the closet. Donna threatened to come back to the house after she died to make sure Gene didn't remarry and have another woman in her bed. Gene was exploring the possibility the kids had wanted to pursue. Was Ghostbusters real?

Gene and Donna filled out their request to be cremated and buried on the Conejos lot. Will it happen? Probably they will never know. At least they did it and relieved the kids of the decision and frustration.

# Darrell

Gene and Donna wanted a son so they decided against the advice of the doctor and tried one more time to round out their family. Donna however did not take the shots prescribed by her doctor when she carried the girls. This caused her to lose sixteen pounds the last two weeks of the pregnancy and initially Dr. F said he could not find a heartbeat. He advised her to allow the baby to be born naturally even though it might not be alive. Donna went home, and she and Gene talked about what to do. Donna was not sure she could do this, but on the next visit to the doctor there was an encouraging sign. The doctor found a faint heartbeat. He suggested she continue with a normal delivery and on February 4, 1965, a baby was determined to come in to this world, and Darrell was born.

When he was three hours old, he had his first heart attack. Donna was holding him on her shoulder when she heard him gasp, and he went limp. All she could think of was to scream for help, and people came running with what looked like an incubator with oxygen. The medical staff got him to breath and his heart to beat. Gene had just left for his office and the doctor told Donna to call him back because they had a little problem.

When Gene got to the hospital, Dr. F talked to them. He said Darrell should be all right but they would keep him in incubation for a couple days. Donna told the doctor, "I can't bear to go through another pregnancy as all three of my children have been born with birth defects of some kind," and she requested that her tubes be tied. She told Dr. F, "You better do a good job because if I get pregnant again you and I are going up to Sandia Crest and only one of us is coming back."

Dr. F replied, "That is what I like about you. You are so much fun."

Gene and Donna realized they were going to have continued problems when the doctors put Darrell in the heart study group right away to monitor his irregular heart. Darrell had heart fibrillation and palpitation the same as Gene had from age five until he turned forty-five. The doctor said they had the same problem as Elvis Presley. The doctor told them when Darrell was ten years old they would do heart surgery, but until then, he would have to live with it. He was a tiny baby at only six pounds and one ounce and didn't seem to grow much.

Darrell had an inverted rib cage commonly called a chicken breast. His breastbones were pushing on his heart; a condition he inherited from his dad. When Gene was diagnosed, it was called an "athlete's heart," a reference to an oversized organ.

When he was four, Donna took Darrell to a chiropractor who manipulated his chest to help it expand. He suggested Darrell start gym exercises such as weight lifting. Darrell had several sessions of various heart problems with serious beat skipping and irregularity. When he was ten, the heart association recommended they to go to Mayo Clinic to find and correct what was wrong. Two other children in the clinic went to Mayo, and they died on the operating table. Donna and Gene thought they would wait and see. When Darrell was three, he was still wearing eighteen-month-old baby clothes.

At age six, Darrell started school at Barcelona; he was on the gym team. He was so tiny he was always on top of the four-story pyramid, and they called him the spider. He was very active, and he was improving his physical condition. When he was seven, he started baseball in the Pee Wee baseball league. He was doing okay until he was nine and a ball hit him in the chest. He collapsed, fell, and his heart stopped. Two of the umpires were paramedics with the fire department, and they ran to Darrell, carried him into the snack bar, and put him on the table. They called an ambulance when they realized his heart wasn't beating normal. He was pale and listless. They got his heart beating, but it still wasn't normal. They took him to the hospital, and after a few hours, all was fine again. The doctor said the next time his heart could just stop.

This was another huge scare, and that night Donna insisted Darrell quit sports. She was very distraught, and she wasn't listening to what Gene was saying. Gene recalled from his childhood when they insisted he drop sports, and he did miss part of his sophomore year of basketball. He never forgave them. Gene would have preferred to continue playing sports, and if he died, he died. Gene insisted Darrell had to live until he died. He and Donna argued until early morning, and Donna finally agreed he could continue sports as long as he didn't play football. Gene's favorite sport had been playing football for four years of high school so he was disappointed. He had also played basketball and track, so he would settle for them. He had finally learned that compromise was the secret to life. Darrell solved the problem by electing soccer and wrestling and tried out for basketball. Gene didn't tell Donna he had gotten hurt many more times in basketball than he had in football.

Donna and Gene agreed from this point on they would treat all the kids as if they had no medical problems. Whatever would be would be. As it turned out, all the children outgrew their early problems and became adults. Darrell was always shorter than others were in his age group, and he was very skinny. At fourteen years, he was five foot two and weighed just over fifty pounds. When he was a sophomore in high school, he became a health nut. He bought cans of protein drinks and came home from school and ate a head of lettuce. He even ate his vegetables without complaining, except broccoli. He became very conscious of bodybuilding and health practices. He was determined to catch up with the rest of the kids. When he was a senior, he began to grow taller and required a new pair of shoes and jeans every month. When he was a senior in college, he was over six foot and still growing. He graduated at six foot one inch but couldn't get his weight over one hundred forty-five pounds.

He and Gene both credit their conquering of heart problems to a very active sport and working lifestyle. Both were probably overactive. Donna complained that both of them were still only when they were in bed and then their feet and bodies continued to move all night.

The hazards of farm life are many; there were old boards lying around with rusty nails, and there was broken glass everywhere. Many old trees on the farm were in an advanced degree of rotting. A big cottonwood tree, which stood in the middle of the yard next to the well house, was mostly dying. A swing was attached to one of the lower branches.

One evening, Darrell was swinging quite aggressively. Suddenly, all heard a large crack and looked up to see the fifteen-inch tree branch falling down just as Darrell was on the downward motion of the arc. The tree crashed to the ground with a huge thud. They had seen Darrell passing under the branch as it fell, and after the thud, there was total silence. Where was Darrell? Everyone ran to the tree suspecting the worst; that Darrell was crushed under the tree.

Upon reaching the tree, they discovered him lying just to the side of the main trunk. He had actually been pushed away by the branch and had some severe scrapes down his back and arms. He was alive but had temporarily lost consciousness. It was a harrowing experience. A split second slower and the tree branch would have caught him directly and crushed him. They loaded him into the car, and Donna sat in the backseat with him while Gene raced to emergency. Arriving at emergency, the employees knew his name; he'd been there before, and it was like old home week. The attendants patched him up and he recovered, but he lost interest in swinging for a few days.

There were many times when Donna had taken Darrell, Darlene, and Denise to the hospital emergency room for stitches. She was now on a first name basis with the doctors and the vet.

One day Donna was in the living room and heard the usual scream of pain. She found Darrell in the kitchen with a huge cut on his foot and blood everywhere. This was a glass milk bottle Darrell was taking from the refrigerator when it dropped on his foot, shattering the bottle and made some deep cuts. She grabbed a big towel, wrapped his foot, then she loaded him in the car and headed ninety miles an hour down Rio Bravo Boulevard on the way to the hospital.

As she drove on Rio Bravo, she approached the veterinary clinic. She looked in her rearview mirror, and there was Dr. A following her to the clinic. She motioned to him as she turned into the clinic parking lot. He recognized something was wrong. The problem was immediately apparent when he saw Darrell in hysterics and the blood-soaked towel. He said, "There isn't time to get him to the hospital because he has lost too much blood." They took him to the operating table and proceeded to clean the wounds and stop the bleeding. He wrapped the foot to restrict the bleeding and suggested Donna take him to her children's regular doctor.

When they arrived at the doctor's office, he removed the bandages and said, "My goodness, Donna, living on a farm has really helped you to put on a professional bandage." She just smiled. He unwrapped the foot. "I need to put some stitches in." The strong smell of horse liniment was beginning to fill the room. Dr. W smiled and commented, "You even used the correct horse liniment." He raised horses himself.

Donna often ran into Dr. W at Victor's Pharmacy down in the valley, and he would ask her, "Well, have you had any more accidents so you could apply your professional bandages?" Donna just smiled and told him, "Not today."

There would be many occasions to apply bandages over the years. Some required the professionals for setting broken bones and for stitches. Dr. A introduced them to Corona, a medical salve for horses. The whole Londene family was raised with corona for cuts and wouldn't be without it. Almost all of the wounds healed with no remaining scars.

Darrell left Barcelona Grade School after the sixth grade and went directly to Albuquerque Academy where Denise was a senior. He was on the soccer and wrestling teams. He excelled in soccer because of his reckless scoring plunges, often going into the net head first, and occasionally to the medics after. He was tough in his weight class in wrestling.

Before his junior year, he tired of the rigorous work overload at the academy and quit to go to Rio Grande High School. After transferring, Darrell dismissed any doubts about being able to excel by graduating close to the top of the class. While at Rio Grande, Darrell was head of the DECCA program for school administration and was awarded a trip to Nationals in New Orleans.

When Darrell was twelve, he danced with the Scandinavian youth group at the midsummer night festival. The family was a member of the Scandinavian Club. Darrell was good enough that Rudy invited him to dance with the university dancers and the Edelweiss Dancers also Rudy's groups. When he was fourteen, Darrell was active in the youth group of the German Club. He was the junior prince of Fasching in 1980.

At the international festival in Kempton, Germany, Darrell was impressed with the German dancers and the country. He thought it was so clean and beautiful he said to Donna, "I would love to live here." Donna informed him he could never live in Germany unless he learned the language proficiently. He was also infatuated with the pretty dance girls from Hamburg. He was very excited about returning to Germany. His parents thought he was more infatuated with the girls and dismissed it as a whim.

When Darrell was a sophomore in high school, Donna was president of Albuquerque Sister Cities. Darrell became head of the youth group of Sister Cities and he and Donna went to the International Convention in Baltimore. While at the convention, the head of German National Library from Stuttgart, Germany, gave a wonderful speech. Donna and Darrell met with him after the speech to congratulate him and to find out more about his topic, "The Carl Duisburg Society Student Exchange Program." The German and American Congress sponsored the program for exchanging professional development students. One from each US state could go each year to Germany and a student from Germany came to each state under a sponsored program. The government would pay all costs for one year plus $125 per month spending money. The applicants had to be in their third year of college and have a chosen profession. After they got to Germany, they must stay one year. If they came home early, the parents must reimburse the cost. When Darrell entered his junior year of college, he was eligible for the Carl Duisburg Exchange Program.

Once in Germany they go to German language school three months to a German trade school three months with the final six months working for a German company in their chosen profession. Donna found he could take a summer course at the Gote Institute of Language in Houston. He drove his 1957 Chevrolet convertible to Houston and stayed with his uncle Raymond for six weeks. When he returned, he could speak and write German better than Germans. When he enrolled in college that fall, he got credit for German by taking and passing the final exam. He began his junior year of college, and at midsemester he got his approval to go back to Germany as a representative.

Darrell went on the year exchange at midyear. He flew to New York where the group went to the United Nations and did a week of various sponsored sightseeing. Then they flew to Germany, and he reported to his first three-month school on Lake Constance in Southern Germany. Next, he went to Stuttgart for the three-month trade school. Gene was a personal friend of the president of a company in Baden Baden, and Darrell went there for an interview to work the last six months. They agreed to hire him. However, somewhere along the way, he met a girl, and he decided to work in her hometown. He ended up working in a butter factory in Koblenz instead of a desk-training job in Baden Baden. Gene and Donna were very disappointed; they had wanted to return to Baden Baden to meet him there. As it was, they only saw Darrell when he took a train up to Helmstedt when they were there for the Sister City exchange that year.

When his tour was complete, he returned to finish his last year and a half of college. Germany now was just a memory, but he did continue studying German; and in the back of his mind, he was still thinking someday he would go. He graduated from the university and the Anderson School of Business with the intention of becoming a CPA. Gene planned that he could take over his business someday. Just before graduation, Darrell told his parents he wanted to go live in Germany for a while and wanted to know how to arrange that. He knew that Gene and Donna knew many business people in Helmstedt, Baden Baden, and other parts of Germany and Gene had tax clients there.

Gene said he had better idea, and he set up a meeting with John, the resident partner of Peat, Marwick Mitchell, and Co, now known as KPMG after merging with their German counterparts. They had lunch, and Darrell presented his credentials and told John he wanted to go to work for a CPA firm in Germany. John said it was wonderful timing as he had just returned from their world conference in Vienna, Austria, and his roommate was a partner from Frankfurt, Germany. John called him on the phone and told him he had an American graduate who would like to work in the German office. The German partner was delighted and said have him send a résumé. Darrell sent it and waited for a reply. Shortly after, the phone rang. Donna answered and realized the party was speaking German and was asking for Darrell. Darrell got on the phone and conversed in German for a long time. When he hung up the phone, he came running down the stairs and told his mother, "They are sending me an airplane ticket to fly over for an interview. The man told me I speak German better than he does." All the classes and efforts to learn German were paying off. Darrell made the grade, and he had earned it.

Donna was heartsick. She never expected it to happen, but she knew once they met him, they would hire him. He looked very Arian, spoke and wrote fluent German, and as a child was blond with blue eyes. He was tall with a great personality and a lot of confidence. The German office needed someone trained in American generally accepted accounting principles and practices to deal with their companies that operated in both countries. They found one, and Darrell caught a plane to Germany.

Two days after graduation, he packed and left. When he left, he said he wanted to stay in Germany for five years and then return to the United States.

He stayed with KPMG for five years, then quit and worked for Phillip Morris in Munich for five years, and eventually opened his own corporate management consulting practice in Germany. Donna knew in her heart when he left he was never coming back.

He married Birgit from Ulm, Germany. Birgit, who the family calls Biggi, was a kindergarten teacher in Ulm. Biggi has a sparkling personality, lots of fun, and a great addition to the family. When the children were born, she retired to being a housewife and mother.

They had a daughter, Madeleine, in 1994 and a boy, Lewis, in 1997. They live in Augsburg. The children were becoming bilingual and could at least converse with their grandparents on a limited basis on occasion. Gene and Donna would always regret that their grandchildren were like distant relatives, but they would see them every year or two for a very short period. Madeleine pursued a ballet dance career, but Gene and Donna never got to see her dance. Lewis lived for basketball, but they also never saw him play. Donna always said she wanted her children to be happy, and if Darrell was happy there, then that is what she wanted for him. Gene finally gave up on him coming home to take over his CPA practice, and he sold it.

Darrell went on to become a very successful CPA and consultant in Germany and provided well for his family. He had occasional assignments in the United States, which made Donna happy that she got to see him. Cheap telephone service and free e-mail helped solve the distance problem.

They would have some adjustment when coming to America. On the first trip Lewis walked out on the porch with his grandpa and picked up an odd contraption that was sitting on the porch rail. He asked his grandpa what it was, and Gene replied it was to keep elephants away. Lewis said, "There are no elephants around here."

Gene replied, "See, it works."

Lewis gave him a strange look, said "Right," and walked away.

The next day, Gene was painting a chair and got some paint on his arm that had dried. As Lewis walked up, Gene was removing the paint with water and using the nearest thing to him, which was a piece of steel wool.

Lewis said, "You are going to take off the skin."

Gene replied, "That's okay, I have three layers of skin, and I only need one." This time Lewis didn't even respond, he just gave his look of distain and walked off. He was learning. He had years of Londene humor to look forward to.

Donna walked from her bedroom into the living room, and here was Lewis hanging upside down from the doorframe. He had crawled up the hinges and door handle, and he hooked his feet over the door trim. Donna was petrified and called for Darrell. However, by the time he got there, Lewis had grabbed the trim and let himself loose to jump down. Darrell said Lewis would run, jump, and do crazy things and was driving him nuts. Donna replied, "What goes around comes around. This is your payback for the agony and anxiety you caused your father and me."

When Darrell was about eight years old, they were at the Conejos River in the trailer. Darrell and the girls went to the little store to play in the recreation room. When they returned, one of the girls mentioned Darrell had some candy and wouldn't share. Gene asked him how he got the candy since he knew Darrell didn't have any money left. After a good amount of questioning, Darrell admitted he had just taken it off the shelf and hadn't paid for it.

Donna lectured him appropriately. Gene simply reached for a piece of paper, wrote, "I am a thief" on it, and pinned it on Darrell's shirt. He gave Darrell a dime and told him he would take the dime to the office and pay for the candy bar, and he was to wear that sign for the rest of the day. Darrell took the dime and wore his sign. They never talked about it again. It was terribly embarrassing for Darrell, but Gene believes it must have been effective because Darrell grew up to be a fine honest boy and a great success in life.

# Donna's Telepathy

Donna was gifted with clairvoyance. She anticipated things that hadn't happened yet. As a child, she often told her mother something was going to happen, and it did.

There were many instances where Donna would suddenly reach for the phone, pick it up, and start talking. Eileen had just picked up the phone to call Donna. The phone never rang, but they were both on the phone talking. This always drove Gene nuts, and to this day, there was no acceptable explanation. It happened too often to be a coincidence.

Donna went to the coffee pot and poured two cups of coffee saying Eileen is coming for coffee even though they hadn't talked that day. Soon the door opened and in came Eileen. Donna and Dana would pack for a fishing trip without discussing the menu. When they got there, it turned out that Donna had brought bacon and Dana the eggs, and between them, they had everything.

Donna and Eileen had a special relationship. Donna would get out a big roast and put it on to cook. Soon Eileen would call and say she was peeling potatoes but hadn't decided what meat to have for dinner. They obviously did the joint dinner.

Sometimes Donna would say Darrell is going to call today from Germany. Gene asked why, "Had he said he was going to call?"

Donna said, "No, but he will call." Within an hour, the phone would ring, and it was Darrell.

One of their old horse playing partners, Anne the artist, lost her husband and she was living alone in the trailer park in the North Valley. They had been neighbors when Donna and Gene lived there back in 1959. Anne had been very despondent, and unbeknownst to Donna, she had developed some health problems. Anne came to the farm in June to bring a spruce tree for an anniversary gift. It still grows on the northwest corner of the house. Later it was a nice day, and Donna was watering the spruce tree that Anne had brought while Gene was trimming bushes. Suddenly, Donna dropped the water hose and came to the porch. She had just had a terrible vision and feeling that her mother had shot herself and was lying on the couch with a blue nightgown on and a pillow over her head. Donna was obviously shook up by the thought. Gene comforted her and told her to call her mother on the phone. She called, and her mother answered. What a relief; it was only a terrible daydream. Nevertheless, what a strange dream it was in the middle of the day. It seemed so real, and Donna could see the blue clothing and pillow and felt she even heard the shot. Shortly after, the phone rang. The call was the neighbor who lived next to Anne. She had heard the shot, and she went into Anne's house to find her dead on the couch. Donna immediately screamed for Gene; she felt guilty that she had not realized it was going to be Anne, and she hadn't acted to stop it. She was beside herself and said she should have known it was Anne, and she should have been there.

Donna recovered and later called them back. She asked, "Was Anne wearing her blue kimono that her husband had brought back from Japan?"

The friend said, "Yes, she was, and she had a pillow over her head where she had shot herself through the pillow." Donna felt she should have realized the blue nightgown in her dream was really the blue kimono that Anne always wore. Donna had a very special relationship with Anne, and she must have received the message from her somehow. When she first came running around the house and told Gene about the dream, it was 9:30, Anne died at 9:45. Once again, how do you explain this? Gene was as stunned as Donna was. This time he had firsthand experience as it happened while he was there. Anne left a note that Donna was to get some special things she knew Donna wanted, like costume jewelry and her teakettle. Donna always called her Teakettle because her last name was similar. Donna would always feel Anne had called to her for help and she had let her down.

In 1972, the family drove to Raton for the horse races; they had a horse running Sunday. They checked into their usual hotel and wanted to leave the kids with the sitter that day. The woman told her, "The sitter is not here, but I will call a friend up on the hill who will watch them." They drove up to the two-story Victorian-style house. As they pulled in the driveway, Donna grabbed Gene's arm and said, "I have been here before. As you walk in the front door, there is a foyer with an upright organ. To the right is a living room with some antique furniture and down the hall on the left is this weird yellow and blue bathroom." Donna had no recollection of ever being in Raton except when they had come to the races. They walked up to the door and the woman let them in. Sure enough, there was the organ and the living room just as Donna described it. She took the kids to the bathroom, and there was the horrid yellow and blue. They never found out the significance of this as Donna had no memories of the house and did not know the woman. She always felt something should be associated with this place. Mac and Gertie were married in Trinidad, Colorado, fifty miles to the north. Maybe they spent some time in Raton.

One day, Donna was working for Heaston Motor Co. and was sitting at her desk when she suddenly realized she had to call her sister; something was wrong with one of her girls. She asked the owner, Louisa, if she could go home and make a phone call. Louisa told her to use the office phone and call. Donna called and her sister answered. Donna could hear the ambulance in the background. Her sister explained she couldn't talk just then as her daughter was lying in the bathroom with a possible epileptic seizure. How did Donna know?

A similar event happened when Donna was in Germany with the Sister City tour. The group had a day off on Sunday to just spend time with their hosts. Her hosts wanted to take her to see more of the border and the wall, which ran adjacent to the town of Helmstedt. They drove north along the border and stopped at a small village northwest of Berlin to have a coffee break at a little outside café. The village was having a fair or fest with tables outside their shops with antiques and homemade items to sell. Suddenly, Donna stopped and told the host, "There is a street around the corner. I have to go up the hill, and there will be a little old stone church at the top of the hill. Across the street will be a big old dilapidated barn with huge red doors." Her host decided to humor Donna, and they walked up the street. They walked around the corner and there was the street, and at the end of the street was the house and church. Across the street was a barn. Her host asked how she knew it was there, and she said, "I remember my grandmother talking to me in German that when she was a little girl, her "Mutter and Vater" (her parents) used to take her to town sell the milk and butter. They walked up the hill to the big red barn on the left with the huge doors, and they went to the church with the big stone steps across the street." Donna knew some German and understood most of what she said. Donna was obviously affected emotionally by the feeling she was standing where her grandmother had been. She felt it very strongly and had tears. Her hosts were so surprised she had described it exactly. The barn was no longer red and was abandoned, but the old doors definitely showed it had been painted red at one time.

When Donna returned home, she did some research and calls to relatives and found out her grandmother did come from old Prussia and lived in the vicinity northwest of Berlin. She always intended to return and check the church records. She did discover her relatives didn't live in the town but in the country, thus no address. She was never able to pursue it further. She did locate the papers where they came over on the ship, but she couldn't trace their home back any further than just Prussia. She could never find out the name of the town they lived near.

There also was the time Donna directed someone to find a product in a store she had never been in before. She found it equally confusing.

One day Gene was leaving to go to the state fair to the horse races. Donna was still recovering from a surgery and lying in bed. She asked if he had a race program yet and he said no. As he was leaving, she said, "There will be a grey horse in the seventh race, bet me two dollars across. He is going to win." Gene went to the track and almost forgot about her bet until he was buying his tickets in the seventh race. Sure enough, there was a grey horse. It hadn't won a race in several years and had odds of seventy to one. Gene knew from prior experience when Donna sent money on a long shot, he had better play it because he would have to pay out of his pocket if he didn't.

This sending of what he called "blind bets" was not an isolated occurrence; it had happened before. He never understood how she came up with these, but he had learned to respect her picks. He turned back to the window and got out her six dollars and bought the win, place, and show for Donna just before the window closed and the race was on. By the time he got outside the grandstand to see the race, they were coming down the stretch. Here was this grey nothing of a horse out in front by several lengths. Now Gene realized it was going to win, and he had no bet on it; he was sick. Donna's six-dollar bet returned her almost two hundred. Now Gene was really sick he hadn't bet the horse, but he was certainly glad he had made her bet. It always seemed to work out that way; he never benefitted from her tips.

On another occasion, they were going to Sunland Park to the races. She told Bud and Joe, "I have to go down to play a horse named Maude." Joe looked in his race form, and sure enough, there was a horse named Maud's Flash. Joe commented he had known a girl once named Maud, but she certainly wasn't a flash. Maud's Flash returned sixty some dollars for the win, and Donna had the only tickets in the group.

On another occasion, Gene was eating breakfast, and Donna commented he should sell all his stocks because they were going to drop. Gene responded but didn't take it serious. This was the morning of what they call "Black Monday" in the stock market. It dropped and Gene lost 40 percent of his values. He should have listened, and she has never let him forget it.

There were many of these "happenings" involving Donna knowing the answer before the event. Gene always thought there must be a way of financially benefiting from them, but it never happened.

While Gene had his office on San Mateo, one day he received a call from an attorney. Donna took the call and transferred it to Gene. The attorney said he was sending over a client with a tax problem and wanted Gene to help him get squared away with the IRS. He told Gene to pay special attention to what this man had to say as he was a person of importance who had already appeared on the Merv Griffin and Johnny Carson shows and was a guest professor of astrology at UCLA and a University in Alabama. His nickname was Cash, and he had a business called Dream Counselors. Supposedly, he could read the energy field aura around people and could tell them everything about themselves and their health and had done so on the late shows. Gene said, "Sure," and prepared to meet this nut.

Cash arrived and came upstairs to Gene's office. He was wearing an open shirt with the top two buttons undone. A large three-sided light-blue stone on a gold chain hung around his neck. He had semilong wavy blond hair and wore very expensive clothes. His diamond rings demanded your attention. He was impressive, and when he spoke, he had the eloquence of a minister. He had eyes that were light blue, but later Donna thought they appeared to be transparent. The first thing he said was "I don't have much time. I am flying to LA to teach a class tonight, and I need to get your attention fast. You have a scar from here to here you got in 1951." The area where he indicated was exactly where Gene's scar was from a stomach operation in 1951. He definitely had Gene's attention. There was no way he or the attorney could have known that. Gene just stared at him, not sure of what he was dealing with. However, Cash definitely had his full attention; now Gene was an intent listener.

Cash explained, "I operate a company called Dream Counselors, and I can read this energy field that encircled everyone and tell certain things about them. I have actually done so on the TV appearances, and Gene could call Johnny Carson and verify this."

Gene was thinking, *Sure, like Johnny Carson was going to accept my call.* As if Cash knew what Gene was thinking, he volunteered to call John and put him on the phone. Gene declined as he was becoming a believer. Cash had his own airplane for going between the universities, and he owned a huge Bluebird brand bus, converted into a traveling motel and office. Apparently, he was doing very well. Later he drove to the office in a new Cadillac. He explained he belonged to a group in Albuquerque that somehow aided his powers. He said, "I was a pilot with the Flying Tigers in World War II in the Pacific, and I acquired this power shortly after while still in the islands." He mentioned crashing his plane in Tibet. All this sounded strange, but he was very believable. Gene later verified he was a "Flying Tiger" pilot from papers in Cash's personal files. There were pictures of him standing beside the plane, and there were articles.

He said, "That is enough of who I am. This is why I am here." He showed Gene an assessment from the IRS for one hundred forty thousand dollars. He went on to explain he had been to

Iowa at this man›s house, and his host was filling out government oil lottery tickets. This was during the long gone years where the government sold ten-dollar lottery tickets on oil leases. The lucky winners actually got an oil lease on government ground, which they could sell to the oil companies. The host entered Cash's name on six of the tickets with him. They would share what they won. Miraculously, they won three leases. They sold the leases for over a half million dollars and Cash got his half. He reported his gain as a capital gain and paid less taxes. Now the IRS said it was ordinary income, and he owed more money. The IRS was correct. Cash pulled out a stack of one hundred dollar bills and pushed ten of them toward Gene. He asked, "Is that enough to get you started?" Gene assured him it was; it was a lot of money in the seventies. Now he knew why they called him Cash. Gene decided that maybe this person wasn't such a nut after all. He may still be a nut, but he was a rich nut and could obviously pay his bill for Gene's work.

Cash had a belief that pyramid power was the thing of the day. The weird stone around his neck was shaped like a pyramid, and it was pale transparent blue like his eyes. He made Gene nervous while talking with him and looking into those eyes. After the tax issues got resolved, and Cash wrote a big check, he came by Gene's office while flying to California. He wanted to set up a company that sold these little six-inch-tall pyramids on three legs to people with the theory that if you placed a list of what you wanted under the pyramid, your wish would be granted. Gene helped him set up a manufacturer in Albuquerque, and they produced hundreds of them. Donna set up the sales organization for shipping the orders, and surprisingly, there were many orders. Their office mailed pyramids all over the world and deposited the money in the bank for Cash.

One day, Cash was flying through from Alabama to California, and he called Gene from the Albuquerque airport. He said he was coming to the office to see what was happening on the making of the pyramids and sales orders. Gene had just returned from the academy where he had to pick up his oldest daughter, Denise, because she had hurt her knee falling down the steps. Gene planned to take her to the doctor. Cash walked in and went straight to Denise, touched her knee with his left hand, and put his right hand above her head. Then he said, "Don't worry, little girl, your knee is only sprained, and it will be fine tomorrow," and he proceeded upstairs. It turned out he was exactly right.

A month later, Donna had her gallbladder removal operation. She was very sick and was not able to get up and walk without pain. She had been home a week and was still very sore. Gene was in his office when Cash called. Cash said, "I am at the airport in Albuquerque flying a commercial flight with a two-hour layover, and I need to see Donna." Cash hadn't been in Albuquerque in a month, and he had no way of knowing Donna had surgery and it wasn't going well, and he didn't ask any questions. He asked Gene to pick him up at the airport and take him to see Donna. Gene thought that was very strange, but he took him to the farm. Cash walked up behind Donna and put one hand on each shoulder. He said, "They removed something from the left lobe of your liver."

She said, "No, they didn't. They took out my gallbladder." He said, "Yes they did, and they also left something undone, and they need to do some corrective surgery. You need to call your doctor." Gene took him back to the airport, and Donna called her doctor. Sure enough, they had removed a tumorous growth from her liver and that is why she was still in so much pain. Later they had to do a corrective procedure on the previous hernia, which they had forgotten was not done. How did he know? It was strange indeed. There was no explanation. Gene told Cash on the way to the airport he didn't understand how he did that. Cash said, "You never will." Now Gene was beginning to believe that maybe Donna did have some special power. Cash certainly did. Gene and Donna were anxious to learn more about this man, but he always said, "Later, when I have more time."

Six months later, Cash showed up in Gene's office. The bubbling feeling of confidence and superiority Cash always exhibited was gone. His always well-groomed hair was a mess. His fascinating eyes seemed dull and listless like maybe he had been sick. Cash began to explain that since he had used his powers improperly to his own benefit in winning the lottery, his powers had gradually gone away, and he could no longer perform his functions. He lost his power to read images. The power just disappeared. He had lost most of the money in bad investments. He said that he could no longer fly his plane and had to sell it. While flying, his eye had burst, and he lost the eyesight in one eye, and he couldn't renew his pilot license. He had lost his contract with the universities, and his health was going. He had to sell his Bluebird bus. He said everything he lived for was leaving. Two weeks later, Cash was boarding a plane in Dallas. As he walked up the stairs into the plane, he had a heart attack and died.

Gene and Donna discussed what a strange association this had been. It is something you usually don't tell people because they wouldn't believe you. Nevertheless, this man really existed, and Gene kept all the brochures and news articles, and he still has them. He also still has a supply of the pyramids. He had met some of the people in Cash's group. They were equally as strange. After Cash died, they all disappeared.

Gene still has a brochure Cash used in his dream counseling business entitled, "Dreams Are You." In the brochure it states, "He was a U.S. Marine, a former test pilot, and a member of the Diplomatic Corps, spending four years in the Far East. It was here, under the supervision of a Tibetan Lama, that he learned to understand the spiritual nature of man and develop his intuitive gifts. In the pursuit of academic knowledge, he attended several universities in the United States. Mr. Bateman resides in Albuquerque, New Mexico, where he is president of Dream Counsellors, Inc. Mr. Bateman is also active in the American Medical Psychic Research Association. Mr. Bateman also helps many individuals in private psychoanalysis, utilizing his clairvoyant gifts and great spiritual perception." Maybe his time in Tibet explained his strange powers. He certainly was a step beyond the ordinary man.

Two years after Cash died, the Albuquerque police called the office. Donna took the call, buzzed Gene on the intercom, and told him he had better take this call. Cash's Cadillac had been registered in Gene's name since he handled a lot of his business. The police reported they found Cash's Cadillac in the Albuquerque airport parking lot. The ticket where it was checked in was several weeks old, and the keys were still in the car. The current registration was in the car with Gene's name on it. How the car got there was never discovered. When Gene tried to trace the call to the police department to verify it was Cash's Cadillac, the main office had no record of the call to the office or the disposition of the car. Who made the call if it wasn't the police? Gene called the Motor Vehicle Department; they showed no record of the registration being paid for two years. How was there a current license? Cash had driven the car to Dallas before he boarded the plane. They never found it. However, knowing Cash, anything was possible. Donna was in the office when the call came in, and she and Gene just sat and looked at each other. They had no explanation as to who made the call or how the car got to Albuquerque. They had been fascinated with this amazing man for two years, now they wondered if he really existed or maybe still existed. Gene had prepared his tax returns, and he definitely had 1099 forms for services from both universities. He most definitely did exist. Gene also had clients Cash had referred him that had meetings and supposedly moved things on a table by concentrating. They were a strange group. Gene asked to go to a meeting, but he never got invited. He was told he was not a "believer." They were right, but both Gene and Donna were fascinated by the whole turn of events. They didn't understand what was behind all this.

Donna continued to have her funny little premonitions, and Gene never figured out a way to profit from them. Maybe he should have believed earlier. He had already tried sitting the pyramid on top of his race form and selections, but it didn't work. He guessed he wasn't sincere enough.

Subsequent to these occurrences, both Gene and Donna paid a little more attention when they watched movies and TV shows on ESP. Cash had made references to things he saw in the sky over the Pacific with the same colors as his stone and implied that was where his stone came from. He referred to his time in Tibet. Again, he said he would tell them about it when he had time. Had Cash contacted UFOs in the Pacific? They will never know, but as Cash said during the first meeting, "I need to get your attention." He certainly did.

Beginning after Donna had her cancer, she would wake in the middle of the night and a form would be standing in the bathroom doorway. Later it appeared in the doorway to the living room. Anytime Donna sat up or started to get out of bed, it disappeared. It appeared to float. It seemed to come as a pulsing light. She described it as tall and dark with an illumination of the head and shoulders. It seemed to appear more often. At first, Gene asked her to quit waking him up as nothing was there, and he never saw anything. He blamed it on the medicines she was taking. Five years later, it reappeared, and Donna kept it to herself. She finally told Gene again in 2007. When she got up, it was always gone.

Gene decided it was Cash coming back for his pyramids and the money in his bank account Gene was still holding when he died. Originally, she told the grandkids, and they were getting afraid to sleep upstairs. They wanted to call ghost busters, so she quit talking about it. Now Gene realized she was really disturbed about these sightings. Maybe it was the ghost, Siri, Gene's mother, saw and it was relocating since the house in Enterprise had burned down, and it wanted to stay in the family.

Gene and Donna wondered how many others had these same weird experiences, and just didn't talk about them because people would question their sanity. Sometimes they even questioned their own. At times, everyone has gone somewhere and felt they had been there before, or they have dreams of somewhere and wake with the feeling they have been there. We only have a few senses, maybe there are other forms we don't know about that have many more. Someday we may discover our few senses only enabled us to understand the tip of the iceberg. Donna often said she feared death as an unknown, and she sometimes feared life for the things that happened in her life she felt shouldn›t have been happening to her. She often stated she was run over by the horse at age sixty, got cancer at age seventy, and wondered what was going to happen to her at age eighty. She feared dying and predicted a loss of her sanity or worse. She scheduled knee replacement surgery in January 2013 and was seriously considering cancelling it, but she decided to do it because she wanted to be able to walk without pain again.

Some people are just closer to the world beyond during their lifetime, and the rest of us lead a dull life as realists.

# Donna's Surgeries

The New Mexico State Fair of year 2002 had just ended, and Donna had finished working seventeen straight days in the Corner Store run by the South Valley Exchange Club. It was all volunteer work with the money donated to "Peanut Butter and Jelly." She delighted at spending time in the booth and meeting people. She knew most of the State Fair employees, and they all came by to talk to her and listen to her stories. Everyone seemed to laugh and enjoy themselves while talking to her. You had to wonder if she was ever serious.

That year she had been exceptionally tired when she came home in the evenings, and she thought that maybe she was just getting old. She had turned seventy and was still very young for her age. Her arm hurt from her elbow to her shoulder, but she thought it was just from the old horse injury. She had stayed home on the night shifts and let Gene and other volunteers run the store. The last few days of the fair, she sent Gene to do the buying and help run the store. Gene thought she was just tired.

The last night came, they closed up the store, and she went to bed to rest. A day or two later, in the middle of the night, she rolled over on her right side. She reached with her right hand to rub her left arm. She was startled that her right hand felt something about the size of an egg in a lump under her arm. She hadn't noticed it before when she was standing up, only when she lay in this position. She woke Gene in the middle of the night and said, "Feel this. I think I have a lump."

Gene felt it and said immediately, "We're going to the doctor in the morning." Donna commented she had just had a mammogram and blood test with her physical recently, and there was nothing wrong. This one was sort of soft, and you could push it around with your hand. When she stood up, it was gone.

Donna called Dr. M, the family doctor, and they went to the clinic the next morning. Doc had her lie down on the table as he examined the left side under the arm. Doc said he didn't feel anything. Doc had gone to school with their daughter, and they had a very casual relationship. Donna told him, "Michael, come to the right side of the table, and I am going to teach you something." Donna rolled over on her right side, dropped her left arm behind her, and told Doc to see what happens.

The grin faded, and he said, "Oh my." He could see the lump now, he felt it, and moved it around. It was like a soft egg or a sponge. He said, "We need to call Dr. Doris, the surgeon, today."

When he returned to the room, Donna lectured him on the ineptitude of modern day doctors relying on mammograms and that she had to show him how to identify a lump. They tell women and give women all these instructions on how to find lumps, but they never have described the method used by Donna to find hers accidentally. They have you check your breasts but never the lymph nodes. Donna had mammograms every year, and they always said there was a small spot on one breast but don't worry about it because it was probably just dormant fatty tissue. Sure.

Doc grinned and said, "I learned something today. I have already called Dr. Doris, and she is expecting you when you leave here now." Donna told him she would send him a bill for the education.

Things moved rapidly. She saw Dr. Michael and Dr. Doris on Thursday. That day she had a biopsy. They told Donna the tests wouldn't be back for a week, but they called her the next day on

Friday and told her to be at the hospital at three o'clock that day. Donna saw the specialist. He told her the biopsy showed she had a cancer of the worst kind and mentioned HRZ 3 and some other language she didn't fully understand. He called Dr. Doris and told her to schedule surgery. Things were happening fast. They went to Dr. Doris office where she explained the seriousness of the situation and that she recommended surgery immediately.

Donna told Dr. Doris she and the family had scheduled a weekend in Las Vegas, and she was going to go. The doctor agreed a few days probably didn't matter. Donna helped celebrate Gene and Randy's birthdays in Vegas, but she and Gene knew before they left that it was cancer. She sat up most of the night just hitting the buttons on the slot machine. She decided to tell the kids after they got home.

Upon returning on Monday, Dr. Doris had a new mammogram and biopsy scheduled. They got the results on Friday and surgery was scheduled for Monday morning. She spent all Friday at the hospital with MRIs, cat scans, pre-op, and tests. Doc told her that the spot at one o'clock in the left breast had spread, and the x-ray showed it had little tentacles like an octopus running down the blood vessels. The minute he touched it with the biopsy needle, it began to spread.

It had already spread to at least the first four lymph nodes and had probably gone farther. They would have to remove the left breast and all the lymph nodes and muscles extending to the middle of the back on the left side complete down to scraping the bone. Even if they did this, they weren›t sure it hadn't already gone into the veins and maybe they couldn't stop it. Both Donna and Gene sat there stunned and speechless. They had suspected a removal of the lump in the breast and maybe one lymph node but not everything. Donna was not sure what Gene felt, but he put his arms around her and they sat in silence for a while. The doctor walked out to the desk and called Dr. Doris, the surgeon, to schedule her for surgery Monday morning. It is a situation feared by everyone, and there are no words to make it better.

Dr. Doris said, "Come to my office, I want to talk to both of you." She gave Donna a brochure and said she recommended a total radical mastectomy, which is a complete removal of the breast and all lymph nodes. It is major surgery and sounded pretty awful to Donna.

Donna said just do it and do whatever it takes to get rid of the damn thing. She didn't realize how completely they were going to remove everything and scrape her to the bone and how terribly sore and sick she was going to be. It was going to leave a huge scarred area and require extensive healing and therapy.

Dr. Doris told her if the reports came back HRZ 3, it was usually fatal. Donna's had come back with a grading of HRZ 2.8. Dr. Doris said she hoped they could get it all if it hadn't gone into the veins already.

Donna called all the kids and told them of the surgery, but she wouldn't mention the severity of the situation, just that she had a lump and they were going to remove it.

On Monday, Dr. Doris performed the surgery for over four hours. It was much worse than she suspected, and they had to take all seventeen of the lymph nodes on the left side. They removed the tissue clear into the center of the back where the muscles started. Donna was going to be a very sore and sick lady.

The surgery seemed to last forever. Gene had gone home to feed the horses as Donna wasn't making too much sense anyway. She was really doped up. Dr. Doris had a great personality and was amazed at Donna's constant sense of humor. She couldn't imagine Donna laughing on the operating table, but she did. Dr. Doris's nurse, Kathy, a Laguna Indian, was very helpful and made things easier. Kathy thought Donna was a nut as she always kept them laughing when she came in for appointments.

Donna spent four days in the hospital until they felt Gene was capable of taking care of her and changing bandages. She got to go home, and a few days later, she realized her problems had just started. The first few days she didn't know where she was.

When they got home, Donna was confined to bed except to make the short trip to the bathroom. She needed help getting up since for a week or so they prescribed those little yellow pills that kept her in "la-la land." She was really out of it. At the hospital, they gave Gene a lesson on how to clean the wound daily and change bandages. Everything was done with plastic gloves and antiseptic while he wore a mask. At the hospital he said sure, he could do it. He knew he had to do it.

At home when he removed the bandage to remove the packing, he almost got sick. He had no idea how huge and totally raw and ugly this hole was. He had never seen bare raw flesh in this magnitude before. He had a sickening pang of pity and sympathy for what Donna was having to go through. He really wanted to call Jack to help on this one, but he knew he couldn't. Necessity drives accomplishments. He wore rubber gloves and kept everything in a sealed sanitary box just as instructed. He may not have done it perfectly, but he did it. The first time was very difficult. When he started pulling the packing out of the hole, he thought it would never quit. You can do almost anything when you really have to. Denise and the kids were the only allowed visitors, and they had to wear masks. The first day, and every day for a while, a nurse came to see if Gene was doing it right and to check vital signs.

About the sixth day, Donna became very lethargic and lost the ability to talk. The next morning, Gene went to wake her after she had slept fourteen hours, and she wouldn't wake up. He called the Dr. and they said to bring her down to emergency immediately. Sure, he couldn't lift her. He looked for the list with the ambulance number. About that time, Randy, and a client from Tucson came by the house. He helped Gene get her into the wheelchair and into the car. He took her to the hospital and readmitted her. They put her on oxygen, and she responded immediately. They sent her home with a temporary oxygen bottle and delivered a larger one to the farm that day. Gene was amazed that he was getting an advanced nursing education in a very short time. The doctors had refused to confirm they thought they got it all, but Gene told a little white lie and assured Donna they did.

The seventh day, the medications were reduced, and as Donna came off the heavy medication, she actually saw the nurse when she wore her glasses for the first time. The first thing she saw was the pin on the nurse's shirt that read, "Hospice." Donna's father had died of cancer a few years before, and Donna knew that hospice only came when you were critical and terminal. She panicked and tried to sit up, and she asked the nurse, "Am I dying?" It was a scary moment before the nurse got her calmed down and explained that she doubled as a hospice nurse, had just come from another patient that required hospice, and she hadn't removed the pin. She took off the pin and assured Donna that her critical period was over, and now she just had to recover. It took a few days before Donna really believed her.

The open wound took over six weeks to heal due to complications. Gene's sister, Joyce, drove down from Denver and assisted with the house chores for a couple weeks. She was a huge help, especially cooking. In about ten days, Donna called the doctor and said something was wrong as the swelling wasn't going down. The area surrounding the open wound was growing. The whole abdomen area seemed to be swelling. Immediately, Gene and Donna thought the cancer was still present and growing. They made an emergency call and went to Dr. Doris's office where she examined her. Donna was sitting on the bed as the doctor poked around the swollen area to see what was going on. Suddenly, the wound broke open and a watery fluid went everywhere. The wound retained water, and when it broke, it covered the nurse and the floor. Donna screamed and thought she had blown up. Another scary moment, but the doctor said this is a normal occurrence, just usually not that much water and coming out with such force.

In two more weeks, she was up and coming to the kitchen to supervise the cooking. Gene had valiantly prepared food and meals by using the recipe book and asking her questions. In her condition, the first few days generated some strange answers. Gene had never cooked except in the early 1960's when Donna was sick.

During this period, he became proficient at several dishes and there were meals fit to eat. He had to figure out little things, like what is a dash and how big is a pinch. By the time Donna began cooking again, he had assembled a recipe book in a language a man can understand, and when the occasion arrives, he can cook a decent meal although limited to what is in his book. When he asked Donna for help, she usually answered, "Oh just put it in until it tastes right." Sure, she had always told him he couldn't taste. He told Donna he was going to publish a book called Emergency Cooking for Idiot Husbands. He got hungry and even learned to make chicken and homemade noodles, fried round steak and gravy, fried squash, eggplant dressing, fried chicken, meatloaf, potato cakes, and many other dishes. His specialty and only cooking up to then had been orange-flavored carrot Jell-O. They ate a lot of Jell-O. The nurse had said to give Donna orange Jell-O and popsicles. They ate so many orange popsicles that they may never look at or taste another one.

Gene's niece, Karen, had just moved to Farmington, New Mexico, and came to help for two weeks. It was a godsend for Donna for the support and help. She helped send thank-you notes and provided some much needed companionship.

As soon as Donna was up and around, the therapy started, and they went to the clinic for chemo treatments. Darlene came home from Germany and took Donna to the doctor for her first chemo appointment.

When Donna was receiving her IVs, they sat and held hands, which was very comforting. Dr. G had been treating Darlene for her refractory ITP illness for years. When they arrived for the appointment, Dr. G at first thought they had made an error in scheduling and the appointment was supposed to be for Darlene. Donna assured him that the appointment was for her and told him if he could see, he would have known. The first day, Dr. G asked her if she would like to keep this chemo as minimum as possible, or if she wanted to treat it aggressively, explaining to her the uncomfortable medical side effects of maximum treatment. Donna told him she wanted it gone and to give her everything he had available. He said okay, they would start out with the maximum, and he would give her prescriptions to help with the nausea and side effects. He cautioned Gene to make sure she drank at least six full glasses of water daily and stayed close to the bathroom.

She went to the first session and sat in the patient chair like all the people around her. She noticed they were all getting intravenous feeding of a clear liquid and some got yellow. Many of them had turbans, but she still had her hair. When they brought her bottles, she got a clear, yellow, pink, dark red, and sometimes another clear one. She was getting it all. Most of the patients were in the chair for an hour or so and finished the treatment. She was sometimes there for several hours. It was very tiring. When she finished the yellow one, they brought the pink one, and then the clear ones. The drip, drip, drip, seemed to go on forever. The red one was the tough one. It made her very sick every time, and she would just barely make it home to take her sleeping and pain pill and back to bed. The girls bought her a CD player and earphones so she could listen to Helmut Lotte, Mario Lanza, and Pavarotti. This lasted for three months.

When she thought she couldn't continue and was to the point of self-pity, Darlene returned the advice that Donna had given her years before and said, "Just suck it up, Mom." They both laughed and went back the next day for more. Donna had never expected Darlene would be around to help her get strength to continue with her treatments. It was a wonderful payback. Darlene's continued illness had created a very strong bond between mother and daughter. They supported each other to accept their condition that neither would ever be totally healthy again. Darlene had a faith in God for her survival that had lifted her many times and was instrumental in helping her mother find her way to recovery.

The end of the first week of treatments, Donna wanted to take her first bath. They had to tape a waterproof plastic bag over the treated area to keep the bandage dry. Right after the bath was bandage-changing time. She lay back in the water while he folded the laundry. All of a sudden, she let out a bloodcurdling scream, and Gene ran to the tub fearing the worst. Surely, she had ruptured the surgery, and he would find a tub full of blood. Instead, she was sitting up in the tub and holding two handfuls of long brown hair. It was all coming out. She had big bald spots and some long strings of hair were still attached. She looked really weird, and Gene wanted to laugh but knew he better hadn't since she was crying uncontrollably. After she calmed down and finished her bath, she sat on the edge of the bed pondering the situation. A look in the mirror told her the hair was gone in places. She thought she looked like a Halloween witch. Gene got the camera, but she told him where to put the camera and refused the picture. Now she wanted another bath and ordered Gene to shave her head to remove what hair was left. He was amazed how bumpy and uneven a head is. It's tough to shave a head because the skin doesn't give, and there are no flat areas. She didn't appreciate his amusement. Now she was completely bald and very demoralized. She sat on the edge of the bed and cried. Her son-in-law Randy shaved his head in sympathy. Gene didn›t because Randy really didn't have much hair left, and he regularly shaved his head anyway. However, it was a beautiful gesture. Denise stopped by often for support.

As the week progressed, she lost her eyebrows and all the hair on her body, except her arms. That means all the hair, even out of the nose, ears, and eyelids. She had always thought she had ugly arms because she was hairy like her father. Now when she lost all her hair from her head and body, the hair on the arms stayed. She was adamant the arm hair should have gone also. Instead, it thrived on the chemo and actually grew. Donna threatened to get a lawn mower for her arms. Gene had bought her a diamond watch for Christmas, and when she put it on, she exclaimed, "I can't even see the diamonds because the forest of black hair covers the watch." It wasn't quite that bad, but to her it was astronomical.

Donna had a wig given to her, and she put it on to go to the doctors. As soon as she was able, Darlene took her to the store and she bought some turbans like those that everyone else wore at the clinic. She bought some nice wigs and had her hairdresser color and set it just like her original hair. A stranger couldn't tell the difference, but she always knew and felt uneasy going out in public. Wigs are so very hot to wear, especially when you have no hair at all, and you are always aware they may fall off at any time. The day came that Gene convinced her to go out to dinner. She didn't want to go because she referred to herself as "the boobless wonder." Now she could add the description of "the hairless woman." She said she was lopsided, and everyone would notice. Finally, they convinced her to wear a heavy jacket and a turban. Arriving at the restaurant, she was very uneasy until she looked around. There sat three other women wearing turbans. The ice had been broken, and it became easier to go out in public.

At the end of the chemo treatments, she had another appointment with Dr. G. This time it was to start the radiation treatments of which she was deathly afraid. She had seen the blackening of the skin, the sunken eyes and the endless vomiting when she took care of her father. She dreaded the radiation, but she had been told it would start as soon as the chemo was finished.

When they examined her to start the radiation, the radiologist requested another MRI and round of tests. Donna and Gene sat in the waiting room for the test results fearing the worst. Had they found more cancer? It seemed like hours. Now they were getting worried, maybe they had found more cancer. Finally, the doctor came in. He had a folder of x-ray and scans, and he looked very stern as if he had something bad to say and didn't know how to start. They expected the worst. He began talking slowly while he looked at the scans some more. Finally, he told Donna they hadn't been able to find a single trace of cancer reoccurrence, and they didn't think radiation was necessary. The maximum chemo had apparently done its job. What a wonderful feeling from expecting the worst news to receiving the best. Donna was smiling for the first time in months and cried with happiness. It was the first time she had been happy for a long time. That night they went out to dinner and really enjoyed themselves for the first time since the surgery.

*Kristen helping her "Gramcracker" recover*

After a few months of constant doctor visits and clinical tests, she was now on a monthly schedule. She complained that she couldn't get around like she used to and got very tired, but the doctor reminded her she was seventy years old and shouldn't expect to feel like she used to. This always made her furious. Dr. Doris had mentioned she wouldn't recommend reconstructive surgery because she was too old. Donna fumed.

The next few years were a constant stream of periodic checkups and constant worry that maybe this was the visit the doctor would say the cancer is back. They had carefully explained the odds of reoccurrence and that if she could make it five years she was probably safe. Every time she had a sore spot or irritation, she suspected the worst. She began taking a drug, which simulates chemo, called Femara. She had tried another miracle drug, but it made her deathly sick. Femara, along with the chemo, has some unpleasant side effects like losing your taste and eyesight, but they insisted it would only be for five years.

Cancer is demoralizing; she went though real periods of depression where she questioned if she even wanted to survive, and the next moment being sure she wouldn't. She went through the normal phase where she started giving her jewelry and possessions to the kids because she knew she was dying. She went around the house putting the children and grandchildren's names on the original oil paintings and china. Gene finally had to tell her, "You know if you die, I may still want to live here for a while. You can't give everything away."

Finally, Donna admitted, "I wanted the kids to get things now so your second wife wouldn't get them." Gene assured her at seventy-five years old he really wasn't interested in a second wife, but she was convinced as soon as she was gone all his old secretaries would line up at the front door. Cancer is a terrible thing to go through, but she had done an admirable job of mental recovery. She is a very strong lady; it is no wonder her children are also survivors. Gene always told people, "She is one tough broad."

They had told her chemo and the Femara would affect her eyesight, but it should come back when she discontinued the pills after five years. By 2006, she had lost enough eyesight that she could no longer read without a magnifying glass, and she could no longer drive. This was a real blow to her morale and feeling of well-being. Now she would be dependent on other people to take her to her appointments and shopping trips. She couldn't even go to the casino anymore as she couldn't tell if she won or lost, and she couldn't read the cards. Again, she was demoralized and felt all she could now do was sit and watch TV or play solitaire on the computer. The kids bought her a casino game for the computer, which she loves. She felt badly because she knew she was taking Gene's time away from his business for the doctor trips, shopping, and other stops. By now, Gene was phasing out his business and could afford the time off so it all worked out.

When the five years were up, she had long planned to start driving again. Now she learned she had macular degeneration and probably couldn't get a license anymore.

After Darlene returned to Germany, the wonderful discovery of e-mail and instant messaging permitted Darlene to visit daily over a cup of hot coffee with her mother and that was a big factor in Donna's recovery. The kids bought Donna a video camera for her computer so she and the children could see and talk to each other while they had instant message computer conversations. That was another marvelous invention. They had coffee breaks together although they were six thousand miles apart. Donna would be up all hours of the night, which was daytime for Darlene in Germany and England.

After Darlene went home, Darrell showed up on the doorstep with Lewis, Donna's first and only grandson. Lewis was just turning four years old, and no one was sure how he would react to a bald grandma. When they came bounding through the front door, Donna was sitting in a double recliner chair. Lewis came around the corner and said, "Hi, Grandma," and just stood there and smiled.

Darrell said, "Mom, Lewis wants to ask you something."

Grandma said, "Oh boy, I can't imagine what this is going to be." She told him to go ahead and ask. He crawled up in the chair and stood beside her. In his partial English, he asked if she would take off her turban. Donna said, "But, Lewis, I don't have any hair."

Lewis said, "I know that, but I just wanted to run my hands over your bald head." Donna gave Darrell a questioning look, and he assured her that all Lewis had talked about on the fifteen-hour flight over was he wanted to feel her bald head. He had to feel it to believe it. Donna took off the turban, and Lewis stood up beside her and ran his little hands all over her bald head as if he were inspecting it and looking for a hole. He was fascinated there were no eyebrows or eyelashes. When he finished, he just said, "Neat," and gave her a big hug. Now he was happy, the subject was dropped, and he didn't mention it again.

*Lewis feeling her bald head*

Denise was very helpful, dropped in daily after taking the kids to school, and sometimes took Donna to chemo and doctor visits. It was a group effort as Gene was now in tax season and had appointments. Denise's oldest daughter, Jennifer, got coffee and iced tea and played canasta on the bed with Donna. Lindsey and Kristen came up, crawled in bed with Grandma to watch Disney videos, and comforted her. Donna had taught them how to play canasta, and they spent many hours of comforting time with Donna. They played canasta, go fish, and watched TV.

The phone calls from the other grandchildren were always welcome. Later when Lauren, Kathleen, and Samantha returned to Albuquerque for college they played a lot of canasta. Madeleine and Lewis only on special trips, but always canasta was on the table for whoever came to the house.

About a year after the cancer surgery, Donna began to feel a growth in her thyroid, and she was having trouble swallowing. She had half her thyroid removed years before because of a tumor. Now something was wrong with the other half. She went to Dr. Doris who referred her to a specialist. They discovered there was a huge tumor growing around the thyroid, and it had to be removed. Their worst fear was that it might be a reoccurrence of the cancer. It was supposed to be a simple one-hour operation. Gene sat in the waiting room for the hour, then another hour, then two more.

Finally, Dr. Doris came out and said it had been more complicated because the tumor was over five inches long and had encircled the trachea and vocal cord and attached itself, and they had a very delicate operation to remove it. The good news was it was not cancerous; the bad news was he was not sure Donna would be able to speak. After a recovery period, Donna was admitted to a room, and Gene could go up. She awoke and asked for a glass of water and a chocolate malt. She could speak. Gene happily commented, "There is no way to keep this woman from talking." Again, it was home for recovery and nursing care. Gene and Denise could do this; they had plenty of practice by now.

In 1974, when they removed the first half of Donna's thyroid, the doctor told Gene it was going to be a very delicate operation, and Donna wouldn't be able to speak for several days and maybe a couple weeks. Gene left the hospital after Donna was in recovery and returned to his office. A few minutes later, the phone rang. It was Donna requesting he smuggle in a chocolate malt, and she had no problem speaking.

Over the years, Donna had every "ectomy" in the books, appendectomy, mastectomy, tonsillectomy, thyroidectomy, hemorrhoidectomy, cholecstomy, hysterectomy, and about every other operation. She finally got to the point that she was convinced she would never get a chance to die; they would just keeping taking pieces until she was all gone. She wanted her epitaph to read, "Never Died, Just Ectomied Away."

There is much data published about growing old gracefully. Regardless of what you call it, Donna and Gene were finding out that growing old has only one description—growing old. Getting old was now becoming their biggest challenge in life. They were restricting their activities to adjust to a lifestyle within their physical limitations. They had lost the ambition to pursue life at its fullest as they had been doing, but what a life they had lived so far.

# Cheating Death: Their Bridge over Troubled Waters

Donna and Gene were both raised in religious families during a time when everyone in Kansas seemed to go to church. It was just understood they would go to Sunday school and church. Many of their activities were church oriented. As children growing up in rural Kansas, there were only three places: school, church, and home.

Donna sang in the church choir and at many special performances. Both attended evening church social functions, like dances, hayrides, bonfires and cookouts, roller skating, and holiday parties. The church was their activity center away from school.

Donna and Gene each have an ingrained belief in God. They took their children to church when they were young, but once the children were able to go alone, they became "holiday" church members, showing up at Christmas and Easter. They got so busy on the farm they just didn't have time to clean up and get to church in the summertime. They made their contributions, but their attendance was spotty.

Donna and Gene seldom prayed at home except at holiday or family dinners. Both admittedly prayed silently within themselves. Why not out loud? No real reason, they just weren't raised to pray aloud. In critical situations, both prayed for thanks or help, however, they had become very lackadaisical about religion.

When Darlene was pronounced terminal, it had an instant impact on both of them. They had survived their parent›s deaths, but to have their own children dying was unthinkable. This had never been in their thoughts, and they were totally unprepared to deal with it. They each reached deep within themselves to recapture their old ability to pray and ask for help for Darlene. They still had to go the extra step to give thanks instead of always asking. Donna lay in Gene's arms that night and each prayed in their own private way. It was early in the morning before they went to sleep.

When they returned home that afternoon after the bad news, Donna had taken the kids for the night so Darlene and Phil could be alone. Gene had worked outside until almost eleven o'clock at night digging a ditch. This was his way of working off frustration and remorse. He prayed for Darlene, and in his own way, he made a pact with God. He asked for Darlene's survival, at least until the children were out of school and they were old enough to go it without her. His next most valuable personal thing he owned after his family was his racehorses. He had this strange thinking that if you asked God for something, you had to give him something in return. He offered his horses and agreed to give up any more wins from his horses in exchange for her survival. This was his way.

Darlene and Donna spent a lot of time reading the bible together as Darlene now relied fully on her faith in God to pull her through. Donna helped her with the children and Darlene read. Donna prayed with her and together they supported each other. When Darlene's eyes bled and she couldn't read, Donna read the bible studies to her. Darlene put her life in God's hands, and relied on Him for her continued life.

A few years later, the horse ran over Donna, and while waiting for the ambulance, when it appeared she might be dead, Gene renewed his pact for Donna. It was a terrible fifteen minutes waiting for the ambulance and not knowing if she would survive. She just lay there in the corral covered with dirt, not moving a muscle. He really thought she was dead, but somehow when the ambulance arrived, she was able to speak.

A few years after that Donna got cancer. The doctor painted such a terrible picture of the severity of the cancer that again they thought they were presented with a terminal situation. Again, Gene tried to comfort Donna, and while sitting in the surgery waiting room, he renewed his pact with God. Again, he privately confirmed he would continue to give up any more wins by his horses in trade for Donna's survival and give his own life for hers. Then he realized he had to keep working to provide money to take care of Donna and the family, and he realized he would have to be around to make this happen. He canceled the part about giving up his life; he had another purpose to fulfill. Both Gene and Donna talked to God as if he was sitting across the table from them as when they discussed problems with their fathers. It made it easier to say what you wanted to say. Seeing God as a fatherly figure took away the mystic feeling, and it was more comfortable feeling as if you were talking to a real person.

Denise and her girls also had some health problems and were in need of some prayers. Her daughter, Lindsey, had an operation, and Denise had several hospital visits. The family was becoming very acquainted with their church minister. They seemed to see more of him in the hospital than they did at church.

Years after their critical times, both Darlene and Donna were still alive. Darlene's kids graduated from high school. She was having difficulty driving, but she was still here and functioning. Donna reached the end of the five-year period after her cancer. Both Donna and Darlene were still around. Gene's and Donna's prayers had been answered and granted. Gene and Donna had graduated from the "help me" stage to the "thank you" stage of religion. They were very thankful that against all odds Darlene,

Denise, Darrell, Donna, and Gene were still there for each other. There was no question in their minds their prayers had been answered. How else could they account for their good fortune?

One beautiful summer Albuquerque evening, Donna brought two ice teas to the porch where she and Gene sat and enjoyed the quiet. The doves that hatched in the garden had learned to fly, and they were now sitting on the rail to the patio watching them. The conversation involved what a road their life had taken, the problems they endured, and how they had survived. Both had cheated death on several occasions, Donna with her cancer, many operations, and illnesses, and Gene with his scares of going under the ice as a child and almost freezing to death, the car wrecks, and the time he was caught in the creek by the logjam where he knew he would never get out. Somehow, they always survived. Why, they weren't sure. Both had faced death and agree with the conception you must almost die in order to realize you really want to live. Donna remembered the time in the hospital when she had the blood clot, and they were wheeling her to the operating room and hearing the doctor say, "We've lost her." She still remembers the feeling of floating, still being able to hear, but seemingly not having a body, and then awaking back in her room. She often spoke of seeing herself lying on the table while they worked on her.

Neither Donna nor Gene understood what all had been working in the background all these years, but both of them knew something special had happened. The family seemed to have cheated death too many times to be just lucky. Then again, maybe they really did understand.

# The Later Years of Gene's Father

No writings about the Londenes would be complete without a chapter about Fred who everyone affectionately called Pop. Gene had called him Pop for as long as he can remember. Both Fred and Siri were the respected parents everyone dreams about.

Siri died in 1972 from a weakened heart. She birthed eleven kids and worked long hours all her life. Fred had depended on her for everything; she even shaved him and always laid out his clothes to wear. Everyone thought Fred, who just turned eighty, was so dependent on her he wouldn't survive but a short time without her. How wrong they were.

Fred lived alone in the Abilene house for a few years but had some problems with the gas stove blowing up and laying a towel on the bathroom heater, which caught fire. The girls decided he needed to go to a home. At the age of eighty-five, he began going to Brown Memorial Home in Abilene and driving the "old" people to their doctor appointments. After a few years of this, the home decided he might as well move in. He lived there for years until he had to go to a nursing home in Chapman.

Fred was always very industrious and had to have something going, card games, pool, checkers, or building something. On the farm, Charlie had always said Gene's hands were usually into something just before his brain got there, maybe inherited from Fred.

Fred and Siri's first trip to the Lexington house set the stage for the future. Gene was at work and boredom set in for Fred. He was home alone and decided Donna needed a step for the rear door for the kids. He found some lumber and a sack of cement. When Donna and Siri got home, she noticed he had built a cement box for mixing the concrete. He said he found some old plywood in the garage and cut it up to make the box. Gene had purchased a very expensive sheet of walnut veneer finished plywood for his cabinets. Now he had a very expensive cement box.

Shortly after, Donna returned from town and asked Fred what he had been doing. He replied he had built something for Denise. Soon the phone rang; it was their neighbor behind them. It seems she had gone out to hang her newly washed clothes on the line, except someone had taken the crossbar that held the lines up. Fred admitted he had decided to put up a bar in Denise's closet that she could reach and had taken the pipe since no one seemed to be using that clothesline. Denise was happy, Donna wasn't. Gene just chuckled to himself and stopped on the way home to buy a new pipe crossbar and repaired the clothesline.

After Siri died, Gene and Donna often picked up Fred when they were in Kansas buying antiques and brought him to Albuquerque for a couple weeks and then flew him home. Gene had to go to work, and Fred was left to invent. Soon Fred had a wheelbarrow and some cement and was building a new cellar door. Then he decided to put some steps on the side entrance. He found some plywood and made some round steps. He was mixing cement, and Donna heard the clink of metal. She thought she better check it out. Fred needed some reinforcement for the cement. She said, "Dad, aren't those Gene's forge tools and horse trimming tools?"

He said, "Yes, but Gene hasn't used them in years." Later he took the floor protectors from the legs of the couch and made Donna a pencil holder out of glue and gum wrappers. It looked very nice, except he put the pencils in before the glue dried and they were permanently stuck. He had been asked to leave Brown Memorial Home because he glued his bed to the floor to keep it from moving. He could solve any problem with glue, cement, or baling wire. It was sometimes welcome to put him on the plane and send him home before Donna lost her marbles.

One time Donna went to buy antiques by herself. She picked up Fred in Abilene and drove to Guymon to spend the night. They stopped at a nice motel, and Fred said, "Now I will go in and get the room." Donna decided she better go along. Fred walked up to the desk holding Donna's hand as he loved to do. When he got to the desk, he told the woman, "I need a single room for me and my girlfriend here." Donna was totally embarrassed and never stopped at that hotel again. Fred was almost fifty years older than her at the time. A few years later when Fred was in his upper nineties, he made his last visit to Albuquerque. Next morning when Donna came home from the store she couldn't find him. She searched the house and yard, no Fred. She started through the buildings and decided to look closer in the pool room. There he was behind the table on a couch sound asleep. The sun had warmed up the pool room, and he lay down for a nap. He was very slow getting up and admitted to Donna he was now on strychnine for his heart, and it wasn't working in the high altitude. Donna took him to ER to have his heart checked. The doctor examined him, and all the while Fred was watching him intently. He had never been to a Japanese doctor before and had never seen eyeglasses that looked like the bottom of a crystal water glass. Soon it came out; Fred looked him square in the eye and said, "Do all you Japs have bad eyes?" Donna held her breath to see what the answer was going to be, but the doctor decided to ignore the question. When the exam was over as they were leaving, Fred turned to the doctor and said, "You are a nice young man, too bad about your eyes." Another embarrassing moment.

When Fred was 103, he drove to the local senior center each day to play pitch or pool. The police contacted the family and said, "Ole Fred isn't seeing so good anymore and is causing some problems with his driving." One was he was doing seventy in town in the thirty zones. Another was he was parking anywhere he chose, parking spot or not. Donna had been with him when he went downtown Abilene and just parked in the middle of the street. He told her, "It's okie dokie. They all know me." The kids told the bureau to not issue him a new license and sold his 1957 Chevy. For someone who owned the first Model T in central Kansas eighty years ago, it was a devastating blow. He didn't speak to the girls for a while. The next trip to Abilene he confided to Donna he really couldn't see anymore, and his driving was scaring him. Donna was very close to Fred and Siri and received the love from them she maybe didn't get from her mother.

*Fred playing pool at farm, at 98*

On his 105th birthday, Willard Scott acknowledged him on national TV and stated, "Fred Londene is still going strong and attributes his longevity to a glass of wine or a shot of whiskey every night and a good cigar in the morning." Fred must have told them that somehow. He never was much of a drinker and hadn't had a cigar in years. The doctor did prescribe him a small glass of wine with his dinner each night, which the home kept in the refrigerator for him.

After his 105th birthday, attended by a huge crowd, Gene and family stopped by the home to say good-bye. He grabbed Donna's hand with those big well-worn hands and said in his usual part Swedish accent, "Shay Donner, you remember when my Siri died I told you I was going to stick around another few years and then I would just give it up and go see Siri. Now you need to give me a big smooch good-bye because the next time you see me I will be pushing up daisies." It wasn't long after when they got the phone call and were told Fred was playing checkers when they came to take his partner to lunch. The nurse told Fred she would be back for him in a minute and he said "Okie dokie" as he always did. When she came back to get him, he was dead. He died doing what he loved, playing checkers.

Fred left five generations of children and grandchildren numbering over 130 and many admiring friends and relatives. The University of Kansas history classes had come to interview him every year as he still remembered almost everything about early Kansas. He will be missed by many. Gene only hopes to achieve some of his accomplishments and respect, but they are huge shoes to fill.

# The Later Years

In 2008, Gene and Donna sat on the front porch approaching their seventy-sixth birthday drinking iced tea. It had been a good summer day with the grandchildren coming over to play pool and go swimming. Donna wasn't able to join in the games. Gene said the volleyball games in the swimming pool were now getting a little exhausting. An eight-hour day of work was more than enough anymore, and he and Donna were happy to retire to the TV by eight thirty or nine, and sometimes they were in bed by nine. He still got up and went to his computer around four in the morning. However, lately, they were sneaking a thirty-minute-or-more nap at noon.

Donna showed the effects of injuries when the horse ran over her and that condition had been aggravated by the cancer removal in 2002 and the Femara medicine she had to take for five years. She had a hard time walking very much, was very restricted in her activities, and could no longer drive because the medicine she took was affecting her eyesight. Donna had lived in pain from rheumatoid arthritis all her life since she was in her teens. Gene had worked all his life, either on the farm or making work out of sports and hobbies. Just after Gene turned seventy-two, they returned from Germany and something was wrong; he was sick and he got worse. He was diagnosed with diabetes II. He went on the recommended medicine for life. Then at about seventy-four, he noticed a substantial downturn in health. He had a small problem the doctor referred to as a TIA or ministroke. He wasn't sick, just getting old.

Both were having eyesight loss, and Donna contracted macular degeneration. Donna had never had use of her left eye and now Gene was losing his right eye. Donna commented, "As long as we go everywhere together, we can each use our good eye and between us we have 20-20 vision."

Gene commented, "I can just see us going for a driver's license." Actually it might work as Donna was very good at backseat driving supported by years of experience. Donna had always told him someday he would understand her pain. She was right as usual.

Gene and Donna went to the cabin to go elk hunting. Dana drove down from Colorado Springs to be with Donna during the day and talk over old times. While they were talking, Donna told her she was sorry they weren't able to go to Don's funeral. Dana said she had Don cremated. Donna replied, "Oh, really, where is he buried?"

Dana said, "Well, he's not."

Donna asked, "What do you mean he's not?"

Dana followed with "He requested his ashes be scattered half in Colorado and the other half in Montana, his home state, and I just can't do it."

Donna asked, "Well, what did you do with him?"

Dana said very sheepishly, "He is in the back of the closet with a blanket thrown over him." They both started laughing. Donna was thinking he didn't really need the blanket.

Instead, she said, "One of these days it will come to you, and you will know what to do with Don."

A year later, Dana came to Albuquerque to visit. Donna's curiosity was killing her. Finally, after two days, she asked, "Dana, where is Don?" Dana said he is still in the closet. Dana had decided to be cremated also and be put in the closet with Don.

She planned to leave a note on the blanket for the kids to scatter them together. Both Donna and Dana could laugh about it now.

Approaching seventy-nine, they began to notice a definite memory slippage. Donna would tell Gene something, and soon he was asking her the same thing again. This was dangerous since her memory loss was right there with his, and she might have forgotten what she asked him to do. Gene bought a GPS so they would be sure to find their way back home.

Finally, Gene made the big admission. He had to admit he was getting old. How could this be, he wasn't done living yet and had lots of things to do. He had no fear of death, but he really preferred living a while longer. Donna was having various health problems and had now developed a small infection of shingles. She never wanted to talk about getting old, and she was still afraid to go to a funeral. She insisted she would live forever just to avoid going to a funeral. Suddenly, they both came to the realization they weren't getting old, they were already old. What they had dreaded happening in the future had already happened. They didn't remember the exact moment, but it apparently came and went without fanfare. There was no question it had happened.

Gene went to buy gas at night and couldn't get his visa card to work in the gas pumps. He swiped it several times, but the pump just wouldn't accept it. He had forgotten his glasses, so he went inside to ring up the sale and showed the man his card. The man was as sympathetic as could be and simply told Gene that was not his visa, but it was his driver's license. The card obviously wouldn't work in the pump. It was very embarrassing, and Gene drove home very dejected.

The next week they came home from the cabin, and the van was almost empty of gas. They preferred to fill up at Costco on their trips for groceries, so the next day Donna made a list and off they went. Arriving at Costco, they realized they couldn't fill the van because Gene had mistakenly driven the Subaru. Donna quickly reminded him of his stupidity. Next, they went in to the store, and Donna realized she had left her list at home, and couldn't buy the groceries. Neither could remember what was on the list. They looked at each other in sympathy, had a good laugh, sat down to eat a hot dog and drink a Coke, and went home. They reminded each other of the old adage, "It only hurts when you laugh." The rest of their lives were going to be interesting, and they just might laugh themselves to death.

Now, when Donna needs something from the store, she makes a handwritten list. Mobile phones were a welcome addition. Now when Gene got to the store she could call him to tell him what she had forgotten on the list, and Gene could call home because he had forgotten to take the list or lost it on the way. They just had to remember to take their phone with them, and it helped to remember to turn it on.

Donna had retired a few years earlier. Gene continued to work until he was seventy-eight because he still felt good. Now he had to admit he was losing his sharpness and couldn't remember all the tax laws necessary to continue his tax business. He finally concluded he had to give it up, and this would be his last tax year, He sold his tax practice, and it was all over except the transition of turning his clients over to a new CPA. They discussed retirement and the things they could do together.

They began to shut down the farm operation. They sold the mares and the young horses. It was a sad picture to look out in the mornings to see the empty corrals. They subdivided the farm. During the filing of the plat, the city officially made the name of the lane "Londene Lane" on the city maps. Soon Donna and Gene may be gone, but now they won't be forgotten.

Someone asked where all the other animals had gone. Donna replied, "Everything that moved we ate! When an animal no longer served a purpose, we ate it. All but the horses and dogs, they never made it to the table."

Gene had met Marty Robbins years before and had played backup to him on a special services tour, and both he and Donna loved his singing. About 1973, Donna was going to the store, and Gene told her to hurry back because soon Marty would be on TV in the Grand Old Opera show, and he was going to sing a song for her. Soon, Marty walked on stage, sat down on a hay bale, and proceeded to sing a new song, a sad but beautiful ballet called "My Woman, My Woman, My Wife." The song recounts the woman's rough life, the two little children lost, the hardships she endured, and their love that survived everything. Gene had heard the song and thought it described Donna's life so closely. When the family had the funeral party, Donna requested this song be played at her funeral.

All their life Donna and Gene had heard of people having problems growing old, and here they were. Secretly, they had to admit to themselves that they just weren't as sharp as they used to be. With Darrell in Germany and Darlene moving to Germany, then England, back to Shreveport and eventually Panama City, they found they could visit all these places and stay with the kids giving them lots of vacation time plus the chance to see the family. One of the things Donna and Gene learned is to keep the family close, love them. and cherish them and their grandchildren. They have transferred the Viola farm into the family trust so all the family will always have a house to come home to.

*Grandchildren at the Farm*

In 2007, Gene and Donna got up early Christmas morning as usual. Gene made the coffee, plugged in the tree lights, turned on some Christmas music, and lit the fireplace as he had done for over fifty years. When Donna got up they sat in the dark, with just the lights from the flickering fire and the Christmas tree lights, as they had done for years waiting for the children or grandchildren to come downstairs. This year they were alone for the first time, and there would be no little feet coming excitedly down the stairs. It was hard to generate any real Christmas spirit. Finally, about daylight, they opened their few presents to each other and some Darlene had mailed home. Instead of the coffee royal, they had another cup of coffee, and they just sat in front of the fireplace in silence, looked at the tree, the fire, and each other. There was no smell of turkey and dressing cooking, and no hustle and bustle to fix the big breakfast with the traditional champagne-orange juice and cranberry breakfast drinks. There was no smell of the usual Christmas breakfast of frying bacon, biscuits, and gravy. There were no candies and no smoked herring. It was awfully quiet, just the soft Christmas music and the occasional snap of the fire. They knew someday it would come to this, but they would never be prepared. They sat and stared at the fire some more, remembering the old days. Even though they weren't there, they still had to smile to themselves thinking about the kids on Christmas's past. They finished a dish of cold cereal, had another cup of coffee, and sat on the love seat holding hands longing for the days gone by. Now they could imagine their parents sitting alone at the kitchen table having coffee and wondering when the children would call home.

Later, they went down to Denise's house for Christmas dinner. Christmas morning was already over and the presents were scattered; they had missed the opening of the presents, but it was nice seeing at least some of their grandchildren. Christmas dinner was excellent as usual, but for the first time ever, there was no turkey. For the first time in Gene's life, there was no roasted turkey, no oyster dressing, and all the fixings for Christmas. Even when Donna was in bed recovering from surgery, he had struggled through making a turkey dinner. This year, Donna didn't feel like it, and Denise had just gotten out of the hospital with knee surgery. They had ham and some of the extras. Even in the military, Gene had turkey for Christmas. He vowed next year he would fix his own turkey. Randy did have a smoked turkey, but you can't make dressing and gravy from that. Christmas away from home would never be the same as Christmas at the farm in the big house with all the family. Both Donna and Gene remembered their first Christmas away from the home they grew up in and thinking the same thing. Christmas night now meant sitting and watching TV until bedtime instead of playing with the new games the kids got for Christmas or playing cards with the family. Christmas day ended as it had started, sitting in front of the fireplace, watching the tree lights and flickering fire.

*With Donna's sister in Las Vegas with "Thumbs Up"*

A fifty-year accounting and tax career had ended. Gene became Donna's eyes for reading recipes when she was cooking, and he could concentrate on his paintings. Retirement for them would just be doing something else. Donna needed some help with the book she was writing. Secretly, they were both thinking, What can we get into now?

Finally retired, they could look back on their lives of achievement, success and failures, happiness and sorrows, big highs and deep lows. They had them all over fifty-six years of marriage. They are hoping when they get to their sixty-year anniversary they can remember what they are celebrating. They have three successful children and eight grandchildren. They have a life full of memories and experiences. Everyone who listened to Donna's stories said she should write a book, and so here you have it.